SONOMA WINE
AND THE
STORY OF
BUENA VISTA

SONOMA WINE
AND THE
STORY OF
BUENA VISTA

Charles L Sullivan

The Wine Appreciation Guild
San Francisco

For Thomas Pinney
the Boss

Sonoma Wine and the Story of Buena Vista

Published by
The Wine Appreciation Guild
360 Swift Avenue
South San Francisco, CA 94080
(650) 866-3020
wineappreciation.com

Text copyright © 2013 Boisset Family Estates

Managing Editor: Bryan Imelli
Copy editor: Margaret Clark
Assistant Editors: Corrine Cheung
Book design: Icon Design Group
Production design: Pete Nixon

Napa Sonoma topographic map (page 139) © Global Graphics: www.mapbiz.net

The CIP catalog record for this book is available from the Library of Congress
ISBN: 978-1-935879-84-8

Printed and bound in the U.S.A.

Table of Contents

Foreword

I can't remember when I didn't love Sonoma county; its rolling hills, its wild sea coast, its redwoods, its unique towns, and its sculptural vineyards. Present in all these places, even at the casual glance, are the bright shadows of history. These historical shadows are so numerous that their presence is hardly noticed, feeling very much incorporated into the now. It is those bright shadows that shape much of what Sonoma County is today and is what Charles Sullivan has captured so well in Sonoma Wine and the Story of Buena Vista.

I can remember coming to Sonoma County as a young man with a somewhat over developed appreciation of horticulture, food, wine, and life. One of my early stops was Buena Vista. At the time it was overgrown. Underneath the glut of green you could still see the remains of what had been, I presumed, a great wine estate. Its imposing stone buildings and its sealed caves all spoke of some glorious, industrious past. Driving up the two lane Sonoma country roads, I encountered vineyards that were considerably older than I, a town with a Spanish mission, the abandoned adobe Blue Wing Hotel and Vallejo's barracks that were surrounded in incongruous fashion by New England style houses from a nearly contemporaneous era. In fact, the Spanish Comandante General Vallejo's house, "Lachryma Montis," would not seem out of place in 19th century New England. It made me wonder about those people — who they were, what they did, what brought them to Sonoma. What made them so energetic and adventuresome that their fingerprints are still etched into the landscape? Occasionally, I would get small bits of information, always somewhat titillating, but fragmentary. Charles Sullivan has, by infusing life into many of the personalities that populated Sonoma and the times that shaped the evolution of Sonoma wine history, given form and animation to these interesting colorful people, the soil they cultivated and the now gnarly vines that they planted.

I moved to Sonoma permanently in 1977. A young wannabe winemaker with the incomprehensible good fortune that allowed me to learn the nuts and bolts of winemaking with Joseph Swan in Forestville CA. I created my own first vintage of Ravenswood Old Vine Zinfandel there in 1976. It would be around Joe and June Swans always socially amiable table that I would meet personalities like Andre Tchelistcheff, David Bruce, Kermit lynch, Tom Dehlinger, and yes, Charles Sullivan who was rarely without his lovely wife Roz. Charles always had a good story to tell, and was a good deal of fun, particularly when he started to get cranky about what he considered mythical historical facts. I suspect that debunking the Haraszthy myth concerning the origin of Zinfandel in California was at least part of what inspired him to write his authoritative work on Zinfandel in 2003. That investigation and historical correction, somewhat ironically, makes Charles Sullivan the best person to give the multifaceted Hungarian his due.

While working with Joe Swan, I discovered ancient vines planted well before prohibition which made exquisite wine. Who, I wondered had the foresight to plant such interesting vineyards, blends of varieties that are found nowhere else in the world in such a unique mélange. With some investigation, I found a few of the answers — mostly New Englanders and Germans before 1900, mostly Italian immigrants after 1900. Charles Sullivan's history of Sonoma County has added many more details to my understanding. Charles's admirable reconstruction has made these ancient vineyards even more interesting as he captures the essence of the human insight, occasional folly and historical events that went into building Sonoma, and California wine into their modern form. Immigration, depression, boom, recession, ambition, chutzpa, luck and wisdom all add to the narrative. Charles rendition of this history contributes to Sonoma wine's foundation, its reason for being, and in the process improves its interest and palatability.

I find that I have much in common with those California wine immigrants of Sonoma's past. Agoston Haraszthy and I came to Sonoma for nearly identical reasons. Good land, lovely climate, great growing potential, and proximity to that very civilized city of San Francisco. It is good to see the legacy of a kindred spirit being revived at the newly reenergized, renovated Buena Vista by a European, French this time, who seems no less intense than Haraszthy himself must have been.

Every morning in Sonoma I wake up and I look out to the west to see the beautiful folded rolling hills with their chameleonic shades changing with the seasons, all the ranges from green to golden. I realize that I am looking at virtually the same scene General Mariano Vallejo, Agoston Haraszthy, Victor Faure, Jacob Gundlach, Charles Bundschu and Emil and Julius Dresel were viewing. There have been few changes save a small communications tower on the ridge. This view reminds me that unburying the past is also unburying the present. I have the good fortune to own a vineyard in the middle of Sonoma valley that is firmly rooted in that past and touches many of those interesting people who populated Sonoma — General Joseph Hooker, Eli Shephard who was the Ambassador to the Far East during the time of the Chinese Exclusion act, and Senator George Hearst with his wife Phoebe Aperson Hearst, the parents of William Randolph Hearst. In fact, about 35 acres of the vines in my vineyard were planted by George and Phoebe in the latter half of the 1880's. My goal has been to learn as much as I can about these vines to ascertain the historical wisdom which they contain. My job is to be the good caretaker of these vines leaving them in better shape than I found them. I too will become one of the characters of Sonoma County wine history, and if I have done my job correctly, these vines will remind the next caretaker of the value of conservation and preservation with their attendant reward which, among other things, is the flavor of great wine.

The majority of the oldest vineyards in California are in Sonoma County. Sonoma County was infested with Phylloxera early and as result was the first to replant with vinifera saving American vine rootstock. As winemakers and grape growers, we have done our best to understand the composition of the varieties in these historic vineyards. Employing DNA analysis we have been able to discover the names of some vines that were not easily identifiable — Castet, Peloursin, Grand noir de Calmette, Mondeuse, Negrette, Tempranillo, Chasselas, and numerous others that are not the current fare of Cabernet, Chardonnay and Pinot Noir. In fact, some of them are so unique you have to wonder how they came to be in Sonoma County vineyards. Certainly there was Drummond's nursery in Kenwood about which Charles Sullivan has much to say. Then too, there was the lost collection of vines that Haraszthy collected on his famous trip to Europe. Could some of these be they? Will some of these vines produce good wine in Sonoma's warmer future? Our ancestor's experiments to find the right vines for Sonoma County have been passed on to us.

As one moves north in Sonoma, from the Carneros, to Sonoma Valley, to Russian River Valley, to Dry Creek Valley, to the Alexander Valley, one is struck by the high proportion of open space and land dedicated to agriculture. This seems improbable given Sonoma's proximity to San Francisco and the fate of other outlying suburban areas like Contra Costa, Santa Clara and San Jose. This miracle is a monument to Sonoma's Open Space District, certainly, but it is also a monument to those early pioneering planters who recognized that the highest and best use for this spot on earth was viticulture and winemaking. Wine and grapes are one of the few crops that have enough value to stay the real estate booms and housing rush. The land has been preserved for the next generation of vintner's to create their own bright shadows. How we got here and how we maintained this amazing county and its viticultural heritage is a fascinating tale well told by Charles Sullivan in his rendition of Sonoma Wine.

Joel Peterson
July 15, 2013
Ravenswood Winery, Sonoma

Introduction

This book tells two stories, one a very important part of the other. It began with an idea of Jean-Charles Boisset, who asked me to write a history of Buena Vista Winery, which he and his family had recently purchased. I saw a chance to write on a grander topic, which I had thought about for many years. I suggested that a history of Sonoma wine, with a special focus on Buena Vista, would be a task I'd like to take on. Mr. Boisset immediately agreed to sponsor such a project.

Buena Vista has a history like no other winery in California. Its "firsts" in the 1850s and 1860s have always been a part of any history of American wine. Its two great winery buildings were constructed fifteen years before any other of California's grand monuments to wine production. Its founder, Agoston Haraszthy, had a profound and lasting influence on the California wine industry. He rightly was one of the first inductees into the state's Vintners Halls of Fame.

Sonoma and its illustrious neighbor to the east, Napa are the heart and center of the greatest wine production region in the Western Hemisphere. But, previous to the publication of this book, Sonoma's wine history had never been set down in a single volume available to the general public.

My wife and I first visited Buena Vista more than half a century ago. But then one look at the grand old winery and a taste of its excellent wines were enough to start my collecting of material on the estate's history. I was able to write much of this book without leaving my own library. But my sources over the years have benefited greatly from the assistance afforded me by the staff at Bancroft Library at U. C. Berkeley, at Shields Library at U. C. Davis and at the library of the Wine Institute in San Francisco. As usual Gail and Ronald Unzelman opened their wonderful historical collection to me. The Unzelman name might be recalled from the dedication to my Zinfandel history. The dedication to this book goes to a scholar who, more than any other person, has assisted and guided my research. As always, Professor Thomas Pinney reviewed my manuscript and, as my daughter once cleverly observed, ""translated it into English." As I earlier wrote, "How could I hope to have a better advisor than an English professor who is also an expert on wine history?"

Boisset Family Estates acquired Buena Vista in 2011 with a view of returning it to its former grandeur. Visitors today to the old winery will see the impressive physical results of the Boisset commitment. The company has made available to me a large amount of historical material for this study. My particular thanks go to Patrick Egan, the company's director of marketing.

And as always, I thank my wife, Rosslyn Polansky Sullivan, for helping me keep some order in the jungle of my historical material, as well as providing the special order particularly salutary to the life of a writer.

Charles L Sullivan
Los Gatos, California
February 15, 2013

Chapter

1

Wine to California, Wine to Sonoma

1783-1850

Wine was brought to California from Mexico almost two hundred years after the great Aztec empire was conquered between 1519 and 1521 by the Spanish under Hernan Cortés. Soon European plant material was pouring into the New World, including *Vitis vinifera*, the classic European wine grape species. These vines did poorly in Mexico, or New Spain, as it was then called. But some varieties that arrived in Peru flourished, particularly the Listán Prieto, which was brought to the New World in 1553 from Spain's Canary Islands. That grape later became useful in northern Mexico, and even later in California, where it is known as the Mission variety. Only recently has DNA research shown California's Mission variety to be genetically identical to the Listán Prieto.[1]

The west coast of North America became well known to the Spanish in the 1600s, but they made no real attempt to learn about the land. They knew that the southern portion of "the Californias" was a long peninsula, today's Baja California. By the 18th century it was known as California Antigua; to the north was California Nueva, today's state.

The Spanish empire moved north from the old Aztec capital by establishing Christian mission communities into which the native people were gathered to form orderly agricultural villages, populated eventually by loyal Spanish subjects and devout Roman Catholics. In theory these missions were meant to be temporary, and eventually, when they were well established, the missionary fathers would move on and the secular clergy would

25

Father Junipero Serra (Courtesy San Juan Capistrano Historical Society)

take charge. This system worked fairly well in northern Mexico. It did not succeed in California.

In the 1690s the Jesuits moved the mission frontier to Baja California, and a few missions planted grapes and made wine. The first vineyard was planted in 1698 near Loreto. A year later Padre Juan de Ugarte began developing nearby the only real agricultural success on the peninsula, at Mission San Javier. For almost a hundred years these Jesuit missions struggled to survive, but only San Javier thrived. It produced wine and brandy, as did four others, from the then-ubiquitous Mission grape.

Suddenly in the 1760s things changed dramatically for California. In 1765 the Spanish crown sent José de Gálvez to New Spain with powers

26

that exceeded those of the viceroy. Two years later he received word from Madrid that all Jesuit priests and officials were expelled from Spain and its dominions. The reason for the decree had nothing to do with Jesuit activities in New Spain, but in February 1768 they were gone. In Baja and most of northern Mexico they were replaced by priests of the Franciscan order, in Baja headed by Padre Junipero Serra. But it was a short-lived assignment for Serra and many of his missionaries.

Alta California lay open to any European country who might take it, and the Russian move into Alaskan waters in the 1760s caused the Spanish crown to investigate the threat. Gálvez did more than that. He decided to move Spain's northern colonial frontier into Alta California by establishing *presidios* (forts) at the bays of San Diego and Monterey and what would become San Francisco. He also ordered Serra to organize his missionaries and to establish a string of missions up the California coast, as he had in northeastern Mexico.

That the Franciscans instead of the Jesuits were in charge of this venture probably changed the history of wine in early California. Most Jesuits in New Spain were not familiar with "the lands where the lemon tree blooms" and where the wine grape thrived. Many were northerners, often Germans. The best personal history of the Baja missions was written by a German priest and published in Mannheim in 1772.[2] Almost all the Franciscans who went north in 1769 were from Spain, a land of vines, and most of these were Cataláns from the region around Barcelona and the islands to the east. This had been wine country since Roman times, and still is today.

The Franciscans were astonished at the land they saw as they moved north. Baja had been an inhospitable wasteland. Alta California, at least in its coastal valleys, was a new Eden. They knew right away that these valleys had the same weather and similar soils as their Mediterranean homeland. Eventually they would plant vineyards up and down the coast, at first for altar wine, and then for their own pleasure and as an item of trade. By the 1790s there was also plenty of brandy, or *aguardiente,* as it was then known.

But they did not bring vines with them in 1769, despite later, oft-repeated claims. For many years they had to get their altar wine by ship from

27

the south. Finally in 1777 Father Serra sent a request for grapevines to the viceroy, and the first shipment arrived in May 1778. Serra had them sent to Father Pablo Mugártegui at Mission San Juan Capistrano. They went into the ground and produced a small vintage in 1782.[3] Within a few years most of the nineteen missions founded by 1804 were producing wine.[4]

In 1805 the most northerly missions were Dolores at San Francisco and Mission San José, south of today's Oakland. North of these missions the Golden Gate and the Carquinez Straits were the northern boundaries of the province. Today's Marin, Sonoma and Napa Counties were as yet unsettled by the Spanish. This was *La Frontera del Norte.*

Between 1810 and 1820 Spain's New World empire unravelled, from Mexico through South America. In 1821 California became a province in the new Mexican Republic, still physically isolated but now open to trade with the rest of the world. And now there was no royal barrier to movement north into La Frontera del Norte. In 1817 a branch of the San Francisco Mission had been established at San Rafael, and in 1820 a small vineyard was planted there.

Mission Dolores, from Two Years in California, *by Mary Cone, 1876.*

Far more important was the 1822 decision by the new Mexican governor of California, Luis Arguello, to advance the frontier by establishing a large-scale mission somewhere between today's towns of Petaluma and Vallejo. The governor developed a plan with Father José Altamira for an expedition well north of the San Francisco Bay to select a site for the mission.

On June 25, 1823 Altamira and a small company of troops set out from San Rafael and marched north to "a place called Sonoma." Altamira kept a diary in which he wondered at the beautiful land and especially at the salubrious weather, almost free of coastal fog that plagued the mission at San Francisco. He was also impressed by the abundance and vigor of the wild grapes there. They marched east to the Napa Valley, where he saw land "quite proper for the cultivation of the vine." But Sonoma won out because of its better water and its easier access to the southern missions. On July 4 the padre had a great redwood cross raised at the site of the "new San Francisco mission," which is now always called the Sonoma Mission. By the end of 1824 Altamira had a thriving operation with more than 600 Indian neophytes. There was soon a small vineyard growing from cuttings sent up from Mission San José. By 1830 there were 3,250 vines east of today's restored mission building, surrounded by a tiled stone and adobe wall.[5]

The Spanish concern about the Russian presence on the California coast had been well founded. In 1811 the Russians established port facilities at Bodega, about fifty miles north of the Golden Gate, and a stockade fifteen miles north, christened Ross for *Rossiya* (Russia). Their purpose was to raise food to supply their Alaskan outposts. Was Arguello interested in heading off Russian expansion to his north by founding the Sonoma Mission? Historians disagree.

In 1834 the Mexican government secularized the California missions, and then established a new pueblo (town) at Sonoma a year later. The result was a little land boom in the Sonoma area as new colonists rushed in. Six years later the Russians abandoned Ross and the ranches they had developed. These ranches had small vineyards whose grapes were used for eating and whose wine was distilled into brandy. There is no evidence of wine production for beverage purposes. But the Russians did plant the North

Sonoma Mission, 1896. The priest's quarters were then used as the "Old Sonoma Winery."

Coast's first wine grape vineyards, a fact that does not always sit well among Sonoma wine folk today.

The secularization process proceeded like a wildfire up and down Alta California. The process placed huge expanses of mission land into the hands of local administrators. In many cases these were the best agricultural lands in California south of La Frontera del Norte. In the Los Angeles area the San Gabriel Mission's land covered more than a million acres. The lands technically controlled by the Sonoma Mission were equally vast. They included the Petaluma and Santa Rosa areas and land to the west, plus the entire Sonoma Valley and Napa Valley to the east. With secularization all this land was placed under the control of a twenty-six-year-old lieutenant in the military, Mariano Vallejo. He was soon appointed *Commandante General* of the Frontera, which accounts for his being called "General" Vallejo ever after, although his highest military rank was colonel.

Vallejo was charged with building a solid frontier against possible Russian expansion. He did this through a continuous series of land grant recommendations to the governor, which were almost always granted. Vallejo placed large swaths of land into his own hands and into those of his numerous family members and friends. He was also liberal in grants to retired military men who had families. Perhaps even more important were his grants to foreign newcomers, particularly Americans. He was sure at an early date that California would eventually be part of the United States. By 1846, when America took control of Mexican California, virtually all of the map of today's Sonoma County had been covered, so far as non-mountainous areas were concerned, by land grant ranchos, although most as yet had few inhabitants.

In 1835 Vallejo began laying out the new pueblo of Sonoma. Under Spanish and Mexican law each official pueblo was assigned four square leagues of land, or 17,712 acres,[6] a large area indeed, but barely one-fourth the size of Vallejo's Rancho Petaluma. All this pueblo land, where most of the early vineyards were concentrated, including Buena Vista, had special legal status that exempted their owners from having to prove title in court under the Congressional Land Act of 1851. Titles to Sonoma pueblo lands were secure and were later given automatic confirmation by the Land Commission.

Vallejo was also liberal in granting town lots to the new settlers in the pueblo itself. Outside the plaza area were thousands of acres of pueblo land, areas considered farm lots (*suertes*). Here was where most of the early Sonoma vineyards were planted, although there were a few close to the plaza.

Sonoma has always been the center of population of the Sonoma Valley, which is about eight miles wide at that point. The valley flattens out to the south into the Carneros region, and narrows as it runs north to the Santa Rosa area. Buena Vista, the subject of our story, is a couple of miles east of the town plaza. In the 1850s the area commanded a "fine view" of the valley and the flatlands south to the bay.

Mariano Vallejo was the pioneer of Sonoma viticulture and winegrowing. Very early he had cuttings taken from the mission's vines, and planted about 400 of them behind his home on the north side of the plaza. These grapes made good eating for his growing family, plus a little wine. In a few years he was making enough wine and brandy to supply all the thirty or so families in the pueblo. An English visitor in 1841 reported Vallejo's production that year as 540 gallons of wine and sixty of brandy, for now he had a little still.[7]

Five years later, the year of the American conquest of California, Vallejo's wine and brandy made history as part of the Sonoma's historic comic opera, The Bear Flag Revolt. On June 14 a group of rough American frontiersmen rode into town and declared for a California Republic. Com-

Mariano Guadalupe Vallejo

mandante Vallejo received them cordially and sat down with their leaders to work out a "surrender." He sent for his brother-in-law, Jacob Leese, to act as interpreter, and ordered lavish amounts of wine and brandy to be sent over from the old barracks he used as a winery. The "Bears" soon became something of a drunken mob. It finally ended peacefully, but Vallejo, who really favored American annexation, was hauled off to Sutter's Fort, a prisoner. Later in 1849, at California's Constitutional Convention, delegate Vallejo argued that if a bear were to be placed on the state's great seal, a mounted *vaquero* should be displayed lassoing the beast.[8]

The general eventually had two vineyards in town, totaling about fifteen acres. Jacob Leese also had a small spread near Sonoma Creek, and there were four more with an acre or more before 1850. But at this date there was nothing yet really approaching a commercial wine industry. In fact, the first real commerce in Sonoma viticulture in the fifties came from the sale of fresh grapes for the table. In the Gold Rush years all fresh fruit was bringing astonishing prices in San Francisco, Sacramento and in the Gold Country. Vallejo made good money in this trade for several years.[9]

Between 1850 and 1856, as the Gold Rush fever subsided, the Argonauts who decided to stay in the Golden State came to realize that there were only four real paths open to most of them to make a good living. They could work in the mines, where getting the gold out was being transformed from a treasure hunt to a serious industrial operation. Or they could become involved in trade, finance or agriculture. The latter was the path most obviously open to the vast majority of the newcomers.

Many headed to the Great Valley and its foothills, but it was obvious to many more that the coastal valleys just north and south of the Bay Area were perfect places to turn the soil. Sonoma County, especially the Sonoma Valley, was soon seeing the arrival of many folks looking for good farmland at reasonable prices. It was obvious to all that just about anything could be grown in this salubrious Mediterranean climate. At first most settlers were interested in cash crops for a quick return, like potatoes and onions. But a few had the capital, the patience and the foresight to plant fruit trees and grape vines, which took a few years to turn a profit.

Peter Storm, who was among the Bear Flag Revolutionaries, with the flag he helped design.

In 1855 one such person, who had been in California since 1849, visited Sonoma. He was an experienced farmer and nurseryman, with a wide knowledge of the ins and outs of intensive agriculture. He had access to capital and held a good government position in San Francisco. He also had a special interest in viticulture, having previously planted vines in both southern and northern California.

This man was Agoston Haraszthy. He visited Mariano Vallejo, looked at the general's vines and tried his wine. The visitor had also been directed to the farm of another local winegrower just east of town. After he saw Julius Rose's handsome vineyard and tasted his good wine, Haraszthy returned to San Francisco with an idea for the future, which included Rose's land, and perhaps even more.[10]

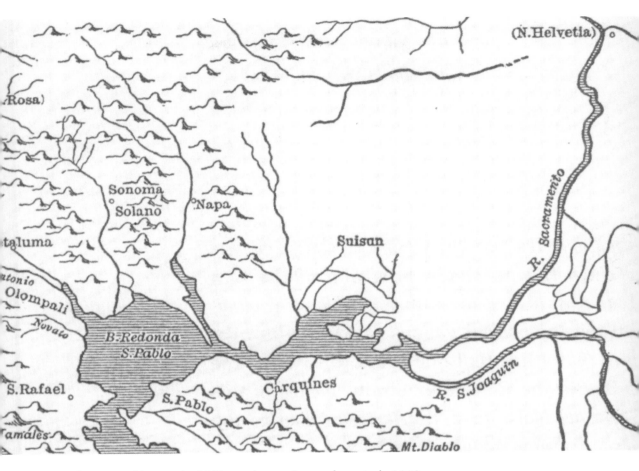

The Frontera del Norte. An 1889 reproduction of a map drawn in the 1820s.

Chapter 1 Notes

1. *American Journal of Enology and Viticulture, 58:2 (2007)*, pp. 242-151.

2. Johann Baegert, *Observations in Lower California*. Berkeley, 1952.

3. Edith Webb, *Indian Life in the Old Missions*, Lincoln, Nebraska, 1952, pp. 95-96.

4. Charles L. Sullivan, "Wine in California, 1698-1846," *Wayward Tendrils Quarterly*, April, July and October, 2010. These serialized articles give a detailed history of California winegrowing in this period.

5. José Altamira, "Diario de la Expedición. . . de 25 de Junio de 1832," Bancroft Library; Robert S. Smilie, *The Sonoma Mission*, Fresno, 1975, pp. 6-15.

6. W. W. Robinson, *Land in California*, Berkeley, 1979, pp. 40-43.

7. Madie Brown, "The Vineyards of Gen. M. G. Vallejo," *California Historical Society Quarterly*, September 1937, pp. 241-249; Ernest P. Peninou, *History of the Sonoma Viticultural District*, Santa Rosa, 1998, pp. 50-51.

8. *Wayward Tendrils Quarterly*, April 2011, pp. 17-19.

9. Irving McKee, Historic Sonoma County Winegrowers," *California-Magazine of the Pacific*, Sept. 1955; Peninou, *Sonoma*, pp. 49-58.

10. Charles L Sullivan, *A Companion to California Wine*, Berkeley, 1998, pp. 146-148.

Chapter

California Wines and Vines

≈◦◦◦◦◦◦◦○◎○◦◦◦◦◦◦≈

1850-1856

Haraszthy was not the only person with an idea for a large scale viti-cultural future for the coastal valleys of the Bay Area. There was activity in the Santa Clara Valley and the East Bay near Mission San José. And Napa Valley would also soon join in. By 1857 there were other areas ready to take advantage of the place, the time and, perhaps most important, the economic situation in the young state. But the leader in the coming explosion was the Sonoma Valley. We need to examine the origins of this historical moment which brought about the beginnings of the modern California wine industry.

When California became a state in 1850, viticulture was overwhelmingly concentrated in southern California, while the state's population was overwhelmingly concentrated in the north around San Francisco and in the Gold Country. In the early fifties grapes in large quantities were shipped by sea from the Los Angeles area to the north; there was virtually no similar trade in wine. Nevertheless this northern area was one of the most bibulous regions in the world. San Francisco, Sacramento and the Gold Country were awash in alcoholic beverages. An Italian diplomat stationed in San Francisco reported to his government on all the major imports that passed through the San Francisco Customs House in 1856: 31,000 barrels of brandy; 25,000 of whisky; 33,000 of beer; 13,000 barrels and 120,000 cases of wine; and 18,000 cases of champagne.[1]

Agoston Haraszthy

A pair of bright young German musicians decided in 1853 to take advantage of this market and bring Los Angeles wine to San Francisco. Flautist John Frohling made and bought wine in the Southland; violinist Charles Kohler continued making money in the evening as a concert musician, and by day sold the wine. By 1857 their trade reached 60,000 gallons. In three years it was double that quantity. Frohling died suddenly in 1862, but when Kohler died in 1887 the firm of Kohler & Frohling was the largest and most successful in California. By that date and for years thereafter, most of their wine had been coming from Sonoma County.[2]

Kohler and Frohling were the industrial pioneers of California wine and in a few years would move the center of their production facilities to the north. But when they were starting out in the Southland there was definitely something in the air in the Bay Area, a sort of a viticultural Zeitgeist. San

Chalres Kohler, second from left, in front of Kohler and Frohling outlet.

James L. L. Warren

Francisco's *Alta California,* the state's most important newspaper, started talking up *northern California* viticulture in 1851 and kept it up for years.

More important was the California Farmer, founded in 1854 by James L. L. Warren, a Massachusetts man who had earlier owned a Boston nursery which specialized in selling grapevines, and who now owned nurseries in San Francisco and Sacramento. He also founded the California Agricultural Society in 1852. His newspaper became a leader in promoting winegrowing with its first issue. A few months later an article on the subject was headed "Cultivators of California! Plant Your Vineyards. Begin Now. . . . No better investment can be made. . . ."[3]

Earlier, Warren began his campaign for Sonoma winegrowing in praise of the same Julius Rose whom Haraszthy would soon visit. Rose's vineyard and his red wine had won special awards at an early meeting of the Agricultural Society.[4]

Warren also actively promoted local agricultural organizations and local fairs all around the Bay Area, the records of whose competitions and awards he enthusiastically published. He early emphasized the successes in the Santa Clara Valley. The early founding of the pueblo of San José there gave that area a forty-year viticultural head start on Sonoma. But that county soon was getting more than its share of the ink, particularly after 1856.

It is difficult to overstate the importance of Warren, his newspaper and his agricultural society in the early development of winegrowing in northern California. This is particularly true of his enthusiasm for what was happening in Sonoma. We can be sure that Haraszthy knew of Julius Rose's winegrowing successes from reading the *California Farmer.* The correspondence between Warren and Haraszthy stored in the Warren Papers at the Bancroft Library begins in 1852.[5]

Haraszthy visited Rose again in 1856 and indicated his willingness to buy Rose's property. In the spring of 1857 he bought the place from Rose for $11,500 and moved there late the following summer.[6]

At this point I want to pop a historical bubble that has been afloat for far too long. It was generally understood that California wine would never reach the potential afforded it by the state's soils and climate until better Eu-

Circa 1950s photos of the Mendocino County Saloon. Bottles were refilled from barrels in the backroom, likely with wine made from the Mission Grape, which, as the author states, if made with care "could easily satisfy the simple tastes of the forty-niners," such as the gentlemen pictured here.

ropean grape varieties could be imported to take the place of the ubiquitous Mission variety brought here by the Franciscans. In the fifties and for years thereafter the Mission variety was called the California grape, sometimes the Los Angeles grape, most often "the native variety." Of course it was not native to California; it was a European vinifera variety earlier grown in Spain, the Listán Prieto. Carefully handled, a barely satisfactory white wine could be produced from this variety, and a less than satisfactory red wine. A quite satisfactory sweet white or red wine was possible when the fermentation process was stopped short by adding a large dose of brandy. The sweet white wine concoction was usually called angelica, the red usually port.

When very careful cellar techniques were employed, producers could easily satisfy the simple tastes of the forty-niners with wines far less costly than the French and Spanish imports. Kohler & Frohling proved this to be true for many years, until they had a dependable supply of better varieties. But everyone with a sense for horticulture and an experienced taste for good wine knew that better varieties were needed.

In the early fifties, men with such horticultural knowledge made good money importing "foreign" table varieties from the East Coast. Commercial nurseries serving potential orchard and vineyard owners popped up all over northern California. Almost always they were founded by Frenchmen or New Englanders. The nursery center was the San José area, where the early leaders were Bernard Fox, Louis Pellier and Antoine Delmas. In the East Bay there was John Lewelling, and in Sonoma and Napa Simpson Thompson. On the San Francisco Peninsula there was Frederick Macondray at San Mateo. The greatest of them all was Col. Warren's friend, New Englander Anthony Smith at Sacramento, who served the Great Valley and the Sierra foothills.[7]

The first shipments from these new nurseries usually came from Boston. They always included grapevines, European vinifera. The gardeners around Boston and Long Island had learned how to raise delicate grapes, in glass nurseries, that were delicious for dessert. Virtually no one in that cold country tried to make wine. All these first shipments of "foreign" varieties, which they certainly were, had been thought best in Boston to serve as table grapes. But everyone who understood horticulture knew that wine could be made

Frederick W. Macondray

from table grapes, and who knew what would work in this new land? At the local fairs all over the Bay Area and the Great Valley, grape and wine competitions were soon being held in two categories, "Native" and "Foreign."

When one reads about these local fairs in the fifties, or studies the nurserymen's lists, one finds that these were the most common "foreign" varieties, except for one I'll focus on shortly: Black Hamburg, Black Prince, White Muscadine, Syrian, Flame Tokay, White Corinth, Black Morocco and numerous muscats. Between 1853 and 1856 no one knew what quality of wine any of them would make, and it would usually take at least three or more years from planting to find out.

A few of these "foreign" varieties eventually proved successful--a very few. There were several muscats that made tasty sweet wine, a muscatel, but they were found most useful for giving the tasteless Mission whites a touch of elegant flavor. The only variety in the scores of these table grapes that proved really successful for red wine was a table grape out of Boston, brought here by New Englanders, who knew it well for its delicious raspberry-like flavor. In Boston they called it the Zinfindal. Eventually in California people came to call it Zinfandel. To this date there is no reliable account of the origin of this name.

When San José's Antoine Delmas made a red wine from this variety in 1858, his friends encouraged him to enter it in the State Fair competition. He did so in 1859 and won first prize. The committee in charge expressed surprise that the grapes for that wine "had been selected more as table fruit than for winemaking." The Zinfandel struck gold in Sonoma in 1862

Antoine Delmas with sons Joseph (left) and Delphin.

when it was again discovered to be an excellent wine grape by Victor Fauré, Mariano Vallejo's wine maker. The vines had been brought in from Boston by Frederick Macondray, a ship's captain who was also a nurseryman. He was one of many who brought Zinfandel to California, but he has picked up most of the historical plaudits in recent years, since his role has been so easily documented.[8]

So what is the historical bubble needing to be popped? People interested in California wine history have been bombarded with nonsense for years by writers who have read about all the "foreign" varieties being tried all over the northern counties in the fifties. They almost never mentioned any specific variety. I believe most of these writers thought that such un-named foreign vines were those such as Cabernet Sauvignon, Chardonnay or Pinot noir. They were not! Only three of those "foreign" varieties made it to the winegrowing finish line: the Zinfandel, the Muscat of Alexandria, and the Muscat blanc (Muscat Frontignan).[9]

But there were several well-documented importations of the truly great European wine varieties, and they are well documented. Antoine Delmas was the first in 1852 with several, including the Cabernet Sauvignon and Merlot. San José's Charles Lefranc, of Almaden fame, imported the Malbec and Grenache in 1856. Francis Stock, also of San José, brought in the Riesling and Sylvaner. Notorious California pioneer Samuel Brannan personally went to France in 1859 and sent home numerous varieties for his Napa estate at Calistoga. And Sonoma's Emil Dresel's 1859 importation included several German varieties including Riesling and Traminer. Most of these imported varieties were shared or sold from time to time, but their spread was very slow.[10] Others imports followed in the 1860s, but a steady flow of the great European wine varieties to California did not take place until the 1870s.

Before I take up the story of Agoston Haraszthy at Buena Vista, I need to make it clear how he got there from his homeland in Europe. He would have been in the history books about pioneer days in Wisconsin and about Gold Rush days in California, even if he had never planted a grapevine or made a gallon of wine.

GRAPES.—*Vignes.*

The abbreviations are as follows:

1. *Form of the bunch:* comp. compact, when the berries are very closely set; loose, when they are loosely set.
2. *Color:* bl. blackish; g. green; w. white; pur. purple; r. reddish; y. yellowish; p. pale; d. dark.
3. *Quality:* 1. first rate; 2. middling; 3. indifferent.
4. * Native; † Foreign.

NAME.	Form of the bunch.	Color.	Form of the berry.	Qual.	REMARKS.
†White Chasselas, - - *Royal Muscadine.*	loose	y. w.	round	1	A superior variety.
†White Frontignac, - *White Constantia, Muscat blanc.*	comp.	w.	round	1	Excellent and highly esteemed.
†White Muscat of Alexandria, - - - *Frontignac Alexandrian.*	long	w.	oval	1	Superb—much esteemed.
†White Sweetwater, - *Chasselas Royal.*	loose	w.	round	1	A hardy foreign sort, and much cultivated in the
Black Hamburg, - - *Red Hamburg, Frankenthal, Valentine's, Admiral, Languedoc, Troller, Purple Hamburg.*	large	b.	round	1	Well known to be one of the most valuable varieties. The berry is uncommonly large and very productive, and is, as it deserves to be, more extensively cultivated than any other variety.
†Black Prince, - - *Black Spanish, Lombardy of some.*	large comp.	bl.	oval	1	A good bearer and colors well.
Black St. Peter's, - - *Black Palestine.*	loose	b.	round	1	Ripens late.
*Catawba, - - -	loose	r. p.	round	2	A very productive, hardy grape, of musk flavor.
†Chasselas of Frontignac, †Constantia, - - -	loose	r.	oval	1	Very good.
†Grisly Frontignac, - - *Muscat gris, Grizeline, Red Constantia.*	long	y. r.	round	1	Muscat flavor and excellent.
*Isabella, - - -	loose	pur.	oval	1	Well known and productive. Hardy variety.
*Jewett's White, - -					
†Miller's Burgundy, - - *Le Meunier, Black Cluster.*	comp.	bl.	round	1	An old variety—a first rate wine grape.
†Oval Malaga, - - - *White Muscadel, White Jar Grape.*	large	w.	oval	1	Excellent for table use—keeps well.
*Pond's Seedling, - -	long	p.	round	1	Sweet, thin skin and very good.
*Schuylkill, - - -					
*Scuppernong White, - *" Black, -	loose	bl.	round	1	Muscat flavor—excellent for dessert.
†Zinfendel, - - -	long, loose	bl.	round	1	An excellent variety, the flavor superior—grows in very large, long clusters of a conical form.

Pictured here is a page from Boston nurseryman James Warren's 1844 catalog.

(Courtesy of William Marchione and the Brighton-Allston Historical Society)

Chapter 2 Notes

1. Frederico Biesta, "The State of California. . .1856," *California Historical Society Quarterly,* December 1963, pp. 318-319.

2. *Alta California,* 6/25/1853; Vincent P. Carosso, *The California Wine Industry. . ., 1830-1895,* Berkeley 1951,

3. *California Farmer,* 1/11/1855.

4. *California Farmer,* 10/19/1854; 5/17/1855.

5. Walton Bean, "James Warren . . . California Agriculture," *Pacific Historical Review,* December 1944, pp. 361-367. Professor Bean called Warren, "a one man agricultural pressure group."

6. McGinty, *Strong Wine,* pp. 295-298.

7. *California Farmer,* 6/8/1854, 8/3/1854, 9/14/1854. 10/17/1855; *San Jose Telegraph,* 8/12/1856

8. Charles L. Sullivan, *Zinfandel, A History of a Grape and Its Wine,* Berkeley, 2003, pp. 25-26.

9. Sullivan, *Companion,* pp. 228-229.

10. Charles L. Sullivan, *Like Modern Edens, Winegrowing in the Santa Clara Valley. . .,* Cupertino, 1982, pp. 15-23.

Chapter

Haraszthy Before Sonoma

When Agoston Haraszthy first arrived in the United States in 1840 he was a young man of twenty-eight years, brimming with ambition and vitality and eager to discover the prospects in a land about which he had read and heard so much. He was born in 1812 into an old but untitled Hungarian family, belonging to what the English call the "landed gentry."

His homeland was part of the Austrian Empire known as Vojvodina, now part of Serbia, with a large Hungarian population. The family estate was near Novi Sad, the provincial capital. He had a good education, with an emphasis on law and language. Philosophically he was an ardent follower of the liberal Hungarian philosopher István Széchenyi. The keys to that man's beliefs were the words "Progress" and "Industry."

In 1833 Agoston married Eleanora Dedinsky. Geza was their first child about a year later. In 1835 Attila was number two. Arpad made it three in 1840. All were named for ancient Magyar heroes.[1]

Bored with the life of a young country gentleman, Haraszthy made his first trip to the United States in 1840, leaving behind his pregnant wife and two young sons. He kept a journal of his trip, from which he produced an American travelogue which was published in the Hungarian city of Pest in 1844. He and a companion made their way eventually to the Wisconsin Territory, which was rapidly being settled. There he spent more than a year establishing impressive and profitable economic roots in what was to become Sauk City, of which he was one of the founders. The annals of

53

Lewis Cass

early Wisconsin history abound with remarkable tales of the Hungarian's achievements along the Wisconsin River. He built a sawmill and a grist mill, operated a brickyard and established a ferry service on the river. He made money in agriculture, raising grain, livestock and hops. But the rugged upper-Midwest climate doomed his attempts at viticulture.

When his roots were firmly planted in Wisconsin, Haraszthy returned home and gathered his family for their voyage to the New World. They traveled to England and sailed for New York on July 31, 1842. They were back in Sauk City at the end of the year. There he continued to prosper and to make his name in Wisconsin's early history.

The year 1848 marked a turning point in Haraszthy's life. Wisconsin became a state that year, and, like most immigrants, he had cast his political lot with the party of Jefferson and Jackson. He had become a close ally of Lewis Cass, the conservative Democratic leader of neighboring Michigan. Cass had been the Michigan territorial governor when Wisconsin was part of that territory. The Michigan leader was the Democratic Party candidate for president in 1848, and Haraszthy was one of his party organizers who helped Cass carry that state. But a fluke in the New York vote gave the victory to the Whigs under Zachary Taylor. Had the Democrat won, Haraszthy would have been a political beneficiary through his close ties to Cass.

When the news of the discovery of gold in California hit Wisconsin at the very moment of Cass's defeat, Haraszthy decided to pull up stakes and join the western migration. He left Wisconsin with his financial affairs in a somewhat complicated and confused condition, a tendency that was to mark his future business activities in California. His family group now had two more children and Agoston's father, Charles.

In April 1849 Haraszthy and his family headed west by oxen train and arrived in San Diego at the end of the year. He had stated that he was not interested in panning for gold, which is confirmed by his arrival in this town so far from the Gold Country.

This family of aristocratic Hungarian gentry must have made quite an impression. Haraszthy had called himself "Count" in Wisconsin, a title to which he had no legal claim. Now he introduced himself as "Colonel" Haraszthy. This honorific made better sense, since he had served as an officer in the Wisconsin militia. He probably had the rank of captain, since he commanded a company for a short time. But "colonels" in state and territorial militias were a dime a dozen in 19th century United States. We have already met James Warren of the *California Farmer*, who was regularly addressed as "Col. Warren" in California, probably in recognition of his non-combatant service in the Massachusetts militia.

Aside from the dusty, yet bustling village of barely two hundred persons, the first thing Haraszthy noticed in San Diego was the climate. The beautiful California spring that had greeted him and his family was followed by a gently warm and dry summer. It was a far cry from the rugged ups and downs of Wisconsin. He planted an orchard and a small vineyard in Mission Valley, just outside town, but agriculture was not the key to quick success here. He was soon operating a livery stable and a butcher shop, and he built the town jail. In 1850 he was elected sheriff of brand new San Diego County and his father was elected to the town council.

Genial weather and personal success could not shield the younger members of the family from the violent and turbulent life of early San Diego. In 1851 Eleanora and the youngest children, including eleven-year-old Arpad, boarded a steamer bound for New York. They settled in New Jersey, where the children could acquire a formal education in a settled environment. Agoston and his family were not again united until five years later in Sonoma.

Haraszthy maintained his close association with the Democratic Party, which dominated southern California politics. One of the chief aims of the Democrats in the Southland was to make the southern portion of the state a separate U.S. territory, divorced from California proper. In 1851 Haraszthy issued a circular supporting the change. The Southland, with a much smaller population, paid far more in state taxes per person than the north; this was Haraszthy's complaint. Next year he ran for a seat in the State Assembly and won. He had previously visited San Francisco, but when he went north for the next meeting of the State Legislature, he got a more complete eyeful. The lively economic activity in the Bay Area convinced him that this was where the action was.

The new legislator spent only one term in the Assembly, and by all reports did a conscientious job. More important, he met many powerful men whose later acquaintance would be of great financial value. Meanwhile he liquidated part of his rather sizeable San Diego holdings. Profit from real estate speculation was always on his mind, ever since the earliest Wisconsin days.

His first northern purchase was a fifty-acre piece of land near the old Franciscan mission, about a mile south of San Francisco. Then he bought a larger tract next door, bringing his total holdings there to about 200 acres. He called this land Las Flores and began developing it in March 1852. Four days after he closed the deal he wrote Col. Warren asking to buy

Out of Missouri, a wagon train makes its way west over the Oregon trail. c. 1846.

"rooted grape vines—the largest vines you have." He also wanted onion and cabbage seed, and closed with "Be sure to take good care of my Roses and Dahlias. . . ."[2]

Anyone who could produce or acquire foodstuff in California in these Gold Rush years was assured a profit. Haraszthy made good money at Las Flores raising vegetables, and perhaps even better money brokering fresh grape deals. The price for this attractive fruit had soared to twenty cents per pound after 1851, that is, $400 per ton for a commodity selling for less than a fifth that sum a year earlier. The source of all these grapes was the Los Angeles area, and by 1852 the steamers *Sea Bird* and *Ohio* were hauling thousands of barrels of grapes north each fall. Haraszthy took an active part in this trade and would continue to do so at Buena Vista after 1856.[3]

A viticultural fact that Haraszthy learned at Las Flores was that it was too cool and foggy there to ripen grapes. In 1853 he had a chance to buy warmer land to the south, in the hilly uplands of San Mateo County, the

San Francisco Mint, engraving c. 1854

so-called Crystal Springs area. He sold off half of his Las Flores acre-age and joined several others in acquiring a huge piece of Crystal Springs land. At first he had 640 acres at his disposal, but this was reduced to 380 acres as the result of a Land Commission decision. On this land he again attempted to develop a diversified agricultural estate and planted an-other vineyard. It is possible that he bought more vines from Col. Warren. Later he transferred a large number of vines from Crystal Springs to Buena Vista in Sonoma. There may have been some East Coast "foreign" varieties among Haraszthy's vines, along with the mostly "native" Mission vines, but there is no good contemporary evidence for this. After he moved to Sonoma he was not able to sell off his Crystal Springs property because of his involvement in a court case, which I shall discuss soon.

Meanwhile horticulture was forced to take something of a back seat in Agoston's affairs. In the 1850s millions of dollars' worth of gold poured continuously through San Francisco. The dust and nuggets had to be trans-

58

formed into bars and coins. After Democrat Franklin Pierce became president on March 4, 1853, pressure to establish a U.S. branch mint in San Francisco mounted; it opened in April 1854. Being a loyal Democrat with good connections in San Francisco, Haraszthy was appointed U.S. Assayer for the mint. We think now that Haraszthy served honestly and efficiently,[4] but he also had a stake in a private smelting firm run by three Hungarian friends, which raised a few eyebrows. The presence of a special Treasury agent in San Francisco then also became a problem for Agoston. J. Ross Browne was already well known in California as the official reporter for the state's constitutional convention in 1849. Now his job was to check out the operations of all Treasury department facilities in the city. When he finally got around to the new mint, Haraszthy's "private affairs" caught his attention. In October 1856 he wrote the Secretary of the Treasury that he considered Agoston an "unsafe man," and recommended his removal.

With his private interest in Sonoma growing after his visit to Julius Rose's ranch in 1856, Haraszthy submitted his resignation to the Mint in January 1857, just before the Buena Vista deal was finalized.

After Agoston's resignation Browne dug deeply into the Mint's accounts and found a shortage of about $150,000. The agent was not totally convinced that Haraszthy was responsible, but they met in June 1857 and agreed that the former employee would submit to a trial. As bond he agreed to transfer the deed to his various properties to his friend and associate at the Mint, Jacob R. Snyder. (We shall meet this man at Buena Vista many times in the next twenty years.) Excluded was the deed to the Buena Vista property, which was not delivered to Haraszthy until December 1857, well after Agoston and his family had moved onto the property and the small 1857 vintage had finished fermenting.

Haraszthy was tied up with the Mint case for three —and- a -half years. He was indicted for embezzlement in September 1857; the indictment was dropped the following March. Then the government tried to recover the mint's shortages by filing a civil suit against Haraszthy. The trial did not begin until February 1861. It lasted five days, at the end of which the judge ended his charge to the jury with these words: "There is no evidence in this case to prove the slightest fraud in the defendant."[5] The jury returned its verdict of "not guilty" within minutes. Haraszthy didn't owe the government a dollar, but his legal costs over the five years amounted to more than $5,000. Later, in the 1860s, Browne and Haraszthy became friends, and the former agent admitted that the case should not have been brought.[6]

All the while during the court case, Agoston Haraszthy was developing and perfecting his plans for a great agricultural estate in Sonoma. By the time the jury brought in its verdict, the press had come to find his work at Buena Vista far more interesting than the dull details of his legal problems.

Haraszthy had started looking around for an alternative to Crystal Springs in 1855. We have already seen his growing interest in Sonoma. One might wonder why he didn't take a closer look at the Napa Valley, soon to be a great winegrowing region. Until the counties of California were formed in 1850, Napa Valley had been part of the Sonoma region governed by Mariano Vallejo. In 1836 he had granted a large rancho in the middle of the valley to George Yount, a famous mountain man who had previously worked for Vallejo. He moved to his grant in 1838 and planted a small vineyard in the winter of 1838-1839. Sonoma was far more attractive than Napa and its small beginnings in 1856. It was closer to San Francisco and it had a small, but established community of vineyardists, even a few winemakers.[7]

It was clear that the Sonoma Valley had a great climate and excellent soils. Haraszthy was obviously interested in viticulture, particularly in the huge profits being made in the fresh grape market. After tasting Mariano Vallejo's and Julius Rose's vintages he knew that good wine was not just a possibility here. There would be excellent profits from such a product, given the demand for imported wine and the continually growing California population. He was also sure that the mild northern coastal valleys could produce better table wine than the warmer Los Angeles area, where the vineyards were now located. And it was obvious that having a production area more than 400 miles closer to the state's population centers gave northern producers a distinct competitive advantage. Haraszthy was determined to follow Col. Warren's call to "Plant Your Vineyards!"

60

J. Ross Browne

CHAPTER 3 NOTES

1. This chapter follows my own serialized biography of Haraszthy in *Vintage Magazine,* February-April 1980. McGinty's *Strong Wine* is much more thorough and is fully documented.

2. James L. L. Warren Papers, Bancroft Library, Box 2, Haraszthy to Warren, 3/29/1852.

3. *Los Angeles Star,* 9/15/1853; *Alta California,* 11/10/1852.

4. It is easier to follow this story in Bryan McGinty's *Haraszthy at the Mint,* Los Angeles,1975, than in his less focused biography.

5. McGinty, *Strong Wine,* p. 291.

6. *Alta California,* 3/3/1861. The *Alta* followed the Mint controversy almost daily in tedious detail

7. Charles L. Sullivan, *Napa Wine, a History,* San Francisco, 1994, pp.10-19.

Chapter

4

Haraszthy To Sonoma

The land Haraszthy bought from Julius Rose in 1857 had a complicated and rather confusing history. It was part of the original Mexican land grant situated east of the town of Sonoma, the Rancho Huichica, covering 18,704 acres. As Buena Vista quickly grew under Haraszthy, part of the estate property also was located on Sonoma's pueblo lands.

Legend has it that Rose's property was first settled by a Christian Indian in 1832. He may have planted a small vineyard, but that part of the story has no documented history.[1] In 1837 this land was acquired by Salvador Vallejo, the general's brother. Five years later it was taken over by a Mexican army veteran, who, in 1841, sold it to Jacob Leese, one of Sonoma's pioneer winegrowers. He also had a vineyard to the west near Sonoma Creek, and probably planted more vines on the new property. He built some of the structures that Haraszthy found there when he moved in. Leese has the honor of being the first California vineyardist to have his vines gain recognition in the press, in 1847.[2]

Julius K. Rose finally acquired the property in 1853 and soon expanded the little vineyard to about twelve acres. Small as it was, it was still one of the largest in Sonoma County. He was primarily interested in taking advantage of the sizzling fresh grape market, but surely made wine in 1854 and 1855, some of which Haraszthy tasted and liked on his first visit.[3]

Rose had his 1856 wine made for him by an "experienced German winemaker." There were 5,000 gallons produced, with an eye, I suspect, to firming up Haraszthy's expressed interest in buying the land for wine production. An article in the *California Farmer* specifically stated that the wine was made at the "Buena Vista Ranch," which suggests that the property had picked up the name before Haraszthy's purchase. Could Col. Warren have heard from Haraszthy earlier that he intended to call the place "Buena Vista"? There is no contemporary evidence to support such an idea; thus the origins of the name are in doubt. Nevertheless, over the years it has been generally supposed and repeated by almost all writers that Haraszthy had given Buena Vista its name.[4]

Besides the twelve acres of well-tended vines on the property there wasn't much else. There was a rather rundown press house, probably built by Jacob Leese.[5] There was also a small distillery, a dwelling house, stables and two bath houses. The best description of the place was in a letter from Haraszthy to the secretary of the State Agricultural Society, dated October 31, 1858. But since he had begun buying up neighboring land on a large scale since June 1857, the description covers more than the original 560 acres.

Buena Vista included large pieces of rich valley land and pasture land running up into the foothills east of Sonoma. There was much oak timber and limestone. Haraszthy described several sulphur springs, one with a healthy temperature of 87° F. Three small creeks coursed through the vineyard and other arable land the year round. But Haraszthy had no intention of irrigating his established vines. There was also a two-acre orchard of apples and fig trees. It is often written that he found one large cellar tunneled into the hillside behind the press house. That is not true. He quickly had his Chinese workers dig one a hundred feet deep, and in the fall of 1858 another next to it.[6]

If Haraszthy had left a diary for these years from 1857-1861, we might trace the evolution of his goals for Buena Vista, but all we have is the reality of his actions. These clearly indicate the dramatic development of his intentions. One of them is sure: he wanted to develop a very large scale, diversified agricultural estate. Almost as obvious is his keen interest in viticulture and winegrowing. By 1861 he was broadcasting views and proposals that might propel California into the role of a world class wine producer.

The Haraszthy family was reunited at Buena Vista in the summer of 1857, but the seventeen-year -old Arpad was soon off to Paris to study civil engineering. On the way he took his eleven- year-old brother, Bela, to New York, to continue his education in Maryland. The two girls were sent to a private school in San José. Attila and Geza stayed home to work with their father.

Living conditions were much safer and more secure in Sonoma than they had been in San Diego, but Eleanora could not have enjoyed living in the roughly constructed frame house on the property. When we think of Buena Vista today, we immediately envision a property with two very substantial and impressive winery buildings, surrounded by a pleasantly verdant land-

An illustration of Haraszthy's neo-classical "villa" from his book Grape Culture, Wines & Wine Making.

scape, with a nice view of the Sonoma Valley. Except for the view, that scene would not have existed before 1861. There was not time nor money for such a project. But Eleanora deserved and wanted something better for herself and her family than these far-from-handsome living quarters.

Within a year Haraszthy had moved to correct this situation. At some distance from the old press house, construction began on an elegant villa. It was built in the style sometimes employed by the famed Italian architect Andrea Palladio. Visitors, and there were soon many, first entered beneath a neo-classical facade, beneath which stretched a broad porch with numerous columns. This would be the family residence, and serve as Buena Vista's office and headquarters. It was a magnet for attracting prominent visitors, and the site of many lavish entertainments and celebrations.

Haraszthy's chief interest from the outset was developing the agricultural estate. The old press house had to be expanded and new winemaking equipment installed. With an eye on his upcoming vintage, he had a storage tunnel dug into the hill behind the press house.[7] He correctly calculated, long before others in our time, that the cost of digging this hundred-foot tunnel would be much less than an equally effective above-ground building. He understood that such tunnels, which he knew so well from his homeland, would provide a consistently cool environment for his wines. This was California's first such tunnel for wine storage.

It must be remembered that from June 1857 until March 1861, Haraszthy's numerous properties, except for Buena Vista, were held in bond by Jacob Snyder. Thus, his expenditures at Buena Vista were difficult to cover because he could not sell the Crystal Springs or Las Flores places, his home in San Francisco, or his several other properties in that city. Nor could he use them as collateral for loans.

In February, even before the family moved to Sonoma, Haraszthy had Attila plant twenty-five more acres of vines near the older vineyard. The vines at Crystal Springs and the few left at Las Flores were also brought up to the ranch.

Haraszthy was intent on having a real vintage in the fall of 1857, making it necessary to upgrade the press house. Rose had made about

This picture of the Buena Vista Press House after renovation is part of a series from famed photographer Eadweard Muybridge titled A Vintage in California *(1870).*

5,000 gallons at Buena Vista in 1856; Haraszthy made about 1,000 more the next year. He also was able to produce 120 gallons of brandy from the little still he had found there. He bought a larger and more efficient one the next year. He also sold fresh grapes as well, since the return on them was still remarkably high.

Haraszthy also reported that he made sixty gallons of Tokay, named for the Tokaji, the marvelous sweet wine of northeast Hungary. He gave a detailed explanation of how he made his California Tokay in his 1858 report on grapes and wine for the State Agricultural Society.[8] Making this delicious wine depends almost totally on the complicated process the Hungarian winemakers employ. The process works, technically, with any variety. Having personally observed Tokaji production in action, I can assure the reader that Agoston Haraszthy had the process down pat, but that he made the wine from Mission grapes probably accounts for his less-than-enthusi-

69

astic praise for the result. (The inexpensive California tokay wine popular in the 1930s is in no way related to the Hungarian Tokaji.)

Haraszthy began his first full year at Buena Vista with his usual energy, but now with a broader view of his own and of Buena Vista's place in the future of Sonoma and California wine. It was an outlook that would expand exponentially in the days to come. Historian Vincent Carosso wrote that the years from 1852 to 1857 had marked "a general period of decay

Jacob Gundlach

70

and depression" in the Sonoma Valley, with the population declining almost fifty percent and land values as low as six dollars per acre. It was soon obvious that the dark economic cloud that had darkened Sonoma spirits in recent years was lightening.[9]

All had changed by the fall of 1858, and the recent viticultural growth in Los Angeles and Sonoma moved the *Alta California* to predict that in ten years wine would be the chief source of the state's wealth. The cultivation of the vine "will make any population permanent, sober and happy, and our State rich." Close to home, a Sonoma newspaper wrote, perhaps tongue in cheek, that the growth of local vineyard acreage might compel growers to depend less on the sale of fresh grapes "and turn their attention to the manufacture of wine."[10]

Haraszthy did not cause this vital change that was coming in Sonoma, but he certainly was its most important leader. Emil Dresel and Jacob Gundlach, who came to the valley intent on winemaking at the same time as Haraszthy, were better businessmen and more successful than Haraszthy in the long run. But the energetic Hungarian was an optimistic dreamer and unbending idealist. He was a natural leader. For years to come this prosperous revolution in Sonoma history was traced to 1857 and Haraszthy's arrival. But that same winegrowing fever was white hot at the same time in Los Angeles, the Santa Clara Valley, and in the Sierra foothills. It would come a few years later to Napa.

In January 1858, sixty more acres of vines went into the ground at Buena Vista. They were mostly Mission, but there was also a sizeable number of "foreign" East Coast table varieties. Haraszthy also began selling cuttings and rooted vines to his Sonoma neighbors and through an agent in San Francisco. By the end of the year there were about a hundred acres of vines on the property, well more than half the number in the entire county. At the State Fair, Buena Vista won "first premium" (first prize) for its vineyard.

When the mint indictment was dropped in March, Haraszthy's financial pressures were partly relieved. He was adding to his cash flow now by running cattle on his foothill property and by planting about 350 acres of grain. Anyone visiting Buena Vista in 1858 could also see an indication of financial savvy by viewing the work force. The acres were planted, the tunnels were dug, and in fact practically all the physical improvements were accomplished with Chinese labor, contracted for in San Francisco. These men were willing to work for less than white laborers. Haraszthy argued, as did many others, that the Chinese were easier to teach, particularly for vineyard and cellar tasks. And they were almost always there the next day, which was certainly not true of white labor in the pioneer days. The powerful California prejudice against the use of Chinese labor in the field did not become virulent until the late sixties.[11]

Agoston Haraszthy made two useful contributions in 1858 to the literature of California wine. I have mentioned his letter to the Agricultural Society describing the structures on the property. This letter and his "Report on

Photographer Eadweard Muybridge's "The Heathen Chinee. Bottle Washer"
from A Vintage in California *(1870).*

Grapes and Wine of California," published in the transactions of the Society, were of special practical interest to the potential vineyardist, available to all in the state, and were copied by newspapers throughout California.

This letter has much specific data about his vines and wine production. He made much of his "foreign" vines and claimed his collection consisted of 165 varieties, which was impossible. This claim was one of the typically wild exaggerations one sees from time to time in his statements and writings about his own operations. In this case there were far less than half that number of such "foreign" varieties in the entire state. Nevertheless, there is no doubt that he did have several, which were seen by the Society's visiting committee in 1858.

Far more important was his presentation of all costs relating to the preparation and planting of a forty-acre vineyard in February. This included such things as the cost of feeding the workers and the hay for the horses. Half the expense was for the rooted vines, $816. The total of $1,642 included the cost for the first year's cultivation.

He gives clear and succinct instructions on how to crush and press the grapes, and a description of the basic equipment needed for a small winemaking establishment. He notes that his instructions would not work for port or champagne. He suggested that a beginner should aim for a "good common wine, and quick returns." The three brief pages made an excellent primer for the beginner.[12]

The report, which had been requested by the Society, gives a brief but inaccurate history of California winegrowing in the mission period. There were sections on soil and climate, followed by technical material on vineyard preparation, training and pruning vines, and harvesting grapes. It is clear that he had brought with him much practical grape and wine information from the Old World. It is also clear that he probably knew more on that subject than any other person in California at that time. There was good advice on winemaking techniques, except for champagne. He called for the grapes to be "over-ripe, sticking to the fingers." If that advice were followed, a winemaker could count on being awakened in the night by the sound of exploding bottles.[13]

Buena Vista covered more than 6,000 acres in the sixties, most of which came from a deal Haraszthy made with Thomas O. Larkin, who had acquired a huge piece of the Rancho Huichica in 1852 from Jacob Leese. Haraszthy struck an agreement with Larkin in May 1858 to buy this more than 4,000-acre piece of land. It ran from the eastern end of the Buena Vista property up into the foothills and across into Napa County. In it was the Lovall Valley, today a beautiful Napa winegrowing area. After Larkin died in October 1858, Haraszthy closed the deal with his creditors and made Buena Vista one of the largest agricultural estates in California.[14]

In the fall of 1858 the second tunnel was dug behind the press house. It was supposed to be deeper than the first, but one searches in vain for a

The distillery at Buena Vista (A Vintage in California, Eadweard Muybridge. 1870)

record of its depth. Buena Vista crushed grapes for 12,000 gallons of wine and made 400 gallons of brandy with the new still. Sixty tons of grapes were sold on the fresh fruit market, but this was twenty-five tons fewer than had gone into wine and brandy.

Buena Vista ended the year with the second largest vineyard operation in the state, surpassed only by the German Anaheim Colony in Los Angeles County. At the State Fair Buena Vista won the prize for the best vineyard in California. But still the financial pinch was severe so long as the mint issue was not resolved.

By 1859 Haraszthy had made the experimental steps necessary to solve a big cooperage problem. He, like others, had tried to use lumber from the redwood groves that flourished in the hills around the northern coastal valleys, but the bitter resins that saturated the wood spoiled any wine that such tanks held. He discovered that scalding water from the brandy would steam the resins from the wood sufficiently to make it perfectly satisfactory for aging wine. At almost the same time in the Santa Clara Valley, Almaden's Charles Lefranc had developed a similar technique for leaching the wood used to construct the puncheons and large tanks essential to a large winery's operations. Since neither man left a record of his work on the problem, the first place award probably should be shared between these two winegrowing leaders. The idea was really a simple one and spread quickly through California's small but growing wine industry.

Redwood cooperage cut his costs, but Haraszthy still needed to boost his cash flow to pay his debts and keep his creditors at bay by good faith attempts to meet his contractual obligations. To ease the pressure he decided to take advantage of Sonoma's growing reputation as a winegrowing area, and the resulting rise in land values. He set about selling pieces of Buena Vista's undeveloped land to others—and if they wanted, he would plant their vineyards for them. They could pay for the land and service in installments.

Haraszthy made several such sales east of town that amounted to more than 300 acres. Two of the buyers' names would later be renowned: Charles Krug, soon to leave for Napa Valley, and John Swett, who four years later would become California's superintendent of public instruction and a wine

CHAS. KRUG,

Vineyards, Cellars,

AND DISTILLERY,

ST. HELENA, - - NAPA COUNTY,
CALIFORNIA.

Sells only the pure produce of
his own vineyards:

☞ Riesling, Hock, Gutedel,
Clarets, Mountain Wine, Port,
Angelica, Sweet Muscatelle,
Sherry. Brandies.

*Charles Krug moved from Sonoma to the Napa Valley in 1861 to build his winery on the
540-acre dowry he received from his marriage to Caroline Bale. By 1876, the date of this
advertisement, Krug's production had surpassed the winery's capacity of 250,000 gallons.
(Courtesy of the Unzelman Collection)*

producer. Later, continuing the program, Haraszthy ran large ads in San
Francisco newspapers, noting the "satisfaction of those gentlemen who
contracted with him. . . last year." He also gave himself a deserved pat on
the back for having "so eminently succeeded in the culture of the grape." [15]
He also added another hundred acres to the vines on his own estate.

We can see Haraszthy's leadership and his expanding vision of
Sonoma winegrowing in his work that spring in helping found the
Sonoma and Napa Horticultural Society. In commenting on this de-
velopment, Col. Warren put forth a suggestion that the master of
Buena Vista soon picked up. Such agricultural organizations at the re-

gional and state level might act as points for collecting, testing, and disseminating world class wine grape varieties. It was becoming increasingly clear that virtually all the "foreign" table varieties being lauded by nurserymen and journalists throughout the state were next to useless for making first class wines. (The exceptional usefulness of the one, the Zinfandel, had yet to be discovered.) We shall see a growing exchange of ideas on this matter over the next two years.

Buena Vista's vineyards continued to grow, but even more spectacularly did the wine grape acreage of the Sonoma Valley. Haraszthy planted about a hundred acres in the winter of 1859-1860, and by summer had about 250. The statistics for the valley acreage are less precise, but the *Alta California* thought that it was at least 500 acres. It may have reached 1,000 by the end of the year; it was well over 1,000 in 1861. In September Haraszthy was still booming his "foreign" varieties, claiming 186 in number now. But we hear little more about these table grape varieties after 1860.

The Sonoma Valley's booming winegrowing interest led Col. Warren to publish the results of a survey of the vineyardists in the *California Farmer*. He counted forty-two vineyard owners and wrote glowingly of the growing sense of community among them. Reading the owners' last names, I can count fifteen Germans, seventeen Anglo-Americans and four Hungarians. Of six I am unsure.[16]

The look of the Buena Vista estate was still less than grand, except for the elegant white villa that looked down on the winemaking facility from a nearby hillock. We also have an interesting picture, supplied by a visiting journalist in June 1860, that suggests a lighter spirit at this place than we might expect.

In the vineyards he saw about thirty Chinese workers hoeing weeds between the vines. But in one of the tunnels he saw "a gay party of gentlemen and young ladies, making themselves very merry in tasting wines." He tasted as well, and particularly liked "the Colonel's Tokay." He expanded on the scene: A fine brook comes brawling down the canyon. . . . On the bank upon a spot shaded by trees of the natural forest, Col. H. has erected a library. . . . I took a book and went to sleep on the lounge beside the rivulet, that talks to itself as it runs, just loud enough to be overheard.[17]

Haraszthy had another idea concerning matters of elegance. For several years there had been talk of making sparkling wine in California, in the style and following the traditional production methods of Champagne. The first important step was taken in Los Angeles in 1855. There the Sainsevain brothers produced 50,000 bottles of their sparkler, and in 1857 they established a San Francisco depot for the sale of their "Sparkling California." By 1862 the venture had ended in failure, despite all the good press the wine had received. Later it was generally admitted that the wine was not very good. But in 1860, for all the public knew, the Sainsevain sparklers appeared to be succeeding. General Vallejo's winemaker had produced a small batch of what everyone now was calling "champagne." And the 384,000 bottles of the Champagne, apparently the real stuff, coming through San Francisco customs in 1860, certainly proved that there was an excellent market in northern California for sparkling wine.[18]

When Agoston wrote Arpad at school in Paris, of the possibility of producing champagne at Buena Vista, his son suggested that he move to Epernay, in the Champagne country, and work as an apprentice in one of the great wine houses there. He was able to get a letter of introduction from a French official and was soon at work at the House of Venoge in the capital of the Champagne country. He learned a lot about producing bottle-fermented sparkling wine, but not quite enough, as we shall soon see.

Vallejo had been winning the lion's share of the awards won by Sonoma wines at northern California's regional and state fairs. Now in 1860, Haraszthy took the plunge, in a big way. His white and red wines won numerous awards, but only the port, tokay and muscats were identifiable. We get a more focused picture from his entries that year at the Sonoma County Fair: port, sherry, tokay, muscats and several brandies. He took first premiums for white wine and brandy. A close look at his entries indicates that he was willing to submit only his sweet wines, or wines laced with muscats. It is clear that he was getting no help from his scores of "foreign" varieties in making acceptable dry table wine.[19]

At the Sonoma Fair that year Haraszthy's more important contribution was his well-received address. He was orator of the day and received

Ho Po, pictured here, was responsible for supplying Haraszthy with his Chinese workforce, skilled laborers he brought in from Guangdong. By the '80s, 80% of California wine and vineyard work was performed by Ho Po's men.

"flattering demonstrations of applause."[20] The topic was agriculture, and he kept his remarks mostly general. But Buena Vista and winegrowing had their illustrative moments.

He advocated crop rotation and the special care of perishable crops, given the state's isolation. He also bemoaned the high cost of labor to the farmer and its current "unbearable disadvantages." He argued for the expanded use of Chinese labor, with Buena Vista as his example. It was cheaper and far more dependable than white labor. They "planted, pruned and cultivated" his vineyards; "my wine was made by them." This idea was well received by the crowd. Twenty years later he might well have been shouted off the podium, so great did the anti-Chinese fervor in California become in the seventies.

He also called for governmental and institutional aid to agriculture. Local organizations, such as he had promoted in Sonoma, should be encouraged and supported by the state. Most important, he called for the state to establish agricultural schools. On this point he expanded, with winegrowing the example. An agricultural school could collect, test and distribute appropriate vines to the varying regions of California, so that potential vineyardists would not be faced with the continuous problem of "What to plant—here!" California would have to wait for Eugene Hilgard's arrival at the University of California fourteen years later to experience the full practical force of this idea. But within a few months we shall see that Haraszthy had developed what he thought was a sure answer to this perplexing problem.

Haraszthy was still selling undeveloped pieces of his great estate. He sold seventy-four acres of neighboring land to Jacob Snyder, his old friend from mint days. He would later have a long association with Buena Vista. About the same time, Haraszthy began developing land in Lovall Valley, located in the vast property he had bought from Thomas Larkin. His idea was to sell ten-acre lots and plant 6,800 vines on each for the owner. Buena Vista would buy the grapes. This project proved successful, bringing in $24,000 to Buena Vista's coffers. Thus did the colonel's vision of a community of winegrowers in the eastern Sonoma Valley advance, though the Lovall Valley is just across the line in Napa County.[21]

Meanwhile Haraszthy was moving ahead marketing and promoting Buena Vista wines. Before the year was out he had set up a depot and retail outlet on Market Street in San Francisco. *California Farmer* claimed that Buena Vista wines were "becoming favorites with those formerly used to the best French Wine."

The 1860 vintage was not all that was hoped for, particularly after a frigid mass of arctic air descended on northern California on September 13 and ruined much of the crop. Haraszthy, however, landed on his feet, since he had just sold 150 tons of grapes on the vine to a San Francisco wine producer only days before the great frost.[22] But Haraszthy's imaginative enthusiasm was unchecked by this temporary setback. Before a few weeks of 1861 had passed he had put together a plan that might bring about the goals he had expressed in his address at the Sonoma Fair.

Chapter 4 Notes

1. Peninou, Sonoma, pp. 56-57.

2. California Star, 10/16/1847; *San Francisco Chronicle,* 1/18/1981.

3. *California Farmer,* 1/5, 6/20, 10/17/1854; 10/17/1855.

4. *California Farmer,* 11/7/1856; McGinty, Strong Wine, pp. 296-298, 539; Paul Frederickson, "One More River," 1961, pp. 242-243, unpublished manuscript, hand corrected by author, in my possession. This biography of Agoston Haraszthy is the result of careful research and contains much useful information. But it must be used with caution on subjective matters concerning Haraszthy's contributions to California wine.

5. The term "winery" did not exist before the 1880s. "Cellar" was the most common term until well into the 20th century. Such structures might be above or below ground. "Press house" was used at Buena Vista. I shall use all three terms. For an explanation of this etymological curiosity see *Wayward Tendrils Quarterly,* October 1997, p. 12; Pinney, *History,* p. 450.

6. Ag. Soc., 1858, pp. 242-243.

7. *Alta California,* 12/r/1857.

8. Ag. Society, 1858, p. 323.

9. Carosso, p. 42.

10. *Alta California,* 9/13/1858; *Sonoma Herald,* 9/11/1858.

11. Sucheng Chen, *This Bitter Soil, the Chinese in California Agriculture. . .,* Berkeley, 1986, pp. 240-249 deals specifically with Sonoma and Buena Vista; *Alta California,* 7/23/1863, 7/28/1863; McGinty, *Strong Wine,* pp. 306-307

12. Ag. Soc., 1858, pp. 242-246.

13. Op. cit., pp. 311-329.

14. Harlan Hague and David J. Langum, *Thomas O. Larkin*, Norman, Oklahoma, 1990, pp. 218-220; Frederickson, pp. 275; McGinty, *Strong Wine*, pp. 305.

15. *Alta California*, 9/9, 10/3, 10/8/1859; *San Francisco Evening Bulletin*, 11/1/1860.

16. *California Farmer*, 9/7/1860; *Alta California*, 2/1/1860.

17. *San Francisco Times*, cited by Frederickson, 291.

18. *Alta California*, 1/9/1861, 12/9/1862; *Atlantic Monthly*, May 1864, p. 603.

19. *California Farmer*, 9/3/1860; *Alta California*, 9/3/1860.

20. The *Alta* and *California Farmer* both printed the complete text of the speech. *Alta California*, 9/2/1860; *California Farmer*, 9/7/1860.

21. C. A. Menefee, *Historical and Descriptive Sketchbook. . .Sonoma. . . .*, Napa City, 1873, pp. 306-309.

22. *California Farmer*, 9/7, 9/14/1860.

Chapter

A European Adventure

1861-1862

In the few months between the fall of 1860 and spring 1861 an optimistic and far-reaching concept developed into a concrete plan that might have had profound and perhaps immediate historical results. At best we can praise the concept as prescient and foresighted. The idea, as put forward by Col. Warren in the *California Farmer,* echoed several of the points Haraszthy had made in his Sonoma address. Warren insisted that the state legislature must start giving California agriculture a strong and helping hand. The state should sponsor and maintain an agricultural college. It should provide for this young state one or more centers for the collection of agricultural plants, trees and vines, where they could be tested for their usefulness. Then the best would be made available to farmers all over the state.

In early 1861 the first steps toward reaching one portion of these goals were taken. Unfortunately we have no diaries or correspondence to give us a clear picture of how and when the plan developed. At the spring meeting of the State Agricultural Society, Agoston Haraszthy presented a resolution calling for the society to use its means to encourage the legislature to establish a viticultural commission. A commissioner should go to Europe to collect varieties of grapevines associated with Europe's finest wines. He also suggested that the legislature fund this operation. The commissioner for Europe should study and report on the successful European practices in the vineyard and cellar. Most important, he called for a state-sponsored system to secure and distribute the vines.[1]

The society passed on these suggestions to the legislature, whose lower house quickly set up a committee to study the matter. Within weeks it reported its support for the proposal, and this report was placed before the whole house. That body passed its supporting resolution, which was soon approved by the Senate. The joint resolution, however, did not authorize the actual collection of vines, nor did it provide for any kind of compensation for the commissioner, who "shall not ask for, or receive, any pay, or other compensation for the performance of the duties of (his) office." Governor John Downey immediately appointed Haraszthy as the commissioner to report on Europe. The whole series of events went off like clockwork. Unfortunately we cannot view the works of the very efficient machine.[2]

The Master of Buena Vista had several motives for setting up this trip to Europe, both altruistic and self-serving. The most obvious was a combination of both. Haraszthy was frustrated that he and almost all other California winegrowers were forced to depend on the ubiquitous Mission grape variety. He, and others before him, like Charles Kohler and Jean-Louis Vignes in Los Angeles, had learned to make passable wines from the "native" variety, but it was clear that most California commercial wines were of mediocre quality, or less. One might ask, "But what about the scores, perhaps hundreds, of 'foreign' varieties planted all over northern California?" The answer was now clear. These were almost entirely vinifera table grape varieties, brought to California from the East Coast. When the *Alta California*, a few months later, listed California's top ten varieties for wine, the Mission headed the field, followed by the Black Hamburg, Black July and seven other table grapes. These did not make high quality wines.

There had already been a few historic imports of first class wine varieties, as has been noted previously, in 1852 when San José's Antoine Delmas imported the Cabernet Sauvignon and Merlot. But such vines spread very gradually from the importer, usually a winemaker, to friends and neighbors. A good example were the Riesling vines imported by San José's Francis Stock in 1857. The vines George Belden Crane brought to the Napa Valley in 1860 came from Stock and produced the first wine that told the world

California Farmer advertisement published March 21, 1861, which gives good indication of the "foreign" varieties available in the year of Haraszthy's European excursion. Note Delmas' claim to "Bordeaux and Bourgogne" stock.

87

in the early sixties that Napa was wine country. When Stock retired a few years later, Charles Lefranc bought his Riesling vines, dug them up, and hauled them down to his winery at New Almaden.[3]

Only one East Coast variety brought to California became a wine star: the Zinfandel. But in 1861 virtually no one was aware of that variety's potential for producing fine red table wine. Victor Fauré, Vallejo's winemaker, got the idea in 1862, but it was not until 1866 that the variety began gaining its general popularity in Sonoma.[4]

On receiving his commission Haraszthy began preparing for his family's adventure in Europe. He naturally wanted Eleanora to take part, and daughter Ida, now eighteen, would certainly benefit from such an experience. Attila and Gaza would supervise activities at Buena Vista, including the 1861 vintage, since Haraszthy wanted to observe European vintage operations firsthand. He also needed to make financial arrangements, since it was clear that the legislature meant for him to act on his own. But he also believed, with his almost naïve optimism, that the state would support him when the marvelous results of the trip were known. He tried to raise money through advertisements in the press which promised specimens of European vines and fruit trees for those who would advance him their cost. He got little response to this "pig-in-a-poke."

The resolution of the mint trial in his favor on March 2 was the key to his ability to raise money to pay for the family expenses on the trip. Now he was able to secure letters of credit based on the return of clear title for all his properties outside Buena Vista. He loathed the idea of carrying bank notes when traveling from country to country, particularly in Germany, since before 1871 the people there lived in a hodge-podge of tiny principalities or city states, if they didn't reside in Prussia or Austria, and it was just such a complicated political geography that contained almost all of Germany's great wine country.

He arranged to send letters to the *Alta California* to keep Californians up to date on the progress of his mission. He also wrote to Harper & Bros., the New York publisher, suggesting that he write for them a book covering the European trip and on the future of California winegrowing. He sent along examples of his already-published material and signed a contract with the company when the family reached New York in July.

Before the family sailed from San Francisco on June 11, 1861, Agoston used the *California Farmer* to tell the people of Sonoma about his objectives. He would promote California business and agriculture, and urge European investment in the Golden State. He also intended to broadcast the future of California as a producer of world class wines,

Cover illustration, Harper's Weekly, May 4, 1861, titled "The Housetops in Charleston during the Bombardment of Sumter."

specifically drawing attention to Sonoma County as the future center of such a development. He concluded with a plea to his Sonoma neighbors: "I beg you to protect. . . my interest, my home, and my children. . . ." One wonders if this plea might reflect something that was on virtually every American's mind in June 1861.[5]

Small wonder that Californians would not be thinking about Haraszthy and his family at this time. At the moment that Haraszthy's allies in the State Legislature were putting through the resolution that would send him to Europe, the entire nation was intently following the drama developing at Fort Sumter. South Carolina had seceded from the Union; other southern states had followed. When the Stars and Stripes was pulled down at Sumter, California appeared to be in a serious political crisis. Much of the state's political leadership was friendly to the Confederate cause. Haraszthy was politically aligned with the Democratic Party faction that believed that America should let the slave states go in peace, but it was not yet clear what Agoston's personal ideas on the subject were.

On the surface it appeared that Haraszthy was oblivious to the national state of affairs. I believe he felt removed from the situation and was totally immersed in his various projects. California politics never appeared to him to be anything more than a way for a good businessman to advance in society. When he returned from Europe in December, the state of California politics had been transformed, and Haraszthy's association with prosouthern politicians would plague him for a while. Later, when attacked as disloyal, he proclaimed his loyalty to the Union, and his opposition to the rebellion and to secession. And even though he thought slavery a cruel institution, he opposed abolition because of its probable social disruption. There was no better evidence of his loyalty to the Union than the fact that such men as James Warren and other solid Unionists later attacked Haraszthy's attackers.

The Haraszthys were on the high seas bound for Southampton when Union armies were routed by rebel forces at Bull Run. After thirteen days at sea they stepped ashore and headed for Paris. Agoston visited an exiled Hungarian diplomat there and explained his mission. He also tried to interest his host in several financial schemes for making profits in California land. As Brian McGinty has written, "The wary exile resolved to keep his distance from the 'reckless' Californian."[6]

Arpad joined the family in Paris, and they were soon off to the Burgundy wine district. Agoston kept a detailed diary which later became the basis for the original portions of the Harper book to be published in the fall of 1862.[7]

The stay in Burgundy was rewarding and thoroughly entertaining. In fact, most of Haraszthy's time in France and Germany amounted to a grand touristic entertainment. His connections and letters of introduction brought him together with knowledgeable men who could explain vineyard and cellar practices in fine detail, and who knew where to find the best restaurants and the most accommodating hotels. That he was a landed winegrower counted for much, but from California as well! This combination would open almost any door.

There was more than good food, fine wine and lively, knowledgeable conversation. In Burgundy, and again in the Rhineland, Haraszthy became totally dedicated to the idea of close planting of vines, on four-foot centers, or even less. He became convinced that this approach would insure more powerful flavors than were then coming from Sonoma's vines on eight-foot centers. He also came to believe that yield per acre could be improved at the same time. Those ideas would lead to dramatic changes in his home vineyards.

That the primary purpose for this adventure was supposedly to collect vines from a large number of established varieties does not come through well in Haraszthy's narrative of the trip. He rarely discusses wine grape varieties in his book. He never describes in any detail how the final collection was put together, nor how the individual varieties were selected.[8] In Burgundy he gave much space to the Pinot noir and Gamay, but he sent only the former home. For Germany he talks only of the Riesling, and yet he reported collecting 103 varieties there, only five of which have ever been reported to grow in California vineyards, and three of these had already been introduced to the state before 1862.

The Haraszthys returned to Paris, where they spent three enjoyable days before taking the newly-built railway to Coblentz. On one Paris evening Agoston took in a musical review with dance numbers by young ladies he termed *grissettes*: "The company was not such as we would like our families to associate with."

Outside Coblentz they stayed at the health spa of Ems, which had a large gaming casino which Agoston visited only as an observer. On their first day he and Arpad joined three ladies for a tour of the countryside on tiny donkeys. The family lingered there for four days before Agoston and Arpad headed by rail for Frankfurt and the wine country.

Their first stop was at Hochheim, today one of the important wine regions of the Rheingau, although it overlooks the Main River, not the Rhine. Their first stop was by far the most important of the trip for Arpad, for it was the site of a large producer of Sekt, the German term for sparkling wine made in the traditional method of Champagne. It soon transpired that their tour guide and the director of the huge manufactory, Herman Dresel, was the brother of Buena Vista's winemaking neighbor to the south in the Carneros area, Emil Dresel. This helped make for a very cordial and informative visit. Little did they know that in a few years Emil Dresel would be the superintendent of Buena Vista. Later Agoston purchased "every kind of implement used in the manufacture of sparkling wine." Arpad would soon be putting these to use at Buena Vista.

On the train down to Frankfurt Agoston learned something about what ordinary travelers in western Europe knew of California. When others in the coach discovered he was from the Golden State, "Everybody in the car looked at me, and I became the lion of the time." They were surprised that he was still alive, so full of California crime was the European press. It depressed him that they knew so little of California's material and commercial progress. "In fact, it is only known for its gold and its crimes." He saw this situation as a serious brake on the flow of productive immigrants to the state.

When the family arrived in the Heidelberg area, Agoston was finally treated to the sight of substantial nurseries where he was able to select about a hundred different varieties for shipment. Since this was just about the number he listed for Germany in his catalogue, it would seem that that day was the only one he devoted to acquiring vines in the German lands.

From there they headed for Basel, and then on to Geneva. He again saw and commented on the close planting of vines, in Switzerland only three-and-a-half feet apart and two-and-a-half between rows. While in Geneva they met Samuel Brannan, the famous California pioneer, vacationing with his wife. The year before, Brannan had imported 20,000 vines from France to plant in his Napa vineyard near Calistoga. This was a fact that Haraszthy did not pass on to his readers.[9]

The Haraszthys spent three days admiring the mountains and lakes of Switzerland before Agoston hired a carriage to cross the Alps and to drop down into Italy, arriving in Turin September 5, less than six months after Italy had been substantially unified, with Victor Emmanuel, the new king, residing in Turin, the new capital. Just as Agoston seemed to be untouched by the Civil War raging at home, he stayed in Turin without mention of the historic events taking place there.

Then it was on to Genoa, where Agoston found a nursery and had vines from eight varieties sent on to Marseilles, one the great Nebbiolo. On his return to California Haraszthy published a catalogue of the vines he collected. Only twelve varieties were collected in Italy, but none was among those from Genoa . No place else in his narrative does Haraszthy supply a list such as this one of Italian varieties.

They steamed to Marseilles from Genoa on September 11. Agoston was not willing to give up any more time in Italy. He wanted to be in France by mid-September for the vintage in the Bordeaux region. As to missing any tips on winemaking in Italy, "God Forbid! They are as far back in this art as are the Mission Indians in California." Haraszthy was probably not aware of the fact that some of southern California's most experienced cellar-men were Indians who had previously made wines at one or another of the old missions. They arrived by train in Bordeaux on September 15.

Agoston visited several cellars and was particular in checking out wine prices in the city. He discovered to be true what he had already guessed.

The "good Bordeaux" sold in San Francisco by the case and barrel was mostly fraudulent, certainly not Bordeaux at all, since prices for such wine were much lower in San Francisco than in Bordeaux. He also toured Châteaux Margaux and Rauzan, which had been named first and second growths respectively in the famed classification of red Bordeaux wines five years earlier. That list is still in effect today and is still respected. Haraszthy acquired a copy of the classification and presented it in his narrative in great detail.

He also gave his readers a good description of the "Big Five" red wine varieties of Bordeaux, but the only plant material he mentioned acquiring in Bordeaux for California were fruit trees. Nevertheless the Cabernet Sauvignon, Merlot, Malbec and Verdot were acquired somewhere in France and appeared later in his catalogue. I find no mention of the Cabernet franc.

On September 19 the Haraszthys turned south, bound for Spain. Agoston looked up a gunsmith at Bayonne and had him load his eight-inch Colt revolver, "for I feared I might have some use for it in Spain." They had to ride in a huge twenty-passenger carriage called a diligence. Their tickets proclaimed that "the company is not responsible for any effects taken by force."

At Burgos the entire diligence, except passengers, was loaded onto an open railroad car. Six hours later they were back in the huge carriage, and finally onto another train that pulled into the Madrid station at one o'clock in the morning. Their ride had lasted fifty-six hours. They soon travelled on, just as uncomfortably, into southern Spain, with little time or interest in the country's wine culture. They passed through Granada, finally arriving in Málaga after six days in the diligence.

There Haraszthy finally found a vineyardist worth a stop. He specialized in raisins, with a 65-ton crop that year. Haraszthy gave considerable space to raisin production at this point in his narrative, since many of the vines he had collected in France were raisin varieties. He had previously promised his readers at home that he would bring back raisin and table varieties. Only six varieties of any kind from Spain were listed in his catalogue, none of them known for good wine. He did list the Mataro, a good Spanish wine variety, but he listed its source as France, where today that variety is known as the Mourvèdre.

94

They steamed away from Málaga after a four-day stay that counted as entertaining but had little to do with the purpose of their adventure. Yellow fever in Portugal cancelled Agoston's intended visit to Oporto and its celebrated wine country. They left Málaga September 29, heading north for Barcelona and thence to Marseilles. They were in Paris on October 5, their almost two weeks in Spain providing them little but discomfort and mostly poor wine.

In Paris Haraszthy found letters "which demanded my immediate return home." We know not what information from home set him on the road to Le Havre nine days after arriving in Paris. And he gave no hint as to his activities during that time in the capital. He had arranged to have all the vines he had ordered sent finally to Le Havre, directed to the American consul there, who had agreed to ship them on to California. Eleanora and Ida stayed on in Paris for a while, and Arpad returned to his Champagne internship at Épernay.

Haraszthy stopped for a while in New York City, looking in at Harper's to exchange ideas about the promised book. Perhaps as important was his visit to the New York depot for the California wines of Kohler & Frohling, run by Charles Stern, whose brother ran the company's depot in Boston. The great success of this San Francisco company, with their Los Angeles wines, encouraged Agoston. K & F had begun plans for their company in 1853, and by 1857 were well established in the northern city, with two cellars on Montgomery Street. By 1860 they had 120,000 gallons of wine in storage, and in that year began shipping wine to the East Coast. Agoston's visit to the depot at 180 Broadway probably helped settle his mind about the future importance of East Coast sales of Buena Vista wines.[10]

Haraszthy arrived in San Francisco on December 5, 1862 and headed up to Sonoma to check out Buena Vista. The vintage had been successful and his sons were getting ready to plant more vines, at Buena Vista and for a few neighbors. He had lots to do. Harper & Bros. wanted the manuscript as soon as possible, and he had to prepare his report for the legislature and the governor. Soon after his arrival it began raining all over California and continued without let until late January, producing

95

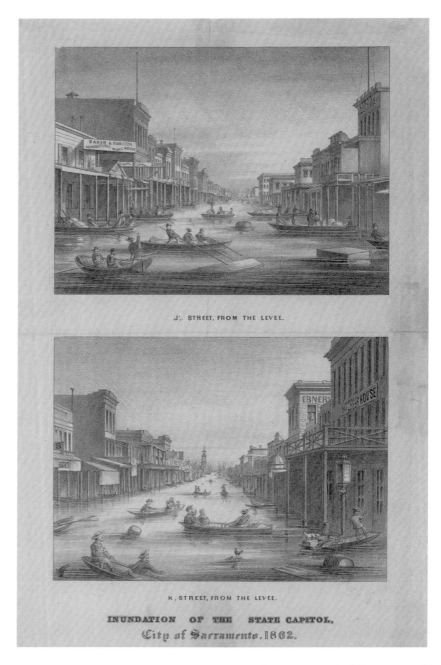

J. STREET, FROM THE LEVEE.

K. STREET, FROM THE LEVEE.

INUNDATION OF THE STATE CAPITOL,

City of Sacramento, 1862.

Views from J and K Street of a flooded State Capital.

the greatest flooding in California's recorded history. Sacramento was destroyed; the Central Valley became a gigantic lake. Sonoma was drenched but escaped serious damage. Agoston had to send his governmental reports to San Francisco, since the legislature and the rest of the state officers had been driven there out of the capital.

California had weathered a political storm and metamorphosis while Haraszthy was in Europe. The press had generally expressed concern that so many of the state's political leaders were southerners, and that the pro-southern wing of the Democratic Party controlled the legislature when fighting began in the East. The governor, John Downey, was of the same mind. But actually only seven percent of the state's population came from seceded states. This fact became clear when Republican Leland Stanford was easily elected governor in September 1861, to take office with a solid pro-Union legislature in January.

Two weeks before Haraszthy's vines arrived in San Francisco, Stanford and the new legislature were sworn in. That Democrat Haraszthy's later plea for financial support to distribute his new vines was met by strong Republican opposition in the legislature is logical. It was a factor, but does not satisfactorily explain the outcome of the situation.

In his report to the governor and the legislature Haraszthy described his huge collection and suggested a plan by which the state could establish an experimental station, similar to the nursery the Sonoma growers had earlier set up. From this state-supported nursery the vines could be distributed. He also argued that a state agricultural college should be part of California's future. And he also asked the legislature to reimburse him for the cost of the vines, perhaps $12,000.

All the right voices in the northern California press supported Agoston's proposals, particularly the importance of setting up a centralized system for distributing the vines. But Confederate successes on the battlefield, and a very tight state budget, put the legislature in no mood to appropriate money to pay for a Hungarian nobleman's family vacation in Europe.

The tone of the debate in the Senate indicates how politically weak was the winegrowing interest in the state. Why should the state support one particular segment of agriculture? If an experimental garden was to be set up for winegrowers, how about a stud farm for race horse owners?

Nevertheless, a joint committee of the legislature visited Buena Vista and reported that the new vines were doing well and recommended that Haraszthy be reimbursed for the actual cost of the vines, $8,457. But in April the State Senate overwhelmingly rejected any compensation, and did nothing to assist in distributing the vines. Biographer Brian McGinty has shown that Haraszthy's association with pro-Southern Democrats influenced the rejection of his proposals. But he argues persuasively that it was more a question of farming representatives being outvoted by mining representatives.[11]

Haraszthy had no claim on state money, and he knew it. His commission specifically forbade it. And, in the first place, it had given him no call to collect vines. He had been on his own. But he had his hopes and should not be condemned for making a good try. The tragedy was not concerned with Agoston's pocketbook; it was that this huge collection of vines eventually came to almost nothing. Later claims that it acted as the basis for the development and growth of California's great wine industry have long since been deposited in the dustbin of history.[12]

But all Haraszthy's stated goals in promoting his adventure in Europe were prescient. After Professor Eugene Hilgard's arrival at the University of California in 1875, virtually all Agoston's hopes for California agriculture were fulfilled by the scholars at Berkeley and their supporters. Without doubt, Haraszthy's ideas and his vigorous promotion of them were well remembered after his death in 1869, and played a part in the formation of Hilgard's successful policies.

What were these vines that Haraszthy brought from Europe, and what happened to them? The catalogue of his imports was published and distributed soon after his arrival.[13] The names of 487 varieties were listed, 94 of which are of wine grapes or synonyms found in Jancis Robinson's authoritative *Vines, Grapes and Wines.* Of these, thirty-one are today well-established varieties in the winegrowing world, and most of them are grown in California. They include such standards as Cabernet Sauvignon, Carignane,

Merlot, Riesling and Sauvignon blanc. It is obvious that this collection had in it varieties that would have been of great value to the state's winegrowers, if they could have been distributed. But Haraszthy's attempt to sell and distribute the vines himself was crippled from the outset by the almost uselessness of the huge list. There would be no useful reason to reproduce the entire list here, but to give the reader some sense of what it contained, I experimented with various combinations of randomly selected varieties. I decided that every twentieth variety was most satisfactory. (F, G and H indicate the countries from which Haraszthy acquired them.)

Azelante, white--F	Kadarka, dreg--H
Somaylölö, blue--H	Bogdány Dinko--H
Kovatsy, white--H	Tokay blanc--F
Chasselas de Florence--F	Majartraube,blue--G
Változo Góhér--H	Cingandi, white--G
Maton --F	Wessenbürgher-- F
Cruchenet, white--F	Morillon, blck--H
Donunrelle-- F	Muscateller, grey--G
Frankenthal, Austrian--F	Pedro Ximan-- Italy
Gránát szagos --H	Piquepoule, rose--F
Gutedel, muscat--G	Riesling, white--G
Jardovany, white--H	Sárfeher, white-- H

Had I chosen the alternate twenty, the list would have included the Furmint, Muscat Frontignan, Orleans and Semillon, all of which are of some importance today.

This giant compendium gave no idea whether a variety was normally used for wine, raisins or for the table. The typical prospective vineyardist would have seen this list as a confusing and indecipherable maze. Again, Haraszthy's catalogue looks like a "pig-in-a-poke." His vehicle to broadcast the contents of his collection was as ill-conceived as his ideas for an organized system of distributing the vines. Viticultural Commissioner Charles Wetmore later wrote that the collection "has not been preserved; the names of the varieties have been confounded in many cases." He had attempted to find winegrowers in the late 1870s who traced their vines to Haraszthy's importation, but could find only two. The imports were "lost to name," and "where they might have survived were inextricably mixed up in old vineyards."[14]

A large number of the vines surely survived at Buena Vista and acted as part of the vineyard expansion there between 1862 and 1865. But we have no idea which or how many imports were planted. None survived the phylloxera destruction at Buena Vista between 1875 and 1885.

Haraszthy was slowed not a bit by the legislature's lack of support. He had several large scale ideas and plunged ahead with them as soon as the Sonoma Valley dried out in March and April of 1862.

Chapter 5 Notes

1. Ag. Soc., 1860, 16-18; *Alta California*, 2/5/1861.

2. Frederickson, "One More River," 304-305; McGinty, *Strong Wine*, 335-340.

3. Sullivan, *Napa Wine*, pp.32-33; Sullivan, *Like Modern Edens*, pp. 25, 31.

4. Sullivan, *Zinfandel*, pp.34-38; *Alta California*, 8/14/1860, 5//6/1867; *California Farmer*, 9/27/1861.

5. *California Farmer*, 6/14/1861.

6. McGinty, *Strong Wine*, 347-348. The author had access to the diplomat's diary.

7. *Grape Culture, Wines, and Wine-Making*, New York, 1862. Portions of the book still make excellent reading, partly for their technical focus on French and German viticulture and winemaking, and partly for their remarkably precise description of travel in mid-century western Europe, when the rail system was new and unfinished. The complete 135-page record of the tour is contained in Theodore Schoenman, *Father of California Wine*, Santa Barbara, 1979.

8. A catalogue of vines collected was issued by Haraszthy after his return. See below.

9. *Alta California*, 8/30/1860; 5/28/1867.

10. *Wayward Tendrils Quarterly*, October 2011, pp.22-27; McGinty, *Strong Wine*, pp.356-357. The Kohler and Frohling early success in the 1850s makes the historian smile at much later claims by wine writers that Haraszthy was the founder of the California wine industry.

11. McGinty, *Strong Wine*, pp.364-369; *California Farmer*, 2/14, 4/3, 4/11/1862.

12. For a thorough examination of this history see Pinney, *History*, pp.279-281.

13. It can be found today in, *First Annual Report of the Board of State Viticultural Commissioners*, 2nd ed., revised, Sacramento, 1881, pp.184-188.

14. Op.cit., pp.65-67.

Chapter

Building a Historic Monument

1862-1863

Agoston's return to Buena Vista in 1862 was quite agreeable. Attila had everything in order and under control. The 1861 vintage was in successfully, and vineyard planting was gradually getting started as the new areas dried some and became workable. The Master of Buena Vista had plenty to do at his desk in the villa; he could count on his son to keep the great ranch humming.

First he had to prepare his reports to the governor and the legislature. The question of the compensation for his trip expenses and the cost of the newly imported vines would not be settled until April, when the State Senate finally put that idea to rest. But $10,000 one way or another was small potatoes compared to the plans he was developing for Buena Vista's future. The final additions to his Harper & Brothers book were quickly prepared and the manuscript was soon on its way to New York. The book was out early the next year, to good reviews from the East Coast and at home.[1]

In April Agoston was elected president of the State Agricultural Society. He took that position very seriously and made it clear that his office would work diligently on behalf of all California agriculture, with no special emphasis on winegrowing. It was when elements of the northern California press questioned his election to that office for what were taken as his "Copperhead" sympathies on the Civil War, that he made his pro-Union position clear. But he continued his association with the pro-Confederate forces in the state. In August a convention of pro-Southern

PREFACE.

I SUBMIT this work to the kind indulgence of the people of California.

The short time allowed me to complete a work of such magnitude and importance will, I hope, serve as a partial excuse for its defects.

To make a tour through a large portion of Europe—examine and collect information—select vines and trees—write the following work, with many of the extracts translated from eminent foreign authors and reports of scientific committees, I was allowed, including my journey to Europe and my return, but seven months and twenty-five days.

The task was augmented by extensive and necessary correspondence with government officials, scientific societies, and eminent writers.

During this time I have allowed myself little time for rest or recreation; and if I have succeeded in fulfilling my duty to my State and to her people, I shall feel myself amply rewarded.

I plead for a lenient judgment on the work on account of my defective English, being a native of Hungary, although a naturalized American citizen, which will, I hope, fully explain this unavoidable defect. That my readers will understand my meaning without difficulty is all that I dare hope.

The translations contained in the work were, in most cases, necessarily literal, and therefore presented difficulties not easily overcome.

With these explanations, the author presents his work to the agricultural public, sincerely hoping that future experience may not belie present promises, but that the matter upon which it treats may prove a valuable and an enduring source of wealth to the American horticulturist and farmer.   A. H.

BUENA VISTA, *Sonoma County, California.*

The Preface to Haraszthy's Grape Culture, Wines, and Wine-Making, as it appears in the original 1862 edition.

106

Democrats denounced President Lincoln for waging an unjust war against the Confederacy. Haraszthy defended his continued membership in this group, arguing that he hoped his conservative Jeffersonian principles might cool the hotheads in the Democratic Party. His forthright statements on the question were enough to quiet his critics.[2]

Haraszthy's chief worry by the summer of 1862 was financial. He was overextended and his personal debts were mounting. Buena Vista income was coming in much slower than he had hoped. He had to take care of the immediate pressures, but his mind became steadily more focused on a long term revolution in Buena Vista finances that he hoped would insure the estate's ultimate success.

To get through the coming vintage he had to raise money quickly. He was able to sell four more vineyard plots in Lovall Valley, which raised about $7,000. He also raised cash by negotiating three mortgages on portions of the Buena Vista property, starting in May 1862. One from French sources brought him about $25,000. With the mint case behind him he was also clear to sell off all his Crystal Springs property. By the first months of 1863 these sales were accomplished.[3]

His long term solution, worked out gradually with financial advisors and friends in San Francisco, was to make Buena Vista into a public institution, which, in Brian McGinty's words, "would dazzle his neighbors and attract the attention of the lovers of wine all over the world." I would add, it would be a physical presence that would attract well-heeled investors, so as to help finance an operation that would make this agricultural estate really look like a large scale, world class wine facility—perhaps the greatest in the world.

Agoston Haraszthy had set his sights on what seemed at first to be a fantastic goal, but by the end of 1863 it was accomplished. Today that great 6,000 acre estate is no more, but what he built over the next eighteen months can still be seen by visitors to California Historical Landmark No. 392. What he accomplished in 1862, still bringing in a successful vintage that year, is hard to believe. We can barely imagine, much less picture, the physical tumult in the area around the old press house during this period,

Arpad Haraszthy (Courtesy of the Unzelman Collection)

for no description of the hectic activity there has ever been discovered. All we have are the excellent, fairly contemporary descriptions of the results.

Arpad returned from France in August and was immediately installed as cellar master. Agoston also gave him free rein to begin experiments in the production of champagne. (This term was almost universally used in California in these years for sparkling wine produced by the traditional methods employed by French Champagne producers. Like burgundy and port, it is still a legal generic term for such California wines, but is rarely seen on bottles of California wine today.) That story is worth special notice later in this chapter.

Before Arpad arrived the three cellars had been finished, dug deep into the hill behind the old press house. By summer, work had already begun to transform the ugly frame structure into the finest winery in California. I shall call it always the "press house," since "winery" was a word not coined for another twenty years. And the tunnels were always referred to as "cellars."

Arpad had to bring in the 30,000 gallon 1862 vintage while the new stone structure was being given the finishing touches by the hard-working and efficient Chinese workmen.[4] Before the vintage, new equipment and cooperage were installed in the cellars and new press house, and there was a new and spacious machine shop built next door. The old distillery was also rebuilt and re-equipped.

Illustration of Buena Vista's grand winemaking operation from the 1864 Harper's Magazine *article* Wine-Making in California.

The great stone press house, and the even larger winery building start-ed just to the north in 1864, would be impressive physical expressions of the vastness of the Buena Vista wine estate. They were meant to produce fine wine and to impress prospective investors. There was nothing like these structures elsewhere in California.[5]

The press house with its three cellars was finished in the spring of 1863. By that time Haraszthy had taken all the preliminary steps to change Buena Vista's financial structure, a process I shall examine in the next chap-ter. When the new look was ready for visitors from the press and for pro-spective investors, the invitations went out.

The *Alta California* printed two long pieces on visits before and during the 1863 vintage. In the first of these,[6] the paper's visiting group of jour-nalists was personally guided on a horseback tour "over the hills and valleys of the plantation." The idea was to impress on them the size of the estate. They covered much of the 6,000 acres, but concentrated on Lovall Valley. There, much planting was scheduled to take place in the winter of 1863-64. They found Attila leading a crew of thirty Chinese workmen clearing land for future vineyards. The visitors were told that 500 more acres were to be planted next winter, including vines of the "celebrated Pino," since the soil there "most resembles the soil on which the Chambertin wine is raised." We never hear more in future years about those 500 acres or of the Pinot noir at Buena Vista.

In the afternoon they visited the almost-finished press house, "an im-posing building, whether seen at a distance or close by," built of massive blocks of sandstone rock taken from the excavations of the new cellars. At that time three additional cellars were being dug just to the north of the new structure. These were to be three stories, with walls up to two feet thick, features meant to help maintain moderate temperatures during the often sizzling September and October months of the California vintage.

A road had been built behind the press house which led up the hill at the rear, to give access to wagons bringing grapes up the road. The visitors were greeted at the great door by Arpad, who now led the tour. At the mo-ment, Chinese workers were bottling champagne for its second fermentation. There were grape crushers and a huge wine press, ready for the coming vintage. Eleven trap-doors in the floor would soon drop crushed grapes into the eleven 3,800 gallon fermenting tanks on the floor below.

Then they inspected the cellars that ran deep into the hill. In one they found rows of used 140- gallon gin barrels used for holding finished wine. On every second barrel a lighted candle had been placed to illuminate their way. Here they also tasted some of the older wines and brandies, dating back to the original 1857 vintage. Before the newsmen left, the growth in future production was emphasized by the three new cellars being excavated. Soon, they were told, another huge wine house would be constructed, even larger than the new structure.

About the same time J. Q. A. Warren, son of the *California Farmer* publisher, paid a visit to Sonoma and wrote an article on the growth of the county's winegrowing industry since 1857. His article centered on the activities at Buena Vista. There, east of town, one had an excellent view of a Valley, "spreading out to the bay, dotted here and there with ntinuous series of vineyards, of all sizes and shapes, and in the shing condition."[7]

was again the tour director, and Warren was able to see many things reported in the *Alta California.* The reporter's description tage activities, well before the grapes had started to come in, obviously were based on Arpad's words concerning the previous year. But in several ways they differed from those of the second *Alta* correspondent when the harvest had begun.

Warren also gave a detailed description of the great wine press, which had been built in San Francisco at the Donohue Foundry. Arpad stated that the pressure, coming from below, was so great that the pomace left resembled a giant "block of black wood, from which not even a drop of juice can be extracted."

The large tanks had been constructed from local redwood, this at the same time the *Alta* in another article was wondering whether redwood had any future for storing wine. In the cellars Warren was also impressed by Haraszthy's wines and brandies. He thought the 1857 white wine from the

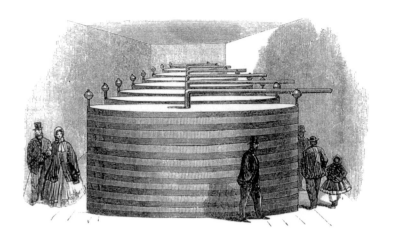

barrel was splendid, "resembling a three year old Chablis." The 1862 white had a bouquet of Sauternes. One cannot help wondering how the Haraszthys were getting these characteristics from the almost tasteless, odorless Mission grape. I suspect the whites had been brightened with a healthy dash of Muscat Frontignan or Malvasia bianca.[8]

Warren did not visit the Buena Vista vineyards that day because of the heavy rain, but he continued his report on Sonoma winegrowing by later visits to several other new wineries, which I shall report on in Chapter 8.

Four months later the *Alta* printed the letter of an unnamed visitor.[9] By then Buena Vista had gone through the process of incorporation, which I shall soon explain. The author was not a casual Sonoma observer who happened to drop in to see how things worked on the estate. He obviously knew a lot about winemaking; there were no hints in the letter that it had been penned anonymously by a Haraszthy. The central point in the writer's 3,500-word epistle was that large scale winegrowing and wine production were the key to the future of the state's wine industry.

The writer covered much of the same ground as in the earlier *Alta* article, but now the vintage had begun, and we get an eye-witness report on how the new press house and its cellars worked. There was also a much more detailed analysis of Buena Vista's soils and natural flora. The low hills of the estate were covered with manzanita, madroña, laurel, buckeye, alder, wild ginger, ceanothus, wild strawberries, wild raspberries and rambling, aromatic yerba buena.

Operations at the press house were not quite the same as previously described. It now had three operating stories, the building covering more than 8,000 square feet. The third story was now used to separate grapes from leaves and stems. The harvested grapes were hauled up from the wagons outside the second story by a steam engine. There they were crushed, falling into the press below, or directly to the first floor into the fermenting tanks, depending on whether red or white wine was the final goal.

For red wines the fermenting tanks each had a movable false top which held down the cap of grapes below the surface of the fermenting must. This increased the color extraction and avoided the necessity of regularly pushing down the constantly rising cap during fermentation. This also lessened the possibility of developing ethyl acetate (vinegar) in the cap. The author added that "Every person who understands wine-making understands the use of the false top, which ought to be employed more frequently than it is." Today such a process is called "submerged-cap fermentation." It was mentioned by Maynard Amerine as promising in 1970, with a description that closely resembles Haraszthy's process in 1863.[10]

Buena Vista got national coverage from a long article in *Harper's Magazine*, probably written right after the 1863 vintage, but published six months later.[11] The authorship, and parts of the article itself, present something

Harpers *Illustrations of Buena Vista's fermentation tanks (facing page) and champagne cellars. The illustrator took creative license with the size and scope of the latter, which seem to recede ad infinitum.*

of a mystery. "A. Haraszthy" was listed as author. But which one? Internal evidence points to Arpad, but there are parts probably written by his father. It is a long article with excellent illustrations of the beautiful villa, vines variously trained, the great fermenting tanks, the cellared champagne bottles and, of course, the new press house, in a fully expressed setting, although the hills behind the building are a bit too majestic. To the left the three new cellars are clearly visible, where the next great wine structure would be built in 1864.

There is a short and moderately accurate history of the place, with a detailed description of its natural beauty, but in the history we can already see examples of Arpad's tendency to fiddle about with events of the past. Buena Vista's first vintage was given as 1856; there were only two vineyards in Sonoma when his father moved there; since 1862 Buena Vista possessed "all known valuable varieties of grape-vines in the civilized world." In years to come, after Arpad left Buena Vista, his supposed memories of the place did much to muddy its early history. In fact, Arpad was there just a little more than a year, for at the end of 1863 he was fired from his posts of cellar master and champagne maker, another story yet to come.

The article takes the reader through all the vineyard and cellar operations: planting and training vines, pruning, cultivation and harvest. The grapes' journey from the picking box to the crusher, press and fermenter is traced in far more detail than in the *Alta's* articles. The processes for making white and red wines are treated separately. There is also a section on fining wine with isinglass for white wine and with fresh egg whites for the reds.[12]

We also see inside the huge machine shop next to the press house, where a great steam engine was operated. Here the green redwood staves were steam cleaned for all the major wine containers. The history of Agoston's experiments with this process are also given in good detail.

In the machine house the steam for the new distillery also was generated, about 300 feet away. Agoston despised the use of fire to heat the distilling material. The building had three redwood tanks, each holding 2,300 gallons. The entire distillery operation was explained in somewhat confusing detail, but the hot gaseous product eventually entered a large

114

copper globe surrounded by cool water, and from there the almost pure wine spirit was further cooled in a 220-foot copper "worm." At the end an "Alcohometer" measured the alcoholic strength of the final product. The whole operation could produce about a thousand gallons of "Cognac" in twenty-four hours.

The article also stresses the cleanliness of the numerous containers and of the facility itself. No oil lamps were used any place, only sperm oil candles. There were also sections on the Buena Vista vinegar factory, which held 6,000 gallons of cooperage, and on its raisin-making operations. The entire article ends abruptly on that subject, noting that raisin grapevines had been imported from Málaga and Smyrna. "In a couple more years there will be forty or fifty tons produced."

The most detailed portion of the *Harper's* article dealt with the production of sparkling wine. Since 1856 there had been numerous attempts in California to produce a sparkler in the style of Champagne, using the traditional methods of that region.[13] In both northern and southern California, winemakers tried to bring out a product that could compete in price and approach in quality the real thing that was yearly flooding the California market in tens of thousands of twelve-bottle baskets. For years it was a seemingly unattainable mirage, a *fata morgana,* in the words of Thomas Pinney. It all started in Los Angeles with the "Sparkling California" of the Sainsevain Brothers, whose operation went under in the early sixties.

In northern California several small scale producers, including Mariano Vallejo, had made worthy, but unprofitable attempts. Agoston had obviously caught the champagne bug by sending Arpad to Epernay in 1860 to discover the mysteries of true Champagne production. When the young man returned to Sonoma, he took over the direction of the cellars and the new press house and made a modest cuvée of champagne, perhaps ten dozen bottles. They apparently sparkled properly and were tasty enough that Agoston entered bottles at the State Fair in 1863. They won Arpad an honorary diploma.[14]

Agoston was encouraged and directed Arpad to prepare between 700 and 800 dozen sparklers. This might be a product that could give Buena

Vista's cash flow a quick bounce. Sparkling wines don't need years of cellaring before they are ready for market.

Arpad and Attila married two of Vallejo's daughters in a dual ceremony during the summer of 1863. It was a great event celebrated with champagne from Arpad's first cuvée, from the 1861 vintage. This took place at the moment Arpad was preparing his huge cuvée from the 1862 vintage. Like his marriage to Jovita in later years, this cuvée was a disaster. Apparently not one of the almost 10,000 bottles of champagne had sparkled. They all had to be emptied, their contents fated for the distillery. All kinds of excuses were provided: It was the over-ripe Mission grapes, or the temperature of the cellars, or not enough rock candy, or even none at all. In later years, and before, there had always been non-sparklers at Buena Vista. But in 1863, all of them?

Agoston was forgiving, but Buena Vista was no longer his to rule by fiat. It was now a corporation, and the board of directors made sure that 1863 marked Arpad's last champagne cuvée and his last vintage as cellar master at Buena Vista. Thus one can see the irony in Arpad's detailed descriptions of successful champagne making at Buena Vista in the 1864 *Harper's* article, penned by "A. Haraszthy" before his sacking.

The champagne disaster also hit Agoston in the pocketbook. The board of directors had previously wondered at the large size of the first commercial cuvée. It was a sizable investment for a first time venture. Agoston's typical enthusiastic optimism won the day; now he felt obligated to cover the losses entailed in the fiasco. The board did not hesitate accepting his injection of $5,500 into the company coffers. On top of this, the projected profits were also gone. The board then hired Pierre de Banne, champagne master for the failed Sainsevain operation in Los Angeles. There were more lively events to come at Buena Vista related to this sometimes sparkling product.

Doubly ironic in this story was the series of events that led to the first truly successful sparkler in California. Isador Landsberger ran a profitable wine and liquor business in San Francisco in the 1850s. Eventually he invested money in Buena Vista, and for a while sat on the board of directors.

Advertisement for Eclipse champagne

He too had a special interest in producing a California champagne, believing correctly that the chief cause of the many failures was related to the use of the ubiquitous Mission grape. He was also convinced that Arpad, with the right varieties of white wine grape, had the knowledge and skill to produce a winner.

They combined forces in 1866, and were soon partners. Within two years they were selling a very good sparkler made in the traditional method of Champagne. It was California's first success in this field, soon to be given the brand name Eclipse. Not surprisingly, the juice from the Mission grape did not dominate their cuvée. The 1868 wine was made from Riesling, Gutedel, Palomino, Mission and Muscat Frontignan. Later white Zinfandel was the dominant variety, with Colombard, Verdelho, Folle blanche and Meunier. There was also a 12% dose of Malvasia bianca, which, like the Frontignan, gave a tasty hint of muscat to the resulting wine.[15]

117

Before we leave the story of the remarkable transformation of Buena Vista in its seventh year, I want to sweep readers through 120 years of time, so that when they visit Buena Vista today they can understand what they are seeing. Between 1943, when the winery's modern history began, and 1982, the two great wine buildings were spruced up to make wine and receive visitors. In 1981 the owners hired architect Reiner Keller, primarily to save the press house. The old winery next door was in much better shape.

For the press house an entire heavy timber structure was designed and built within the old stone building. It was internally braced and bolted to the two-foot-thick stone walls. The grouting between the stones of the old walls was badly decomposed. Thus, the walls were re-grouted to insure the physical integrity of the building. Balconies on three sides of the building's interior were reconstructed, and another added to the fourth side. A heavy concrete retaining wall was constructed behind the press house to protect it from hillside movement.

Two old tunnels were reconstructed with concrete and lined with stone and bricks to recreate the original appearance. The roof was removed and rebuilt with shingles that resembled the heavy old slate roof. Inside, a large portion of the old stonework remained uncovered. Additions were made to afford visitors both a sense of history and a comfortable place to taste wine.

Keller's achievement won him the 1982 Centennial Honor Award for Architectural Excellence from the American Institute of Architects. Opening ceremonies took place May 15, 1982.[16]

Although there are places in California today where one can point to an old wall once part of a building where wine was made before 1863, and thus claim an earlier founding date for a winery, these are not old wineries. Today, California's oldest working winery operation is the 1863 press house and the neighboring 1864 winery, together a great historic monument.

Chapter 6 Notes

1. *Alta California*, 2/2/1863.
2. Charles L. Sullivan, "A Man Named Agoston Haraszthy," *Vintage Magazine*, April 1980, pp. 15-16.
3. Frederickson, "One More River," pp. 361, 383-384; McGinty, *Strong Wine*, pp. 292, 392-393.
4. Richard Steven Street, *Beasts of the Field*, Stanford, 2004, pp. 249-256. The author of this history of California farm workers gives a detailed description of the contributions of Chinese workers at Buena Vista. He has not consulted standard histories of California wine for his observations on Buena Vista history in general.
5. Several years ago, in a conversation about the winery buildings of the world with historian Thomas Pinney, I wondered where in the world was the finest collection of truly great old winery buildings. We enjoyed our exploration. The great châteaux of Bordeaux and the castles on the Rhine did not make the cut, since these were really magnificent residences. Even though many of them had good-sized cellars underneath, they were not wineries. We looked closely at the viticultural landscape of South Africa's historic Cape Colony, but it was clear that the elegant edifices there were mostly manor houses. Obviously we settled on northern California, where we decided the largest concentration of wineries that could be considered historic monuments were located. In Santa Clara County there was Paul Masson, Stanford and the great Wehner Winery in Evergreen. Livermore had Olivina. But Napa and Sonoma Counties overwhelmingly had the

lion's share. The gold medal had to go to Napa for Inglenook, Greystone, Trefethen, Far Niente and Chateau Montelena and a few other possible nominees, all five the creations of Hamden W. McIntyre, who also designed the Stanford Winery in Palo Alto. Sonoma obviously scores with Korbel, Buena Vista, Simi and perhaps Fountaingrove. And, of course, a special award has to go to Buena Vista, California's first great winery, built more than twenty years before any of the other vinous masterpieces mentioned above.

6. *Alta California,* 7/28/1863.

7. *California Wine, Wood and Stock Journal,* May 1863, pp. 78-79.

8. Napa's Jacob Schram was the first to spell out this technique, in which he raised the flavor of lowly Palomino whites with a dose of muscat. These wines he termed "verbessert," or improved. Sullivan, *Napa Wine,* pp. 40-41.

9. *Alta California,* 9/21/1863.

10. M.A. Amerine and M.A. Joslyn, *Table Wines. . . ,* Berkeley 1970, p. 603. Recently an article appeared booming the invention of a submerged-cap fermenting tank in 2001. *Wines & Vines,* January, 2005, pp. 28-32.

11. "Wine-Making in California," *Harper's New Monthly Magazine,* June 1864, pp. 22-30.

12. Isinglass is a transparent form of gelatin derived from the air bladders of certain fishes. Amerine, op. cit., p. 539, considers this the best fining agent for white wines.

13. There had also been successful production of carbonated wine, years later referred to as the "soda pop" technique. Usually marble dust was introduced to an acid solution in a closed container, producing carbon dioxide under pressure, which was then injected into the wine. Inexpensive and fairly popular, such wines were generally looked upon with contempt by lovers of Champagne.

14. Peninou, *Sonoma,* p. 62; McGinty, *Strong Wine,* pp. 400-401; Frederickson, "One More River," p. 383.

15. *San Francisco Bulletin,* 11/9/1867; *Alta California,* 3/19/1869,

12/16/1877; Ag. Soc., 1866/67, p. 203; 1868/69, pp.105, 384-395; Sullivan, *Companion,* pp. 98, 185; Brian McGinty, *A Toast to Eclipse,* Norman, Oklahoma, 2012; *Wine World,* September 1974, pp. 41-46.

16. Reiner Keller press release, 5/10/1982; "Buena Vista News," 5/17/1982.

Chapter

B. V. V. S.

1863

The financial pressure on Agoston Haraszthy in 1862 moved him to seek advice from friends in the San Francisco business world. By the end of the year he had determined that incorporation of the estate was the best way to ensure its future and to settle the gathering claims on his personal fortune. But there were legal hurdles to overcome.

In the early fifties the flood of newcomers to the state encountered a frustrating land situation. The huge Spanish and Mexican land grants had placed much of the state's best agricultural land in the hands of the few. A pro-settler point of view, often termed "squatter mentality" by landholders, colored much of the early state legislation. An example was a law making it illegal for enterprises of a predominantly agricultural character to incorporate. In 1858 such operations were legalized, but limited to 1,440 acres of agricultural land.

Nevertheless, Agoston's lawyers put together articles of incorporation for what would soon be named the Buena Vista Vinicultural Society (BVVS). The document was signed March 27, 1863 by Haraszthy and eight other San Francisco businessmen, most of whom were well-to-do members of the city's influential French community. Two were not: one the aforementioned Isador Landsberger, and the other Herman Michels, who was elected president of the board of trustees.

The source of the money to get the new corporation off the ground was never openly disclosed, and, of course, no large sums were needed until

Bank of California advertisement from The Salt Lake Daily Telegraph, *May, 1869*

it became possible for the corporation to buy Buena Vista from Agoston and his wife. Many writers on this subject have supposed that the bulk of the first funds came from William C. Ralston, who was on his way to being one of the most important financiers in California. Ralston's most famous creation was the Bank of California, which opened its doors in 1864. That Herman Michels was one of the original trustees of this powerful institution certainly supports the idea that Ralston was an active influence in BVVS affairs from the very beginning.[1]

Now it was necessary to make it legal for the new corporation to purchase Buena Vista and its 6,000 acres of potential agricultural land. For that to happen, the 1858 law had to be changed. In 1863 the state legislature, under Republican control, was far from anti-business. To be a Republican did not simply mean that a man was pro-Union. Many were former Whigs, like President Abraham Lincoln, and were quite comfortable helping to promote the growth of corporate enterprise.

124

It took but twenty days from the signing of the articles of incorporation for both houses of the state legislature to act. The next day Republican governor Leland Stanford signed into law a bill which now made it legal for a corporation to own and cultivate "any number of acres of land, not exceeding. . . six thousand." It is obvious that this was a well-orchestrated and well-oiled series of events that rushed the bill through the legislature. The magical 6,000- acre limit makes it quite clear whom the law was intended to benefit. It also suggests who probably was conducting the orchestra.[2]

A week after Stanford signed the bill into law, Agoston and his wife deeded the entire Buena Vista estate to the new corporation. To the Haraszthys' great advantage, part of the conveyance to the corporation included the mortgage obligations executed by Haraszthy during the recent months.

The BVVS capital stock was set at 6,000 shares, each originally valued at $100. The company paid Agoston and Eleanora 2,600 shares for the Buena Vista property. In future months Agoston was able to raise cash for his own purposes by pledging portions of these shares as collateral for more personal loans.

Seen in retrospect, the corporation's prospectus, intended to attract future investors, was an almost laughable exaggeration of its future prospects. But seen in the light of the frenzied spirit of madcap investment that characterized San Francisco's business community in the years before everything came crashing down in 1873, few doubted the numbers projected by the BVVS given below.

The company's assets were obvious: The huge estate covered 6,000 acres. Already there were more than 400 acres in vines, the largest such vineyard holding in the world. Great steps had been taken since the previous year to make the wine and brandy production facility the greatest and most modern in the world, as symbolized by the new and marvelously equipped press house. The company's projection held that in ten years the vineyards would cover 3,000 acres. By 1873 the annual wine crop would be more than two million gallons, with 100,000 gallons of brandy. The *Alta California* published the ten year prognostications in detail, for each year: receipts, expenditures, profits. The *Alta* was soon running ads for BVVS shares.[3]

Placard which, judging by board members, dates to the early 1870s.

...TURAL SOCIETY'S ...D VAULTS ...OUNTY. California.
...R & CO. ...ISCO. ...TS.

J. G. KLUMPKE.
ROBᵗ C. JOHNSON.
J. C. MEUSSDORFFER.
G. DUSSOL.
B. E. AUGER.

BOARD ∞ TRUSTEES

A complete inventory of all Buena Vista property involved in the transfer of ownership was made public when the BVVS trustees made their first annual report covering activities of 1863. A valuation was presented for each entry. What follows is a very partial list. I have excluded many common items such as twine, tools and lumber.[4] The entire value of the inventoried items was given as $583,273.

BUILDINGS

1 Stone press house

1 Granary

6 Large stone cellars (tunnels)

1 Fruit House

1 Adobe barns

9 Divers outhouses

3 Stables

2 Dwelling houses

VINES AND FRUIT TREES

400 acres of vines on 485 acres of land

90,000 vines in nursery

8,359 fruit trees

6,000 acres of land variously valued, including vineyards and orchards

EQUIPMENT

1 Large Press

3 Wagons

1 small press and crusher

2 circular saws

1 grist mill

1 Turning lathe

1 Distillery, complete

1 Steam chest

1 Steam engine

6 Large tubs

1 hydraulic ram

2 copper syphons

1 Large force pump

29 champagne stands, each of 3,500 capacity

3 corking machines

1 Platform scale

2 Wire makers

1 large bell

1 cork softener

Stock, etc.

22 Horses

3,924 lbs. rock candy

2 Cows

18 Casks of corks

120 tons of hay

14,000 separate corks

20,000 lbs. wheat

Product Containers

12x3000 gal. vats

16 Hungarian casks

21x4000 gal. vats

40 Bordeaux casks

194x125 gal. casks6x500 gal. casks

10 Demijons

15x20 gal. barrels

1163 bottles

PRODUCTS ON HAND

23,736 gal. white wine

16,000 gal. red wine

1500 gal. California burgundy

400 gal. white wine from foreign grapes (muscats)

804 gal. brandy

129

There was never specific mention made as to whether the Haraszthy villa was included in the transfer. That the two dwelling houses together were valued at only $7,000 suggests that the beautiful Palladian mansion may not have been included in the transfer. A few years later it was destroyed by fire.

We have already seen the highlights of the 1863 season, particularly the heavy building program and the champagne disaster. All observers applauded the day-to-day management of the estate by sons Attila and Bela. In April Geza headed east and received a captain's commission in a New York cavalry regiment. He saw lots of action in Louisiana, but in May 1864 he was captured and sent to a Texas POW prison. After peace he returned to his outfit, a major. He was back in Sonoma in June 1866.

The 1863 vintage at Buena Vista was short of what had been hoped, about 65,000 gallons of wine. All Sonoma had felt the effects of the dry, hot weather that year. The BVVS total was about a quarter of the Sonoma County total. There was also a lot of brandy made in the new distillery, and not all from grapes—there was also peach brandy and applejack. Also important was the large amount of fruit drying, particularly raisins. And, as usual, a good part of the crop made it into the fresh grape market, but here the returns were far below average due to low grape prices.[5]

Part of the financial problem triggered by the short crop was a slump in the market for California wines, but southern California was hurt far more than the north coast counties. This situation in the Southland helps explain the slump in fresh grape prices in Sonoma, as southern vineyardists were forced to dump their oversupply of grapes by shipping them north, and selling dirt cheap.

More hurt was done by the federal war tax on wine and brandy. The latter, at two dollars per gallon, was a serious problem, since any drop in the demand for wine could always be met, partially at least, by upping the production of brandy from the lower quality wines. There was also the threat that federal gaugers might impose the tax on brandy used to fortify sweet wines, but this did not happen until much later.

130

In December Haraszthy, with the support of many wine industry leaders, took the California tax grievance to Washington, D.C., surely the West Coast's first wine lobbyist at the national capitol. He made the trip again in 1864, both visits coming years before the transcontinental railroad was finished in 1869. It is not clear whether he traveled cross country or by sea, to Panama and then up to the East Coast. That had been his route in 1861.

Haraszthy appears to have persuaded the Congress to modify tariff regulations so that imported wine was taxed not on its value, usually understated, but by volume. This move made it easier for California producers to compete with foreign imports, particularly on the East Coast. Since 1861 the amount of California wine in that market had steadily risen, and the BVVS public statements always pointed to the growing importance of the company's East Coast sales. The brandy tax did not come down until the fighting ended in 1865. For the Golden State's brandy producers the new level of twenty-five cents per gallon was a pleasant relief.[6]

In 1863 the Sonoma County Fair was celebrated early in the year, during the vintage. The speakers' emphasis on wine and the lively wine competition were clear indications of the exponential rise of winegrowing interest in the county since 1857. The *Alta California* gave a long and detailed account of the wine competition, which was dominated by BVVS and Glen Ellen's Joseph Williams. One premium was granted to the best entry in each division. Williams won seven premiums, BVVS four. No one else won more than one. The BVVS awards were for the 1857 and 1861 white wines, the 1857 red, and Arpad's "Sparkling Sonoma" from the 1861 cuvée. This award came before it was discovered that the huge 1862 cuvée had not sparkled. BVVS also won an award for the best brandy, and a special award for its peach brandy.

Wine competitions in the early days at regional and state fairs in California often produced dubious outcomes. The awards often tended to falsely magnify the quality of certain producers' wines, partly because fair officials often did not know how to run wine competitions. The most common flaw was the tendency to allow judges to know the names of the producers before submitting their results. Another unhappy but not

Published by W. O. Hoeker, Sonoma, Cal.—Expositor Print.

RHINE FARM, Sonoma, Cal., the Home and Vineyard of Carl Dresel.
This is the home of the man who planted the vineyard that raised the grapes that made the wine that took the Grand Prize at the St. Louis Exposition in 1904, and the Gold Medal at Portland in 1905.

Rhinefarm postcard dated 1906. (Courtesy of the Unzelman Collection)

very common tendency was for producers to submit specially prepared lots which were not taken from the general supply of a certain wine. There is even evidence that on occasion a producer would submit a noted European wine disguised under his own label. But the detailed record of this particular Sonoma competition is very convincing: The tastings were blind; judges were not allowed to communicate before submitting their results; and according to the *Alta* reporter, who was one of the three judges, the votes for the winners were unanimous in almost every case. Emil Dresel's partner, Jacob Gundlach, was another judge. That their soon-to-be-famous Rhine Farm won no award also speaks well of the judges' work.[7]

Haraszthy made his report for 1863 to the BVVS board of trustees early the next year. He had good reason to be positive about the estate and its operations, less so concerning financial matters. More vines had been planted in the winter. The physical plant was new and successfully operational, perhaps the finest in the world. A new stone wine building would soon be built in front of the newly-dug cellars. He predicted correctly that 1864 would see a steep drop in capital expenses. He believed that profits would soon appear on the company's balance sheets. He closed on an optimistic note: the condition of the BVVS "is in every respect in an admirable condition."

132

President Michels' report was not so cheerful, but just as optimistic. They had hoped to raise cash by selling many more shares to the public, but in this hope they "were disappointed and as a consequence many designs set forth in the prospectus could not be carried out." Receipts from wine and brandy sales were less than expected, but non-construction expenses were also less than expected. Technically there was a profit on the books when production costs were weighed against cash flow. The drought and the general economy made 1863 a year of "financial difficulty and confusion," but "the future can have little danger for us."

Michels then went on to count BVVS's many advantages. The sale of new shares in the corporation was inching up. He gave a convincing picture and in no way distorted or otherwise misrepresented the prospects for 1864, except for one omission. His booming optimism concerning the future of champagne production did not mention the recent disaster. His contention that such production "will pay a handsome profit and give a return within a year," suggests that he knew nothing about how champagne was produced, or that he believed that M. de Banne, the new champagne master, was a magician.

Before we shift gears and look closely at the fascinating history of Sonoma wines in the sixties and seventies, I don't think it unfair to glance ahead at a snapshot of a few confusing words from the BVVS president's next annual report: "heavy expenses," "serious financial difficulties," "increase in debts," and then a glimpse into the future, "a most brilliant success after a short time. . . ." [8]

Chapter 7 Notes

1. David Lavender, *Nothing Seemed Impossible*, Palo Alto, 1975. Ralston's financial empire collapsed in 1875 shortly after the opening of his Palace Hotel in San Francisco. The main cause was the national depression heralded by the so-called Panic of 1873.

2. McGinty, *Strong Wine*, pp.395-397.

3. *Alta California*, 7/28/1863, 9/21/1863.

4. *Reports of the Board of Trustees. . . of the Buena Vista Vinicultural Society*, San Francisco, June 24, 1864, pp.13-15. Hereinafter, *Reports.*

5. *Sonoma Democrat*, 1/16/1864; *Alta California*, 12/24/1863.

6. Peninou, *Sonoma*, p.66.

7. *Alta California*, 9/19 and 9/20/1863.

8. *Reports*, 1864, pp.4-9; 1865, p.3.

Chapter

Sonoma Leafs Out

1855 - 1875

When the State Assessor reported, or better guessed, in 1855 that Sonoma County only had about thirty acres of grapevines, his number was probably low, but not by much. Three years later the visiting committee of the State Agricultural Society didn't find much in Sonoma County to visit, at least so far as winegrowing was concerned. They looked in at Buena Vista, and later found no one at home at General Vallejo's place. This group's report reflects their view that there was much more action, agriculturally speaking, in the East Bay, in Santa Clara County, and in the Sacramento area. And yet twenty years after the Assessor's report, Sonoma County had become the state leader in wine production, finally edging out Los Angeles.

Today, Sonoma and neighboring Napa County dominate the Treasury Department's official North Coast Viticultural Area, almost universally recognized as the greatest fine wine producer in the Western Hemisphere. Overall, Sonoma County's geography is much different than that of its famous neighbor. The Napa wine country is really one large valley, flanked by low but picturesque hills dotted with numerous small winegrowing areas. Similarly, the Sonoma Valley, where this story begins, has many of the same physical characteristics as the Napa Valley. It opens out to the great bay to the south and gradually narrows in a northwesterly direction toward the city of Santa Rosa. Its upper portion, above the old town of Sonoma, is also referred to as the Valley of the Moon, a name popularized by Jack

London. The town looks out toward the bay and the rather flat Carneros area, today a noteworthy viticultural area in its own right. To the east of town are Buena Vista and its neighbors. Up the valley, on the road to Santa Rosa, are the villages of Glen Ellen and Kenwood.

What makes the county so much different than Napa can be seen in diverse areas to the north and west. Beyond the hills to the west of Sonoma Valley is a large region once commonly referred to as the Santa Rosa Valley. Today the names of several towns act as the geographical labels for the area's important winegrowing areas, notably Windsor, Healdsburg, Forestville and Occidental. To the west of Healdsburg is the famed Dry Creek Valley. Another winegrowing area today is the Alexander Valley north of Healdsburg. It stretches out to the east of the Russian River and to the Napa County line. Geyserville, and Cloverdale to the north are the main towns. Between them is Asti, on which we shall focus a lot of attention in a later chapter.

The county's real viticultural pioneers were those who contributed to the thirty or so vines in the 1855 count. If we overlook the historically unimportant and anonymous Russian farmers who planted a few vines at their ranches outside the Ross settlement before 1830, Mariano Vallejo is *the* Sonoma pioneer. After he established the town in 1834, he planted a few hundred vines behind his adobe residence on the Plaza. He later planted a larger vineyard just west of town, and nearby, in 1851, built his fine mansion, Lachryma Montis. In 1840 he granted the Rancho Cabeza de Santa Rosa to his widowed mother-in-law, Maria Lopez Carillo. She planted the first vineyard in the Santa Rosa area, and ran her rancho "with a strong hand," according to historian Ruth Teiser.[1]

For years Vallejo's best moneymaker was his fresh grapes, sold in the San Francisco market in the 1850s. But some time before 1856 he met Victor J. Fauré, a French homeopathic physician with an excellent knowledge of wine chemistry. Vallejo also had an experienced vineyard manager in Pietro Giovanari, for a while the partner of Arpad Haraszthy after he lost his job at Buena Vista. For the next few years Vallejo's wines won numerous awards for high quality. Fauré even made a creditable champagne, but it never became a commercial product.

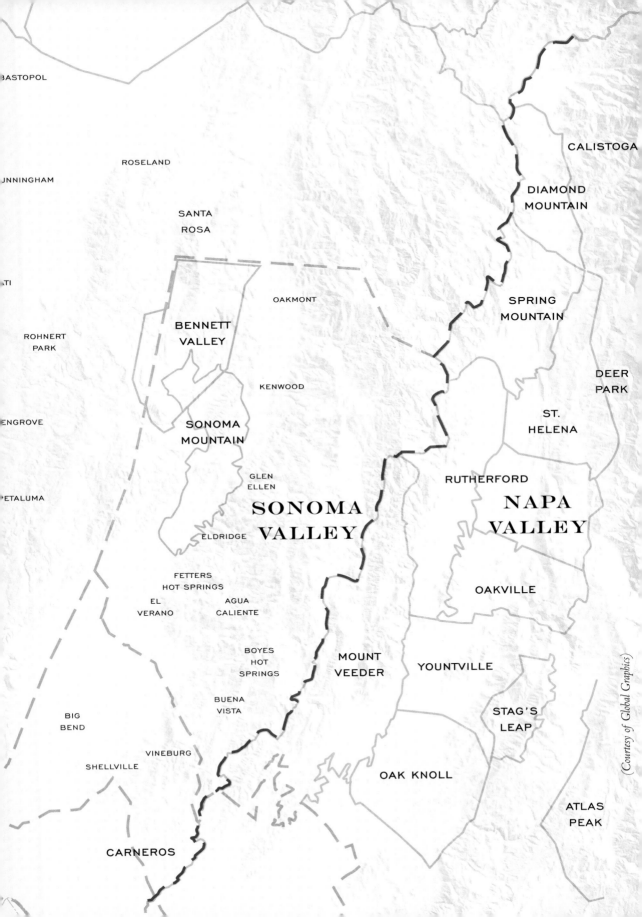

SEBASTOPOL

CUNNINGHAM

ROSELAND

SANTA
ROSA

TI

ROHNERT
PARK

OAKMONT

BENNETT
VALLEY

KENWOOD

ENGROVE

SONOMA
MOUNTAIN

PETALUMA

GLEN
ELLEN

ELDRIDGE

SONOMA
VALLEY

FETTERS
HOT SPRINGS

EL
VERANO

AGUA
CALIENTE

BOYES
HOT
SPRINGS

MOUNT
VEEDER

BUENA
VISTA

BIG
BEND

VINEBURG

SHELLVILLE

CARNEROS

CALISTOGA

DIAMOND
MOUNTAIN

SPRING
MOUNTAIN

DEER
PARK

ST.
HELENA

RUTHERFORD

NAPA
VALLEY

OAKVILLE

YOUNTVILLE

STAG'S
LEAP

OAK KNOLL

ATLAS
PEAK

(Courtesy of Global Graphics)

Mariano Vallejo surveys his Sonoma estate from horseback. His majestic home, Lychryma Montis ("mountain tear"), towers in the background.

The Frenchman is also partly responsible for discovering the potential of Zinfandel as a fine red wine grape. In 1859 William Boggs, the director of the short-lived Sonoma Horticultural Society, bought a collection of "foreign" vines from Napa's Joseph Osborne. They were the usual table varieties, mostly useless as wine grapes, but they included the so-called "Zinfindal." Most of the cuttings died, except for the Zinfandel. Boggs planted these and in 1862 took some of the grapes to Fauré, who thought they might be a good red Bordeaux wine variety. He made a very good wine from them and the word was soon out. In 1863 Giovanari planted Zinfandel for Vallejo, and within a few years there were not enough cuttings in the Sonoma Valley to meet the demand.[2]

Vallejo's name immediately brings to mind that of his brother-in-law, Jacob Leese. We have already seen that he had owned the piece of vineyard land that eventually became the original Buena Vista site. In the mid-1840s Leese also had a small vineyard along Sonoma Creek, and a shed he used

140

as a winery. He was probably the first American to make Sonoma wine, but his interest in winegrowing was short-lived. In 1862 he and his family were off for Texas, but in 1847 he had set another young man on the road to winegrowing when he sold cuttings to Nicholas Carriger, who came to California in 1846.

During the war Carriger served with the U. S. forces at Sonoma and carried the mail between the pueblo and San Rafael. No sooner was he discharged than gold was discovered, and he was one of the earliest at the mines. He had already acquired some vines from Leese and had planted them near the Plaza. By the summer of 1848 the male population of the little town was almost zero, and the local cattle were free to roam the streets and eat what they liked. The mission's vineyard was almost destroyed and Carriger's vines had disappeared.[3]

With his mining profits he was able to buy a large piece of land west of town, near Sonoma Creek. There he built the first redwood home in the valley. His main interest was running cattle, but in the winter of 1848-1849 he planted a vineyard that expanded throughout the fifties. For a while he sold most of his grapes fresh and made small amounts of wine, then larger amounts. By 1863 he had ninety-five acres of vines; only five vineyardists in the county had more. The next year he began building a large winery, and when finished it was surpassed in grandeur only by Buena Vista. According to a contemporary historian it was "a magnificent building of three stories in height, the lower one being built of stone quarried out of the hillsides."[4]

He later added a distillery, but concentrated on producing red table wine. His was the best red at the Sonoma County Fair in 1871. Earlier, New York author Charles Loring Brace had written that Carriger had "succeeded remarkably" with his Zinfandel, "which was one of the best red wines in California (for in general the red wines here are miserable.)"[5] By the end of the seventies his estate covered 1,000 acres and his winery had a capacity of 180,000 gallons. His vineyard covered 150 acres. Most of his production was bought up by the large wine houses that developed in San Francisco in the late seventies.

The Carriger estate, as it grew, maintained its diversified approach to agriculture, but it was known mostly for its good wine and the pioneer efforts of its founder. Carriger died in 1885, but his son continued operations into the next century. Most important historically is the fact that his was the only one of Sonoma's earliest pioneer wine operations that was able to stay the course and thrive.

By far the most important Sonoma wine pioneer was a graduate of the University of Pennsylvania who later served as a customs official in Philadelphia, before coming to California in 1849. William McPherson Hill made enough money as a San Francisco commission agent to buy in 1852 a large tract of Sonoma land near what became Glen Ellen. He began farming in 1854, starting with a peach orchard on the west side of Sonoma Creek; vines came soon thereafter. These were table and raisin varieties, part of the wave of "foreign" vines that poured into California nurseries from the East Coast in the 1850s. That a very common one was called Rose of Peru has led some writers to believe that some of Hill's vines came from Peru. They did not.

Among them was the Zinfandel, which became Hill's particular favorite in the 1860s. In fact, he was the first winegrower to become famous for his Zinfandel. He was particularly fortunate to have captured the attention of Edward J. Wickson, publisher of the *Pacific Rural Press,* and later head of the University of California's viticultural research. Wickson wrote in 1871 that a group of wine enthusiasts, he being one of them, had proclaimed Hill's Zinfandel red wine "superior to any they had seen in the State." A year earlier, the *Alta California* claimed that his Zinfandel "would take first at a National Exposition."[6]

In 1882 Hill helped solve a historical mystery concerning Zinfandel. Among the "foreign" varieties imported from the East Coast was a vine named the Black St. Peters (BSP). Years earlier J. Fisk Allen, the noted Massachusetts grape expert, had observed the remarkable similarity between the BSP and the popular Zinfindal, both grown in hot houses as table grapes in New England and on Long Island. Both came to California in the 1850s. San Jose's Antoine Delmas had won a gold

Sketch of the Carriger estate. The stone and redwood cellar can be seen at the far left.

for his BSP wine at the 1859 State Fair. He sent cuttings to Mariano Vallejo, who gave some to Hill.

In 1882, at a San Francisco symposium of winegrowing savants which included George Husmann, Professor Hilgard and Charles Wetmore, among others, Hill explained to the group that years earlier he had planted the two varieties in adjoining plots and today, "the two are identical, and both are Zinfandel." A vineyard owner in Santa Clara had the same experience.[7]

Hill continually expanded his estate, which eventually approached 1,800 acres in size. He was ever attached to a widely diversified approach to agricultural production, but he loved producing fine wine, even though his vintages rarely exceeded 10,000 gallons. In 1875 he was elected to the State Senate and there fought successfully to support financially Professor Hilgard's program for phylloxera research. In the 1880s he was an

143

early supporter of Julius Dresel's campaign to employ resistant rootstock to save Sonoma's vineyards.[8]

In 1889, at age sixty-seven, Hill sold a large part of his land to the state to establish a childrens' hospital. Today it is the Sonoma Developmental Center, covering almost 1,000 acres. Hill kept two vineyard parcels, one on Sonoma Mountain, which his son later sold to Jack London. The other covered sixty acres and is today the home of the Old Hill Ranch. The vineyard was mostly untended after Prohibition, but in 1981 the Teller Family found old vines worthy of resuscitation. Since then, wines from Old Hill Zinfandel grapes have received the same kind of praise awarded those of William McPherson Hill more than a hundred years earlier.[9]

The post-pioneer growth of Sonoma winegrowing is often pictured as a sort of frenzy set off by Haraszthy's acquisition of Buena Vista in 1857. That the county acreage of vines grew from about fifty to almost two thousand between that year and 1862 is important and merits close inspection, but in relationship to Sonoma's total agriculture it was a drop in the bucket. It was less than one twenty-fifth of the county's current wine grape acreage.

Haraszthy was certainly the leader of the early Sonoma development, but the Sonoma phenomenon in that period was part of a statewide movement that was equally rapid in Santa Clara County, the East Bay, the Sacramento area and Los Angeles County. By 1855 it had become increasingly obvious that grape crops had a multiplicity of money-making outlets. Most obvious then were the profits from fresh fruit. And there were also table wine, fortified sweet wine, brandy and even raisins. If anything triggered the post-1855 wave of vineyard plantation it was Col. Warren's continuous advocacy of viticulture in his influential *California Farmer,* then the state's only periodical devoted to agriculture. He set off his campaign with his articles in 1855, headed "Cultivators of California! Plant Your Vineyards. Begin now. . . . No better investment can be made. . . ."[10]

It is easy to determine where to start this part of the Sonoma story. All one needs to do is to look at Buena Vista's neighbors east of town, who by 1862 made up a small, but noticeable winegrowing community. Chief

144

among these were a pair of Germans who formed a partnership and in 1858 bought about four hundred acres of land about a mile south of the Buena Vista property, much of it today within the Carneros Viticultural Area. Emil Dresel and Jacob Gundlach called their spread "Rhinefarm," although each held title to his individual land. The partnership, Dresel & Co., lasted until 1875. Emil had died in 1869 and was succeeded by his brother Julius, who ran the company until his death in 1891. His son Carl carried on until Prohibition. The other portion of Rhinefarm became the property of J. Gundlach & Co., also a power in North Coast wine until the founder's death in 1894. Previously Carl Bundschu had married his boss's daughter, and after 1894 the firm operated as Gundlach-Bundschu until Prohibition. The Bundschu Family kept part of the old vineyard, and in 1973, descendants of the founder revived the Gundlach-Bundschu Winery, which still prospers on historic Rhinefarm land.

Emil Dresel had come to Texas in a wave of German immigration there in 1849, a year after Julius arrived in the state. Theirs was a wine family; we have already met brother Hermann in 1862, when he hosted Agoston Haraszthy at his Hochheim wine operation. Emil brought Riesling grapevines with him to Texas, which Julius planted and unsuccessfully tried to grow in the hill country near San Antonio. Emil traveled overland to California in 1851. He had been trained as an architect, and he teamed up with C. C. Küchel. Their firm employed Emil's sketches from all over California and Oregon for a profitable series of lithograph collections, today prized by lovers of early California art.[11]

During the winter of 1858-1859 Gundlach, Dresel and two other partners (soon out of the picture) were listed in the local press as planting eighty-five acres of vines, mostly German varieties which Gundlach had sent back from Germany in 1858. He had operated a very successful brewery in San Francisco before becoming a winegrower and was apparently the financial brain behind Dresel & Co's success. Emil was soon the winemaking expert. When Agoston Haraszthy lost his job at Buena Vista, Emil was hired in October 1866 to run the operation. I shall touch on that story in the next chapter. Julius will come to Sonoma after Emil's death in 1869,

Küchel and Dresel lithograph titled "Lone Mountain Cemetery, San Francisco [California], view towards the bay." c.1857.

and we shall meet him as an industry hero in the chapter on the phylloxera battle of the 1870s and 1880s.[12]

Haraszthy sold pieces of Buena Vista land to two of his friends, but they did not stay long in Sonoma. Both are deservedly famous, with long histories in wine. One was John Swett, a San Francisco schoolteacher who in 1859 planted seven acres on his forty-acre property. In 1862 he was elected California's Superintendent of Public Instruction, and served until 1867; he kept his Sonoma place long enough to win an award for his red wine at the 1865 San Francisco Mechanics' Fair. Later he moved across the bay to the Alhambra Valley, where he lived until his death in 1913, the master of Hill Girt Winery, famed as a producer of fine wines. He is best known today as the "Father of California Public Education" for his continued work in that field until his retirement in 1895.[13]

The other neighbor was gone within two years. Charles Krug had known Haraszthy since their years at Crystal Springs. He bought his Sono-

146

ma land in 1859 and planted twenty-five acres of vines on his Montebello Ranch, but within a year he was advertising to sell this spread, noting that it was a neighbor to Haraszthy and Dresel. In his ad he announced, "Having in view to commence a more extensive plantation, this place will be sold cheap. . . ." He had previously made wine for three Napa vineyardists. One was Bismark Bruck at the Bale Ranch, where Krug met Carolina Bale. He married her on December 26, 1860; her dowry was 540 acres of Bale land ready for "more extensive plantation." There the Charles Krug Winery stands today.[14]

Jacob Snyder became a neighbor of Buena Vista in 1859 when he bought seventy-four acres just to the north. He had come to California in 1846, and became involved in almost every important event leading to California statehood. He was drawn to Sonoma by his earlier good relations with Haraszthy at the mint. By 1862 he had thirty acres of vines and had made his El Cerrito Ranch one of the county's most impressive estates. His approach to winemaking was careful, deliberate and scientific. By the late sixties his red table wines were famous, having won first prize at the 1868 State Fair.

In 1869, after Emil Dresel's sudden death, Snyder was hired as superintendent of Buena Vista. Previously he had served as president of the California Wine Growers' Association. Snyder's vineyard had already begun to droop from phylloxera infestation before his demise. Within a few years the estate was the site of dairy farming and turkey raising.[15]

Before we head up-valley to look at the rest of the post-pioneer wave, we should examine the first good survey we have of Sonoma's pre-1863 winegrowing. Rightly disgusted by the often laughably inaccurate official statistics released by the Assessor's office, the county's leading wine men combined to record an accurate statistical picture of the local wine scene. It was published in the proceedings of the 1862 State Winegrowers' Convention.

The county had eighty-one vineyardists with more than an acre of vines. Of these twenty-nine, or 36%, had vineyards exceeding ten acres. These growers were now seriously involved in commercial viticulture.

Averages can be misleading. The mean average holding for all was twenty-three acres, a number that would have been 19.5 without Buena

Vista's overwhelming 338 acres. But the median average was only 7.2 acres, which indicates that for most of these farmers, grapevines were not a large part of their operations. In fact, twenty-eight of them had less than five acres of vines each.[16] It was not until the 1880 U.S. Census that a really complete picture of Sonoma viticulture could be found.[17]

In these early days, ten acres of vines would probably yield about 7,000 gallons of wine, but not every vineyardist with that many grapes had the capital to build a winery and properly equip it. Thus, many vineyardists had to find a market for grapes that they could not sell fresh for the table. Such sales were nowhere nearly as profitable or even available as they had been in the early fifties. Some simply sold their grapes to local winemakers; others were able to sell large amounts in San Francisco to such large scale producers as Gottlieb Groezinger, Charles Kohler and Isador Landsberger. There also developed something like today's "custom crushing" operations. Vineyardists could contract with a local winery to make up their grapes on shares, and then sell the resulting wine where they could. In and around the town of Sonoma there were several operations where this was the system for producing the bulk of their production. After Vallejo created a winery by converting the old soldiers' barracks on the Plaza, winemaker Victor Fauré made a considerable amount of wine on shares, as did Attila Haraszthy at his place near Vallejo's home. The leading producer in town was Camille Aguillon, with a large adobe winery on the west side of the Plaza, but he didn't own a single vine.[18]

In 1872 the Agricultural Society's visiting committee asked Jacob Snyder to give them a tour of the Sonoma Valley's wineries. They wanted to see a representative cross-section of producers, after he had shown off his own place and Buena Vista, where he was then the boss.[19] He first selected Oliver W. Craig's operation west of town, right next to Carriger's land. Craig's ranch was a perfect example of a working vineyard and winery of modest size on a fairly large estate, about 225 acres. He acquired his land in 1851 and fell victim to the wine fever in 1859. Within a few years he had thirty acres of vines, and in 1865 had built a solid stone winery.

Craig was best known for his white wines. He had acquired Riesling vines from Emil Dresel and blended their wines with the neutral-flavored Palomino.[20] His total production was about 25,000 gallons. He also made brandy. Craig was always in the market for good grapes from his neighbors with small vineyards. At age eighty-one in 1890 he closed his winery after having exhibited his wines at the 1889 Paris Exposition.

No comprehensive work on California wine history ever fails to mention an event in Craig's vineyard, one he probably did not relish. Many Sonoma vineyards had witnessed small areas of declining vines by the late sixties. On April 19, 1873 Craig and Horatio Appleton, armed with magnifying glass and scientific text, identified the small bugs on the roots of Craig's vines as the *Phylloxera vastastrix*, "the destroyer." Historian Ruth Teiser named this event "the incident that triggered the opening shot in the two decade war to control the scourge."

Land to the north is often called the Valley of the Moon. Viticultural development took off here in the seventies. Beyond Hill's property we come to an area known today as Glen Ellen. Here in 1856 Joshua Chauvet, a Frenchman from France's Champagne region, bought a large tract, built the county's first flour mill, and prospered. He planted grapes around 1872 and had a small vintage in 1875. By 1880 he had production up to 100,000 gallons, and in 1881 built a huge 250,000 gallon winery, which still stands in Glen Ellen village. He expanded his Sonoma vineyards and went heavily into resistant rootstock in the nineties. Meanwhile, he built a 400,000 gallon winery in Santa Rosa.

That one can produce "good wine, but not lots of good wine" is a worn-out adage that Chauvet early disproved. After 1880 San Francisco's Schilling wine house, noted for its emphasis on high quality, bought every gallon Chauvet could produce. The best description of Chauvet and his wines comes to us from Australian wine master Thomas Hardy after his 1882 visit. In rare detail for that early year, Hardy takes us step by step through the operations of this "splendid new stone-built cellar." He was impressed by Chauvet's refusal to use over-ripe grapes, drawing the line at 23.5° Brix (Baume 13°) and 12.5% alcohol for his reds.[21] He also used submerged cap fermentations for these wines. The "jolly old Frenchman" invited Hardy to sample "from any cask I liked." This Australian wine expert knew good wine when he tasted it. He was also impressed by the entire wine scene in the Glen Ellen area, where there was no sign yet of phylloxera.22

Chauvet's neighbor, and everyone's friend around Glen Ellen, was "Captain" Charles Justi, who gained the honorific from owning the little steamer *Georgia* for one year (1853-1854) and running it from San Francisco to the embarcadero south of Sonoma. He came to the Golden State in 1849 from Saxony via New York City. In 1854 he settled on a piece of Glen Ellen land up the road from Chauvet. He planted eight acres of vines and made about 4,000 gallons of wine per year. The Glen Ellen Tavern was his best customer, he being the owner. The village got a post office and officially acquired the Glen Ellen name in 1871. Justi was the first postmaster.

A cartoon published in the satirical weekly Punch, *September 6, 1890, with the caption, "The phylloxera, a true gourmet, finds out the best vineyards and attaches itself to the best wines."*

Charles V. Stuart, Justi's far larger viticultural neighbor, bought a large piece of the old Agua Caliente land grant in 1858. He had come to California in 1849, leading a mule train. He planted vines and had forty acres by 1863, ninety by 1880. He sold almost all his grapes to neighboring wineries. Ellen Mary Stuart was his Scottish-born wife, and he honored her by calling his estate Glen Ellen. He later changed it to Glen Oaks when her name took on its grander meaning. Mrs. Stuart continued managing the estate after her husband died in 1880.[23]

Shortly before his death, Stuart was a Sonoma delegate to the 1878 California Constitutional Convention. His famous speech there gave him a special place in the history of California's very gradual struggle against racial discrimination. His was the only voice raised in opposition to the convention's discriminating planks against the state's Chinese.[24]

By the time Thomas Hardy visited Glen Ellen, it had become the terminus of the railroad line from the south and a favorite Sunday resort for San Francisco folk. Round trip by steamer and narrow gauge railroad cost $1.50. Hardy marveled at the verdant beauty of the setting.

Another Stuart neighbor was Jacob Warfield. After completing his medical studies in Ohio, he came to California in 1849. He practiced in the Gold Country until 1859, and in that year bought his land in Glen Ellen. In 1862 he planted about sixteen acres of Mission vines. His production grew steadily, but his Ten Oaks Winery did not gain much fame until after his death in 1878.[25]

In the next few years Catherine Warfield, always called Kate, became one of the most famous winery owners in California. By 1880 she was expanding her vineyards with Riesling and Sylvaner vines. She hired a French winemaker, but she was the boss, very much in charge of the business. By the late eighties she was experimenting with Tannat and St. Macaire varieties to blend with her Zinfandel, and had grafted over to better varieties most of the vines her husband had planted. At the 1886 San Francisco Mechanics' Fair she exhibited Cabernet Sauvignon, Sauvignon Blanc and Syrah, among others, "the finest collection ever seen at the Fair." And she was a leader in the eighties in the upper Sonoma Valley in the use of resistant rootstock to combat phylloxera.[26]

151

The Warfield neighbor up the road was a real pioneer in the area. William Hood acquired a large part of the Los Guilicos land grant in 1849 and started building a remarkable mansion in 1857. Sonoma's buildings then were either wood frame or adobe. Hood's home was built with bricks produced on the spot. It still stands today, Historic Landmark #692, as part of the Sonoma Regional Parks System. Hood had about forty acres of Mission grapes by the early sixties, and built a large winery. By the seventies he was averaging vintages of about 30,000 gallons of ordinary wine. More important was the distillery he had in place in 1861. His brandy became famous, but it may have been his personal downfall. By 1877 his alcoholism got the best of him, and to top it off the government charged him with illegal distillation.[27]

In 1858 Hood had married teenager Eliza Shaw, and in 1877, in her early thirties, she took over complete control of the Hood estate. Contemporary sources politely avoided mention of her husband's fate. She immediately hired a French winemaker and began grafting over most of the vineyard, except the Zinfandel, to varieties such as Cabernet Sauvignon, Riesling and Semillon. The Missions that survived went into the brandy still. By the mid-eighties her brandy was nationally famous, and her Cabernet won the praise of European wine expert Frederico Pohndorff, who had assisted Professor Hilgard at the university. Hard times in the nineties forced Mrs. Hood to sell her property in 1897 with its 230-acre vineyard. It was then managed by the Italian Swiss Colony. She died in San Francisco in 1914.[28]

Eliza Hood, Kate Warfield and Ellen Stuart form a historically remarkable viticultural triumvirate. They were friends and associates, together in the early eighties successfully petitioning the Sonoma Superior Court to confirm their right to operate their wineries as "sole traders." In winning this petition they secured their perfect legal right to manage their wineries strictly in their own names. [29]

If travelers returning from the Hood mansion turned right at Glen Ellen, they would take a rougher road headed over to Bennett Valley, and eventually to Santa Rosa. Several small vineyards were planted in this valley in the sixties, but its place in Sonoma wine history rests on the accomplishments of one man who settled here in 1859. Isaac De Turk came to California from Indiana, where as a boy he had helped his father make wine. He had sixteen acres of vines on his Yulupa Ranch in 1862; by 1867 he had a 100,000 gallon winery, and after 1878 he was the largest wine producer in Sonoma County. He later built an even greater winery in Santa Rosa. We shall pick up his story as part of the California wine boom of the eighties.[30]

Today the bulk of Sonoma County's almost 60,000 acres of wine grapes is located in the vast and varied region of valleys and foothills from south of Santa Rosa to the county line above Cloverdale. But in the 1860s this area was just beginning to fill up with large farms devoted mostly to extensive, rather than intensive agriculture. There were vineyards scattered about the region, but commercial viticulture was not yet important. This situation changed dramatically in the late seventies and eighties.

There are several reasons to think of 1875 as a turning point in Sonoma wine history, most obviously the announcement throughout the state's wine industry that this northern county now led California in wine production. In 1875, almost in symbolic recognition of this event, Charles Kohler bought 800 acres of Sonoma Valley land west of Glen Ellen, moving the center of his gigantic pioneer Los Angeles company to the North Bay. He had been making Sonoma red wine for several years at his massive cellars in San Francisco, but these were from purchased grapes, mostly Zinfandel. He clearly saw correctly that the future of California fine wine lay in the coastal valleys around the Bay Area. And 1875 is also the year we start to see a significant interest in planting more wine grapes around Santa Rosa, Windsor and Healdsburg. The wine industry was still suffering from the economic woes associated with the 1873-1877 national depression, but these would soon end.

CHAPTER 8 NOTES

1. Madie D. Brown, "The Vineyards of Gen. M. G. Vallejo," *California Historical Society Quarterly,* September, 1957, pp. 242-244; Teiser, p.28.

2. *San Francisco Evening Bulletin,* 5/1/1885; *Napa County Reporter,* 7/4/1884; *St. Helena Star,* 6/8/1885; Sullivan, *Zinfandel,* pp.32-34.

3. Hubert Howe Bancroft, *History of California,* San Francisco, 1889, II, p.743.

4. J. P. Munro-Fraser, *History of Sonoma County. . .,* San Francisco, 1879, pp.460-461; *Sonoma Democrat,* 6/10/1865; Menefee, pp.298-299; Peninou, *Sonoma,* p. 286.

5. *The New West or California 1867-1868,* New York, 1869, p.264; *Alta California,* 10/7/1871.

6. *Pacific Rural Press,* 12/23/1871; *Alta California,* 5/20/1870.

7. J. Fisk Allen, *Practical Treatise on the Culture and Treatment of the Grape Vine,* New York, 1855, p.24, pp. 93-97, pp.135-139, p.308, p.311; Sullivan, *Zinfandel, pp.27-19; Pacific Rural Press,* 9/30/1882.

8. *Sonoma Democrat,* 3/28/1876, 10/6/1877; *San Francisco Merchant,* 10/9/1885.

9. Tom Gregory, *History of Sonoma County,* Los Angeles 1911, pp.303-395. This book has a very useful history of the Hill family. Hill's son, Robert Potter Hill, in 1897 became steward of the huge hospital.

10. 1/11. 3/29, 4/5/1855.

11. Peter E. Palmquist, *Pioneer Photographers of the Far West,* Stanford, 2000, p.355.

12. *Alta California* 8/18/1860, 12/13/1862; *California Farmer,* 9/26/1860; Peninou, *Sonoma,* pp.71-77; Teiser, p.75.

13. *Alta California,* 8/13/1865; McGinty, *Strong Wine,* p.325; *Pacific Wine & Spirit Review* (PWSR), 12/20/1892, 2/26/1895, 10/31/1902. Earlier this important trade journal appeared under other names, particularly *San Francisco Merchant.* All will be cited *PWSR; American Wine Press,* 9/1/1913.

14. *San Francisco Evening Bulletin,* 8/28/1860; Sullivan, *Napa Wine,* pp.25-26; Peninou, *Sonoma,* p.52.

15. *Alta California*, 12/13/1862; 11/2/1865; Ag. Soc., 1868 and 1869, p.105; Munro-Fraser 683-685; Menefee, pp.306-309; Peninou, *Sonoma*, p.54.

16. *Alta California*, 12/13/1862.

17. Peninou, *Sonoma*, pp.293-312 presents all the names and numbers.

18. *Alta California*, 12/24/1863; *Napa County Reporter*, 3/22/1873.

19. Ag. Soc., 1872, pp.193-198.

20. In Sonoma and Napa the Palomino was usually called the Golden Chasselas. Charles Krug knew better. *PWSR*, 1/26/1891; *San Jose Mercury*, 6/16/1907.

21. In 2009 the average Brix for Sonoma Cabernet Sauvignon and Zinfandel was a whopping 25.1°.

22. Thomas Hardy, *Notes on Vineyards of America. . .*, Adelaide, 1885, pp.20-22; *St. Helena Star*, 5/29/1908; *Cloverdale Reveille*, 2/5/1881; Peninou, *Sonoma*, pp.92-94.

23. Erwin G. Gudde, *California Place Names*, Berkeley, 1969, p.145; Peninou, pp.100-102; *Sonoma Democrat*, 8/21/1880.

24. Timothy Sandefur, "Charles V. Stuart. . .," Pacific Legal Foundation, Economic Liberties Project, Sacramento, 1/29/2008 contains a detailed description of Stuart's presentation and the reaction to it.

25. *Alta California*, 12/13/1862; *California Farmer*, 8/3/1871.

26. Ruth Teiser and Catherine Harroun, *Winemaking in California*, New York, 1983, p.80; Peninou, *Sonoma*, pp.100-101;Frona Eunice Wait, *Wines & Vines of California. . .*, San Francisco, 1889, pp.142-143; *Sonoma Index-Tribune*, 11/27/1887; *Napa County Reporter*, 5/13/1887; *PWSR*, 11/6/1885, 3/16/1888.

27. *California Farmer*, 12/19/1862, 8/3/1871; *Alta California*, 5/20/1870; *PWSR*, 3/21/1892; Redwood Rancher, 7/1/1980,p. 57.

28. *PWSR*, 8/15/1884, 1/29/1886, 2/28/1899; California, *The Vineyards of Sonoma County*, Sacramento, 1893, p.28. Hereinafter *Sonoma, 1893.*

29. Edith Sparks, *Capital Intentions*, University of North Carolina, 2006, n.254.

30. Teiser, pp.74-75.

Chapter

Spaced Out

1864-1869

After Arpad's departure, Attila was in charge of the day-to-day tasks at Buena Vista. Agoston was away from Sonoma during much of the year, but activities on the great estate were lively and gave every appearance of a well-organized and complex operation. No visitor would have seen any sign of the underlying financial instability that was gradually increasing in intensity.

Work on the construction of another stone wine building in front of the three new tunnels was well underway. The first of its eventual three stories was finished by the end of the year. There was also a large dwelling house built for the Chinese labor crew. They now numbered about fifty men, and were active in almost all aspects of the cellar and vineyard work.

During the fiscal year 1864-1865 they performed 12,686 days' work. Agoston's statistics for the period show how essential this hardworking and efficient crew was to all areas of Buena Vista production. They provided 532 days' work in the cellars, 144 in the distillery, and 219 making champagne. Of course, most of their work was in the vineyards, where they put in more than 9,000 days' work.[1]

The spring of 1864 brought too little rain and some sharp frosts after the vines started leafing out. Nevertheless, the vintage came in without problems and was a good one, considering the poor weather conditions. There were about 42,000 gallons made in 1864, and after things quieted down the new champagne master, Pierre De Banne, laid down about 40,000 bottles of (hopefully) sparklers.[2]

On October 28 the Haraszthys put on a costume ball at the villa to celebrate the harvest. It was a huge and lavish affair, with scores of notables from all over the valley. Quite a few guests came up to Sonoma by steamer from San Francisco to the embarcadero south of town, then by carriage to Buena Vista. The trustees were pleased to underwrite the costly event. They hoped to publicize the glamorous side of Buena Vista life and show off the facility and the grounds. There were still more than a thousand unsold shares, and no profits or dividends in sight.

Agoston was on the East Coast in February, "on business." There he visited a meeting of the Farmers' Club of the American Institute in New York. He was recognized by one of the members and agreed to give an extemporaneous talk on California winegrowing. He covered many topics of interest to his listeners, and answered questions on California in general and on Buena Vista specifically. It was a good talk, accurate and forthcoming, without the bloated production and profit predictions that had become standard in official pronouncements emanating from Buena Vista.

One item in Haraszthy's talk deserves special attention. It concerned a matter of great importance which, in the next eighteen months, would greatly affect Agoston's future at Buena Vista.

He talked about his 1860 trip to Europe and focused on one of his observations there. We have already seen that he was impressed by the common practice in many of the great vineyards of France and Germany of planting vines closely together, often referred to as "close-spacing." He noted that eight feet was the preferred spacing in northern California and at Buena Vista, resulting in 680 vines to the acre, but in many of Europe's most famous vineyards the spacing was often only about three feet, sometimes even less. He told the group that the matter was "still a mooted question," that is, undecided, but it would be clear by the 1864-1865 planting season that Haraszthy was definitely not undecided.[3]

Well before the end of the year Agoston had developed his own special plan for close spacing at Buena Vista. His logic seemed sound, given the European successes employing this system. He contended that European grapes acquired better color, better maturity, and better flavor when grown

IN this example of layering, the parent vine is on the left, its cane giving rise to the nascent vine on the right. In 1865, BVVS trustees reported the layering of over 350,000 vines. (T. Proffitt, courtesy of Patrick Iland Wine Promotions)

on vines closely spaced. This result was attained by pruning each vine to fewer buds, thus producing fewer grapes per vine. But overall the total yield per acre was about the same as, sometimes even greater than, when vines were spaced on eight foot centers.

The *Alta California* wrote in February 1865, after the planting season had begun, that "one of the most common topics of conversation now among the wine-growers of Sonoma is the distance at which vines should be planted." The paper presented the arguments on both sides. It seemed that Haraszthy's idea "appears to gain converts," but that the Colonel was at present in the minority.[4] Haraszthy also presented his views in a paper prepared for the State Agricultural Society, claiming that "Careful experiments at Dijon (Burgundy)" proved that better wines resulted when vineyards were planted at 2,500 to 3,000 vines per acre.[5]

Haraszthy added a special twist to the Buena Vista changes. Where possible he had ordered that new vines were to be propagated by layering, a standard practice in the vineyard, but unheard of, I think, on the scale Haraszthy was undertaking. In his authoritative work on viticulture, Professor Albert Winkler contends that there is only one good reason for vineyard layering, that is, to replace *occasional* missing vines in an established vineyard. The only exception would be in cases where the variety to be propagated is almost impossible to root by cuttings, which was not the case at Buena Vista.

Layering is achieved by selecting a long, vigorous cane from the parent vine and bending it down into a hole or trench in the open space beside the vine. The tip of the cane, with two buds, projects from the ground exactly where the new vine will grow. As much as possible of the living cane is buried. The buried buds produce roots. Above ground the tiny new vine leafs out. The new vine should not be allowed to produce for at least two years. It is thus able to devote its energies to the growth of the new stems and roots. When secure and healthy in its place, the new vine is cut away from its parent, and is genetically identical to it.[6]

Close spacing is a standard practice in many winegrowing areas today, including California. But it is always done after careful experiment with small plots at first. So it had been in the European areas Haraszthy had observed in 1860. It is also important to have vineyard tools and equipment specifically made to work in such a densely planted space. Work crews and their supervisors must be carefully trained in the special techniques required to maintain such vines. Of course, cultivating by horse and plow in large areas of vineyard expanded from 680 to 2,722 vines per acre by layering would be virtually impossible during the first two years. It would still be very awkward in later years as the closely spaced vines grew and reached out. In France today one sees tractors that ride above and straddle the closely spaced vines (*tracteurs enjambeurs*).[7]

In June 1865 the report of the BVVS trustees indicated that after the 1864 vintage the vineyards expanded by layering covered 173 acres; that is, 2,040 layered vines were added to each acre. Thus the rows in all directions were cut into four foot intervals and layered. The partially buried canes criss-crossed the pathways straight across and diagonally. The report added

160

that at this early date the new vines were "now equal in size to three year old vines." The report also claimed that 646,000 new vines had been planted on close centers. These new vines would have covered 237 acres. It was not explained how this enormous expansion could have been accomplished unless huge areas of old vineyard had been ripped out. What varieties were involved in this great effort was not revealed.[8]

In 1865 financier William Ralston's heretofore guarded influence on the Buena Vista trustees became more obvious and effective. He was determined to take steps finally to make Buena Vista a profitable company. He and several others came to Sonoma in March 1865 on an inspection tour. One of the visitors was Frederick Law Olmsted, the noted landscape architect, who, with Calvert Vaux, had laid out New York's Central Park in 1858. Later in 1865 he formulated the master plan for the grounds and buildings of the College of California, soon to be the site of the great university.

Olmsted wrote the group's report, and Ralston had it ornately printed by a respected San Francisco publishing house.[9] Of course, the physical presence of the Buena Vista estate and the bustling atmosphere in vineyard and cellar impressed Olmsted, and his experienced eye as a landscape architect led him to praise the estate in the highest terms. The entire operation was "well adapted for the accomplishment of a large amount of work, with great economy of current expense." Olmsted did not repeat the extravagant prediction earlier made by the trustees, but generalized that, "the business is one promising extraordinary profits." This was just what Ralston wanted the public to read and hear. The unsold shares needed to be sold.[10]

Three months later the president of the board wrote in his annual report that the enormous interest payments which BVVS was obliged to pay on its debt had moved the trustees to open a new subscription list in March, at the time of Ralston's visit. A total of 1,387 shares, valued at $110,000 was offered. President Walter Rockwell went on to state that as of June, "a large number of shares" had been subscribed for. He predicted that all the BVVS mortgages would soon be paid off. Yet hidden in the numbers of the secretary's June report was the fact that 1,145 shares were still unissued, and 250 more had been sent to their New York agent, to be sold, if possible.

The Master Plan for Stanford College, Stanford, Ca. Frederick Law Olmsted, 1887. (Courtesy of Department of Special Collections and University Archives, Stanford University Libraries)

The president's opening words had complained of the "serious financial difficulties, and heavy expenses" of BVVS in 1864-1865. He closed with, "the prospects of a brilliant success after a short time under proper management is indisputable." Did this indicate that a new manager might come on board?

By the end of the year the chief dispute at Buena Vista, muted though it was, concerned the adequacy of Haraszthy's superintendency. Many of his neighbors considered his close spacing and layering program disastrous, and he had been absent from Buena Vista for much of the vintage. Attila had written his superintendent's report for him. This and other long absences suggest to biographer Brian McGinty that Agoston was once again growing restless. "Was he incapable of maintaining his focus for any appreciable length of time?"[11]

One can imagine that the 1865 vintage was nothing if not awkward at Buena Vista. How were the experienced Chinese harvesters to race up and down the rows, as was their custom, with the vineyards criss-crossed by still connected layered vines? There was surely a lot of unaccustomed hopping about. Still the grapes came in to produce 43,000 gallons, about the same as in 1864; it was still tops in the county. Emil Dresel was second with 20,000; eleven others made 5,000 gallons or more, including Carriger, Craig, Snyder, Fauré for Vallejo, and Attila at his own place.[12]

During the summer of 1866 the BVVS trustees became increasingly aware of a rising tide of criticism leveled against Haraszthy's management. One searches in vain for specifics in the press, but the annual report in June spelled out the charges in general terms. He had been accused of "extravagance and unfaithfulness in the performance of his duties. . . ." The trustees' investigation of the "constant malignant attacks" against Haraszthy "found none of them substantiated . . . ." President George Johnson expressed the board's "full confidence in his capacity and his integrity," but there was no mention of his management ability. The success of BVVS was "wholly due" to Haraszthy. This was not great praise, since the corporation's success as a profit-making endeavor so far was nil.

The specific relations between Haraszthy and the board between July and October 1866, whether recorded or publicly discussed, appear to be beyond the reach of historians. The record is mysteriously non-existent, but the discernible facts hint at what probably happened. The hard facts of the situation remain undocumented.

Beyond Agoston's apparent loss of interest in the personal management of the Buena Vista estate, his personal finances moved from stressed to shambles between 1863 and 1866. He raised money through personal loans totaling $52,000 between 1863 and 1864, more than 80% of it backed by his personal BVVS shares. Between August 1865 and January 1866, he negotiated five loans from San Francisco businessmen, totaling about $20,000. There is no record where the money went.

Agoston also moved to secure a piece of land so that Eleanora could be secure, whatever happened. In January 1866 he had Attila buy four adjoining vineyard properties west of town, totaling 126 acres. The cost was $21,000 and Attila signed a mortgage for $20,000, which Agoston co-signed. Attila then deeded the property but not the debt to his mother, solely in her name, as a gift.[13]

The 1866 vintage at Buena Vista came off successfully, yielding again about 43,000 gallons. But the vineyards were far more tangled than in 1865. It is clear that the board had had enough of Haraszthy's layering scheme, and some time during the vintage it was decided that he would be replaced as superintendent. One of the local winegrowers who had continuously questioned both the layering and the close spacing was Emil Dresel, Buena Vista's neighbor to the south. In October 1866 he was offered the job and he took it, with the understanding that the vineyards would be restored to 680 vines per acre under his supervision.[14]

Dresel was a perfect choice. The Rhinefarm that he and Jacob Gundlach had developed over the last ten years was a leader in Sonoma wine production, and arguably *the* quality leader in the large scale production of white table wine. He was no charismatic figure, but he was an excellent businessman and expert winegrower.

There was no public firing of Haraszthy, and he remained on the Board of Trustees until June 1867. He obviously stayed on in some probably advisory capacity after October, for in December he was seriously injured at the distillery when one of the steam tanks exploded. He settled down on his wife's property, and for two years he and Attila made wine and lots of brandy, about 10,000 gallons in 1867. In September of that year he solved his problem of personal indebtedness by successfully filing for bankruptcy.[15]

He still had ideas for a large venture. In February 1868 he headed south for Nicaragua, and later in May was joined by Eleanora. Two months later she died of yellow fever. They had settled on a hacienda where Agoston hoped to distill spirits from the local sugar cane, but in July 1869 he mysteriously disappeared. The family accepted the idea that he had attempted to cross a stream on a large tree branch, which collapsed, "and then the alligator must have drawn him down forever," in the words of Otelia, Agoston's daughter. There was never clear evidence to explain his disappearance.[16]

The mysterious and apparently dramatic end to this wonderful Hungarian fits nicely into what has come to be called "The Haraszthy Legend," and much of this legend is based on good historical evidence. Biographer Brian McGinty asks a question to which I unhesitatingly answer "Yes!"

"Was he one of those men who are suited to launch businesses with great promise, but never see them through to their greatness—a gifted, even brilliant entrepreneur but an erratic, undependable manager?"[17]

He was also the most important individual to affect the course of California wine history in its pioneer days. He was a great publicist, and was the industry's conscience, promoting better wines from better grapes through rational cellar practices. In the 1860s he advocated and widely explained some vineyard and cellar practices considered prescient in the 1880s. California wine leaders in those later years understood and praised him for these accomplishments, but none called him the "father" of the California wine industry. It was agreed that that honor went to Charles Kohler, who had founded his great and financially successful wine house even before Haraszthy settled in Sonoma.

Haraszthy's lasting legacy is most obviously the Buena Vista estate today. The buildings and grounds are the first example of the physical

Buena Vista Vinicultural Society,

OFFICE, 409 BATTERY STREET,
SAN FRANCISCO.

VINEYARDS AND CELLARS,—SONOMA.

ORDERS RESPECTFULLY SOLICITED FOR

WHITE AND RED WINES, AND PURE BRANDY.

SPECIAL ATTENTION IS CALLED TO THEIR

SPARKLING NATIONAL GRAPE,

Which received Honorable Mention at the Paris Exhibition in 1867.

An 1870 advertisement touting the Honorable Mention awarded to the 1864 Champagne vintage. Though only 10% of the bottled product sparkled, it was Buena Vista's most successful attempt at a style that would prove to be a costly, ten-year boondoggle. (Courtesy of the Unzelman Collection)

grandeur that years later became common in the California wine country. Nothing else like it survives from the sixties and seventies, because then there *was* nothing else like it.

Emil Dresel's job as new superintendent was not to undo any of Haraszthy's work, except to un-clutter the vineyards. The work continued on the huge "cellar building" next door to the press house. But no new planting was envisioned, with the new vines from 1865-1866 not yet in bearing.

A noteworthy element of continuity was the continued efforts in champagne production, even though only 3,000 of 1864's 30,000 bottles had sparkled. Nevertheless, those 3,000 turned out to be quite

166

good. Dresel sent some to the 1867 Paris Exposition, where it won an honorable mention, and "appeared to be much liked," according to the American delegates.[18]

That Buena Vista continued its attempt to crack the California sparkling wine market flies in the face of the contention that William Ralston ruled the roost on the Board of Trustees before 1873. The noted financier thought large scale champagne production at Buena Vista, before a solid market for it was established, was too costly and quite unprofitable. He was correct. In 1866 De Banne got 5,000 good bottles from the 40,000 laid down; in 1867 the results were almost as bad and M. DeBanne "resigned." In all, after Arpad left, Ernest Peninou has counted six champagne masters at Buena Vista before the firm finally saw the light and ceased production in the mid-seventies. It was serious mismanagement in a company desperately attempting to turn a profit. The bottles that came through were generally well received and won several awards, but they could not stand up to Arpad Haraszthy's popular "Eclipse."[19]

Dresel did not last three years at Buena Vista; he died suddenly in August 1869. But he left the estate in good shape. Nothing that met the eye would suggest the underlying financial problems. His first vintage in 1867 was surprisingly small, a mere 24,000 gallons, only 14% of the county total; in 1866 it had been 21%. In 1868, when the 1865-66 vines began bearing, Sonoma had a record crop, almost double that of 1867. And Dresel produced a record 98,000 gallons, fully 28% of the county total. The quality of his wine was never doubted, and wine prices in general were on the rise.

After the 1868 vintage an *Alta California* reporter visited the estate and revealed the extent of the change in the vineyards since 1863. Only 126 acres were fully bearing, and 236 partially. This meant that only sixty-four acres remained with vines planted before 1864. A few months later he returned and inspected the vines remaining since the closely spaced thousands had been ripped up. He found the "foreign" varieties terribly mixed, and most "of inferior value." He meant that, except for the Zinfandels, they were almost all useless table and raisin varieties that for years had been touted as "foreign" varieties. He also noted that the 1868 harvest of the vines that had been re-centered had been "very difficult," and that it had been "almost impossible to get enough grapes of any one kind to make a barrel of wine." Nevertheless, there were almost 100,000 gallons of wine in the cellars, the 1867 wines already sold. It is also worth noting that he did not report any sign of serious vineyard decline.

By 1869 close spacing was a settled matter in the Sonoma Valley. It had cost Buena Vista dearly to plant the new vines and to have the layers set. It was even more costly to plow up what amounted to almost a million vines to restore order. It has been suggested that Dresel opposed close spacing because he thought it caused the deteriorating condition of the Buena Vista vineyards. In other words, he attributed the vineyards' initial decline from phylloxera to close spacing. The great vineyards were not yet obviously in decline; there were many spots where a few vines had to be replaced for unknown reasons. But Dresel was reacting to the clutter, the disorder, the trustees' concern and the workers' discontent. The huge vintages in 1868 and 1869 show there was not yet a general decline. There were still a few years before the phylloxera infestation became serious, and then it was the entire area east of town that was in sharp decline.

That Haraszthy had been successful in spreading the fame of his great estate is attested to by Charles Loring Brace's visit to California in 1867. The noted social reformer and prolific writer on many subjects made it a point to visit Buena Vista and record his impressions of Emil Dresel's recent accomplishments.

In the Sonoma Valley he found "the most carefully managed vineyards in the State." The town he thought was a "wretched run-down-looking village," but the valley was "filled with beautiful vineyards, to which is generally attached a neat villa or farm-house." During his stay he visited Craig, Carriger, Snyder, Rhinefarm and Buena Vista. He obviously had a very knowledgeable guide.

Brace's observations covered all aspects of winegrowing, both cellar and vineyard. He was especially interested in vineyard layout and spacing. At Buena Vista he noted Haraszthy's gigantic and failed close

168

spacing project. He wrote, "Mr. Dresel had been obliged to take up thousands of vines, to the great loss of the (BVVS). . . as the division cost so much in hard-labor, and diminished so much the product." Dresel told him that Buena Vista was getting about three tons of grapes to the acre, with 370 acres bearing or partially bearing. The large 1868 vintage and subsequently larger later vintages suggest that many vines had not yet come to full bearing.

Brace was particularly impressed by the valley's cellars, "the best in the State," and Buena Vista's, the best of the best. Jacob Snyder's cellar, with its partly underground and constant temperature of 60° F., received special notice. He thought Snyder's wines excellent, partly because of his wealth which allowed him to withhold them from the market until mature. He thought Snyder's whites were among the best in the state, produced from the Riesling of Johannisberg, "a great favorite in the valley."

He also loved the Zinfandel wines produced around Sonoma, particularly Carriger's. He noted that at this early date there were already various opinions as to the European birthplace of the variety. None that he suggested was correct.

At Buena Vista he found Dresel's white muscat to be "one of the most delicate wines made in California." He added that Buena Vista had never shown a profit, "perhaps never will." For Brace this was of no importance. The estate's excellent wines were what counted, not dividends, and he was convinced that "under its present skillful superintendency," more celebrated wines were on their way. But, of course, in a year Dresel would be dead.[20]

A reader of Brace's book, published just before Dresel's demise, would not have been surprised to read in the *Alta California* two weeks after the sad event, that Jacob Snyder had been appointed the new superintendent at Buena Vista.[21]

CHAPTER 9 NOTES

1. *Report, 1865, pp.6-7.*
2. *Alta California*, 2/16/1865.
3. *Annual Report. . .American Institute. . ., 1863, '64,* Albany, 1864,p. 284.
4. *Alta California*, 2/15/1865, 1/16/1865.
5. Ag. Soc., 1864/1865, pp.290-295.
6. A. J. Winkler, *General Viticulture*, Berkeley, 1962, pp.156-158. For the 1974 edition, pp.203-205.
7. Richard E. Smart, "Vine Density," in *The Oxford Companion to Wine*, I Oxford, 1994, pp.1031-1032. At p.48 see one of these remarkable tractors at work.
8. *Report*, June 24,1865, pp.4-7.
9. F. L. Olmsted, et al, *The Production of Wine in California. . . Buena Vista.*
10. McGinty, *Strong Wine., pp.409-411.*
11. *Strong Wine*, 423.
12. *California Farmer*, 3/1/1866.
13. McGinty, *Strong Wine, pp.431-436.* The author's research into these financial matters is definitive.
14. *Report*, 1867.
15. Peninou, *Sonoma, pp.67-68.*
16. *Alta California*, 8/6/1869, 8/26/1869, 8/27/1869.
17. *Strong Wine,* pp.423.
18. *Alta California*, 11/29/1867; Ag. Soc., 1866/1867, p.330, p.539.
19. *California Farmer*, 1/26/1871; *Alta California*, 3/5/1872, 6/30/1873, 10/22/1876; Peninou, *Sonoma, pp.65-69.*

170

20. Charles Loring Brace, *The New West: or California in 1867-1868*, New York, 1869,pp. 260-266.

21. *Alta California*, 8/2/1869, 8/23/1869.

Chapter
10

Running in Place

1870-1879

The 1870s may have been the most complex decade in American history, particularly for Californians. It was a time of marked prosperity and rock-bottom depression. Although the 1869 rail connection to the east had given Californians great hope for rising prosperity, it instead gave them an overpowering monopoly, the Southern Pacific "Octopus." Although the Civil War had ended slavery, racism triumphed all over the country. In California the anti-Chinese movement was viral, capped by the national Exclusion Act of 1882.

For California winegrowers the seventies was a time to survive or get out. By 1878 massive numbers had given up. Most of those who survived into the eighties prospered. The names of many survivors are enshrined today among the heroes of the state's wine history: Krug and Beringer (Napa), DeTurk and Dresel (Sonoma), LeFranc and Pellier (Santa Clara) are six of the most illustrious.

California wine men and women also had unique problems. Would Congress never get rid of the stifling Civil War tax on wine and brandy? And there was a continuous conflict over the tariff on cheap foreign-produced wine, which was eventually eased when the national government finally passed helpful protective legislation.

And there was the phylloxera, finally identified for sure in California when it was discovered in a Sonoma vineyard in 1873. I shall give a more detailed picture of the fight against this bug in a later chapter, but for now

The Workingmen's Party of California was an influential 1870s labor organization. "The Chinese must go!" was their official motto. (Courtesy the California Historical Society, CHS2099.002)

the "destroyer's" advance was slow but deadly, and the area where it became the deadliest and the earliest was around the old town of Sonoma and a few miles to the east, the land of Buena Vista. It was the deadly vise of economic depression and phylloxera infestation that finally squeezed the Buena Vista Vinicultural Society to death in 1878. Ironically, this moment also marks the date when a Sonoma man named Dresel showed the rest of the state how to successfully combat phylloxera, just before California and the nation rose out of the great depression and into the prosperity of the 1880s. Without doubt, bad luck was a good part of the reason for Buena Vista's demise.

What was *not* a cause of the winery's troubles was a continuation of the extravagance and bluster that had marked the years from 1857 to 1867. Sober business principles were the new rule. Extended debt was not countenanced unless the need was overpowering, even if the goal was grand. Good wine, and lots of it, was the continued overriding goal, as evidenced by the production statistics of the seventies. The public image the trustees pro-

174

moted was of a large and famous production facility producing good and dependable products, and Buena Vista won more than its share of awards at the several international expositions held in the 1870s.

One element of Buena Vista's production that defied this policy was the company's continued and costly production of sparkling wine. Even after announcing an end to its money-losing champagne venture in 1871, two years later they were at it again, and again without profit. But it would be incorrect to point to these losses as a significant cause of the company's troubles.[1]

Wine and grape prices between 1870 and 1872 rose slightly, partly because of the decline in French and German wines available on the East Coast due to the Franco-Prussian War of 1870-71. The 1871 vintage at Buena Vista was enormous, now that all vines planted in the late sixties were fully bearing. With the wine left over from the 101,000 gallon 1870 vintage added to 1871's 160,000 gallons, there were 230,000 unsold gallons in the cellars. The new board could sniff the possibility of profits in the offing. William Ralston now sat on the board, as did the former president's son, Robert Johnson. Six years later he would own all that was left of the Buena Vista estate.[2]

In an attempt to work against the external forces hurting the local wine industry, in 1871 the short-lived Sonoma and Napa Grape Growers Association was formed.[3] Their number one objective was to lower or remove the Civil War taxes on their products. They also discussed ways to pressure the Southern Pacific railway system to ease up on their hurtful rates on wine and brandy headed east. The "Octopus," as it came to be called, owned 11,588,000 acres of California land, and a pure monopoly in the rail traffic going east. By the mid-seventies the company had tightened the noose by making rate-fixing agreements with the company that controlled most of California's ocean commerce. There was little that the state's agricultural interests could do legally to effect relief from the SP's rigid policies.

One of the leaders of the local association was a relative newcomer to the Sonoma wine scene. When Emil Dresel died in 1869, his estate went to his brother, Julius. He had lived several years in Texas and had a thorough understanding of viticulture and wine making. Most important, he had a powerful interest in the phylloxera and had developed an idea from his previous contacts in Missouri on how successfully to fight the "destroyer."

A sign of better times at Buena Vista was a contract struck by the company in late 1871 with a famous photographer. English-born Eadweard Muybridge had settled in San Francisco in 1866, and became famous for his outdoor California shots, particularly of Yosemite. At Buena Vista he created what has come to be accepted as the greatest nineteenth century collection of winery and vineyard photos in the world. The stereoscopic views were on sale in San Francisco in the spring of 1872. Unfortunately the economic disaster that descended on California and the rest of the nation over the next five years dampened the hoped-for publicity dividend that might have resulted from the collection. The reader can well appreciate that potential from the Muybridge photos on the accompanying pages.[4]

The failure of a great New York banking house in September 1873 triggered, but certainly did not cause, a national depression that lasted until 1878. The railroad boom after the Civil War had led to a speculative bubble in securities, and over-expansion of productive capacity in agriculture and industry meant falling prices, vanishing credit, unemployment and general suffering. It took a while for the full force of the great wave of depression to crash down on the Pacific Coast.

At Buena Vista in the spring of 1873, and again in 1875, vines were grafted over from lesser varieties to Burger and Gutedel, to complement their already good stand of Riesling. More and more since the Dresel days, the emphasis here, and generally in the Sonoma Valley, was on white wine in a German style. But there was lots more Zinfandel grafted in 1873 and planted in 1875. In the latter year the advance of phylloxera meant fairly large spots of at least a quarter acre had to be replanted. At that date there was no solution to the problem in sight; for now, it was replant and pray.[5]

For Sonoma in general, wine grape acreage, even in the face of bad times, rose from 5,200 acres in 1873 to 6,300 in 1875. This expansion was mainly north of Santa Rosa around Windsor and Healdsburg, an area as yet unaffected by the phylloxera spread and one where good land was

176

Illustrated by MUYBRIDGE.

A VINTAGE IN CALIFORNIA.

Published by BRADLEY & RULOFSON.

—Buena Vista Vineyard, Sonoma. Cellar, and Wine for distillation.

Samples from Eadweard Muybridge's series of Buena Vista photographs.

still relatively inexpensive. But Sonoma was still not heavily planted wine country, by any means. That 5,200 acres of wine grape was less than 10% of the county's total planted acreage in 2011.

Buena Vista in 1873 got a new manager in Adam Kitz, touted to be a champagne expert. He did produce good sparklers, one of which won a medal at the 1876 Philadelphia Centennial Exposition. He also won medals there for red and white table wines. But in a depression, bread consumption stays fairly steady, while champagne consumption plummets.[6]

In 1875 the wave of depression really hit California. William Ralston, with his Bank of California, had invested in numerous shaky enterprises. He had also started construction of San Francisco's great Palace Hotel. Buena Vista was actually one of his least unsound ventures. On August 26, 1875 his financial empire collapsed, and the Bank of California closed its doors on its customers. A month later wine prices collapsed, with most of Buena Vista's gigantic 205,000 gallon 1874 vintage still unsold. The county headed state wine production with its 1,800,000 gallons.

Before 1875 Buena Vista had depended on its brandy sales to bolster income. The brandy tax had been lowered to fifty cents per gallon, but in that year the government changed its rules, and now required distillers to pay the tax while the brandy was still unsold under bond. This was an impossible load dumped on all brandy producers. Kitz wasn't making any bad wine at Buena Vista which had to be sent to the still, but around the state that was standard procedure. The result was huge amounts of poor wine, that normally would have become brandy, being dumped on the market at ruinous prices. Buena Vista felt the pain, for a sinking sea brings down all boats. And just when smaller grape crops might have been welcome, Sonoma's total production soared.[7]

Later, in a speech to a large group of Sonoma winegrowers, Eugene Hilgard, the new Professor of Agriculture at the university, looked back on these days between 1875 and 1877 as a time when it was more profitable for vineyardists to turn the hogs into the vineyards than to pay to have the grapes harvested, when wine was selling at ten to fifteen cents per gallon. It was not quite that bad all over Sonoma, but it was very bad.[8]

178

For almost two years the northern California press bemoaned what looked like the total economic destruction of the Bay Area wine industry, an area now understood to be the center of fine wine production in the state. "Full cellars and empty pockets," was perfectly illustrated at Buena Vista, which, even in the face of vineyard decline from phylloxera produced 158,000 gallons in 1877.[9]

The lack of rain in 1876 and 1877 accelerated the killing effect on Buena Vista's phylloxerated vineyards, but by no means had these more than 400 acres of vines lost their ability to produce fairly large crops. By the fall of 1877 a clear and deadly fact faced the winery's board of trustees: Buena Vista was the center of phylloxera destruction in the Sonoma Valley. Even the large plantings of 1864-1866 were developing noticeable areas of decline and death. With the industry tottering and the destruction of its vineyards accelerating, the company's leaders saw that they could not afford to replant its dead and dying vines, and even if they did, the new vines appeared to be doomed. In 1878 there was no reason to believe that ten years down the line there would even be any vineyards left in northern California. There was still no remedy for the gradually expanding menace, and somehow the deadly bug had even appeared in the Napa Valley.

On July 22, 1878, the Buena Vista trustees, still faced with several mortgages to be settled, announced their intention to disincorporate the BVVS. There were still 6,000 acres which would continue to have economic value, even as bare land, which seemed possible with the advance of the phylloxera.[10] At first, ads appeared simply announcing that Buena Vista Vineyard was for sale, the entire property with real improvements, equipment and vineyards, "undoubtedly the finest single property in the county of Sonoma."[11]

This approach got nowhere, so the real estate, land and buildings, was placed at auction and sold to Robert C. Johnson for $46,501 in January 1879. It is not clear whether any of the Society's mortgages were passed on to Johnson, but the tiny price suggests that this was the case. As was traditional, the contract price given was in gold coin, "and other valuable consideration," which could mean almost anything.

Beuna Vista Castle, Sonoma, Cal.

Early twentieth-century postcard featuring Robert C. Johnson's mansion, referred to by locals as "Beuna (sic) Vista Castle."

Johnson had been a member of the board, and George Johnson, his father, was its president when Haraszthy left Buena Vista. He had made his money in a large San Francisco iron works and had one of the largest fortunes in the city. Robert and his brother inherited this fortune.[12]

The next step for the now-unincorporated society was to sell as much of Buena Vista's "goods and chattels" as possible. This auction was announced in a huge ad in November 1879, at the end of the vintage. For sale were 120,000 gallons of red, white and sparkling wines, "with all the appliances necessary for their production." There were tanks, presses and crushers; casks, vats and tubs.

180

There were a lot of horses and other livestock offered.[13] The corporation had followed a common practice over the years of raising small amounts of money through regular mandatory assessments on the stockholders; before the auction a huge list of delinquent stockholders appeared in the press.[14]

It is clear that Robert Johnson and his wife, Kate, did not have a powerful interest in vineyards and wine production, but there was still activity at Buena Vista for a while. Even though the vineyards were now "totally infested," in what the *Sonoma Index* called "the valley of death," the vines were not all dead. Johnson had 57,000 gallons of wine made in 1879, the fourth largest producer in the county. After that the *Index* reported that the cellars were empty, and "The future of the place is a mystery to all." In future years Buena Vista grapes were shipped to San Francisco wine producers.[15] Historian Ernest Peninou has written that wine was made on the property each year, through 1883, but none thereafter.[16]

Epilogues normally appear at the end of historical works, but Buena Vista did not die in 1883. Viticulturally speaking, the great property slept until awakened in the 1940s by Frank Bartholomew. Nevertheless, it certainly had an interesting history during the next sixty years.

Robert and Kate Johnson did nothing after 1883 to pursue winegrowing at Buena Vista. More than anything else, they were art lovers and collectors. As for their new real estate acquisition, more than anything else, they wanted to expand on the area's natural beauty and on human aesthetic development of the land begun by Agoston Haraszthy and continued to a lesser degree by the BVVS.

Johnson gradually sold off his mostly-undeveloped land, well over 5,000 acres, keeping for his family about 300 acres, including the historic winery buildings and the elevated land area above these works, where Haraszthy's villa had been located. That elegant structure had burned to the ground in the seventies.

The Johnsons had a great three-story mansion built, with a two-story observation tower rising above the main structure. It was a perfect place to experience the *buena vista* of the Sonoma Valley and bay that had given the place its name. After 1883 they set about expanding the gardens that were already there. Lawns were planted, as were groves of tropical trees. There was even a Japanese tea house.[17]

By this date the decline of the vineyards was so complete that it would have been financial folly even to have pruned the poor vines still living. In 1884 Thomas Hardy, the Australian wine expert, passed through the Sonoma Valley and found the Buena Vista vineyards, "nearly all gone to ruin" from phylloxera. They had "a sad and disheartening appearance after seeing the luxuriant Napa Valley." Had he returned to Napa twelve years later, he would have witnessed a similarly disheartening landscape.[18]

By the end of the eighties the Johnsons had created the most beautiful country estate in the North Bay area. After Robert died, in 1891, his obituary emphasized his art collection, "mostly rare and costly statuary and paintings."[19] Kate Johnson lived for two more years, being best known for her collection of Persian and Angora cats. John Gottenberg, the manager of the property, must be credited for having preserved the two winery buildings and their tunnels, where he kept and bred carriage horses.

The Johnsons' heirs controlled the estate until 1905, when most of it was subdivided. The mansion, usually referred to as "The Castle," and the winery buildings were purchased in that year by Henri Cailleau, who sold the property to the state in 1915. Eventually the great residence became an annex to the Sonoma State Home at Glen Ellen; then it was a home for delinquent girls. It burned to the ground in 1923, in a fire supposedly set by the girls themselves.

The 1906 earthquake had damaged the old winery buildings and also brought down portions of the tunnels. Buena Vista had to wait until 1943 for full resuscitation, when Frank Bartholomew fixed up the old winery and replanted some of the vineyards.

＊　　　　　　＊　　　　　　＊

182

Buena Vista's demise was due more to a perfect storm of bad luck than to bad management. In 1878 the prospects for successful winegrowing were bleak, and the sale of the property, after fifteen years without a penny of profit, is understandable. But if the trustees could have seen events and conditions over the next twenty-four months, they might have hung on.

Vineyard planting in the northern Sonoma Valley and north of Santa Rosa had continued in a small way after 1877. But who would have thought that the county's wine grape acreage would more than double between 1877 and 1882?

In 1877 the press had bemoaned "full cellars and empty pockets." Before the end of the 1879 season the same newspapers were reporting almost empty cellars in Sonoma. Wine and grape prices were on the rise, and it seemed that every new settler crowding into the Healdsburg and Windsor areas was planting at least a tiny vineyard.[20] At the end of the 1878 vintage the *Pacific Rural Press* wrote, "A winemaker's face these days is a joyful thing to behold." This journal was published and edited by Edward Wickson, who some years later would succeed Eugene Hilgard as the Professor of Agriculture at the university. During the 1880 vintage Wickson visited Sonoma and reported happily that "all along the road to Cloverdale men, women and children might be seen gathering grapes." Four years earlier in the same area, vineyardists had been turning in the hogs to harvest their vines. Soon the San Francisco press was reporting that land prices were booming in Sonoma County.[21]

Between 1878 and 1879, people were happy that conditions had improved, for the first time since 1871. But no one was predicting the coming wine boom all over the state, which would help change the face of Sonoma and Napa, permanently.

Chapter 10 Notes

1. *Alta California*, 6/30/1873, 10/22/1876; *California Farmer*, 1/26/1871; *San Francisco Bulletin*, 1/8/1876.

2. *Pacific Rural Press*, 3/2/1872; *Sonoma Democrat*, 3/9/1872; Peninou, *Sonoma, pp.*68-69.

3. *Sonoma Democrat*, 12/2/1871.

4. Muybridge became even more famous in 1874 when he shot and killed his wife's lover, an act a jury determined was "justifiable homicide." For an interesting take on this "father of the cinema" see Rebecca Solnit, *Infinite City*, Berkeley, 2010, pp.23-30.

5. *Alta California*, 2/17/1873, 3/15/1875, 10/4/1875.

6. *Alta California*, 6/30/1873; *San Francisco Bulletin* 7/24/1876; Peninou, *Sonoma*, p.69.

7. Carosso, pp.95-97.

8. *Pacific Rural Press*, 11/30/1878.

9. *San Francisco Bulletin*, 7/13/1877; *Alta California*, 8/28/1876; *Santa Rosa Democrat*, 6/6/1877.

10. *San Francisco Post* and *Bulletin*, 7/22/1878.

11. *Alta California*, 7/24/1878.

12. *Sonoma Index*, 1/8/1879.

13. *Alta California*, 11/10/1879.

14. *Santa Rosa Democrat*, 6/16/1879.

15. *Sonoma Index*, 7/17/1880, 11/27/1880.

16. Peninou, *Sonoma*, p.70.

17. *Saga of Sonoma*, Sonoma Historical Society, 1954; Robert M. Lynch, *The Sonoma Valley Story*, Sonoma, n.d., p.59.

18. Hardy, pp.17-18.

19. *Sonoma Index,* 5/30/1891.

20. *Healdsburg Weekly Enterprise,* 11/22/1877; *San Francisco Bulletin,* 8/25/1879.

21. *Pacific Rural Press,* 11/30/1878, 10/26/1880; *San Francisco Bulletin,* 9/10/1883.

Chapter
11

Sonoma Wine Boom

1879-1890

Between the spring of 1877 and the fall of 1878, a hopeful glow developed all over the northern California wine industry. The press led the way, at first with a mild optimism; by vintage time in 1879 a bullish roar of confidence had engulfed all of California agriculture. Land prices began to soar. Lines of credit were now easily established. It was boom time in the wine country, particularly in Sonoma, Napa and Santa Clara Counties.

In Sonoma there had been vineyard expansion on a small scale, even in the bleak mid-seventies. This took place mostly in the broad and open land around, and particularly north of Santa Rosa, where land was plentiful and cheap. But there had been no large scale development. In the Sonoma Valley, particularly in the southern area around the town of Sonoma, fear of phylloxera almost precluded planting in these years.

Of California's fifty-eight counties Sonoma is larger than average, covering 1,576 square miles, about one million acres. It is about twice the size of Napa County. Approximately 400,000 acres have a useful agricultural potential, mostly range lands. Today the county has about sixty thousand acres of wine grapes. In the early 1870s a person ballooning over the county might have had trouble locating vineyards, for they covered only about five thousand acres. Two years into the wine boom, in 1880, there were about ten thousand. When planting leveled off at the end of the decade, there were almost twenty-three thousand acres of wine grapes, double the county's total would be in 1970 at the beginning of the modern wine

This card, wishing "Compliments of the Seasons" from CWA and its seven founding members, bears the Association's trademark, a young Bacchus being rowed through the Golden Gate. (Courtesy of the Unzelman Collection)

boom. And just like the 1880s, the 1970s saw Sonoma's acreage double in five years, finally in 1976 exceeding the record set in the 1890s.

The pattern of the winegrowing explosion in the 1880s tells us a lot about how this really new industry would eventually develop. Large scale wine producers would raise grapes but buy a large percentage of their crush from small scale vineyardists. No longer would a sizeable portion of vineyard owners make their own wine. It was a matter of capital expenditure. It was far more efficient financially to produce and sell wine on a large scale, than for large numbers of individual farmers to amass the capital to pay for the facilities and equipment to produce wine. Historian Vincent Carosso contended that the wine boom developed largely because California wine quality greatly improved in these years. Actually, the wine boom, following the pattern I have described, was largely responsible for the rise of California wine quality. The economic environment of the seventies depression had knocked many small wine producers, mostly ill-equipped novices, out of the wine making business, even though most kept their vineyards. Many of these new producers were responsible for California wines' poor reputation before the eighties.

188

Men like Napa's Charles Krug, San Jose's Charles Lefranc and Sonoma's Isaac DeTurk made lots of wine in those years, and lots of good wine. And in the worst of times they prospered.

To get a picture of this bucolic transformation in the eighties we should take a leisurely tour up the Sonoma Valley, then cut across to Santa Rosa and move north toward the county line near Cloverdale. In doing so we would pass many of the pioneers introduced in Chapter 7. In and around the town of Sonoma and to the east toward the Napa County line, the vineyards were dead or on their last legs by the mid-eighties.

The land was still fertile and productive as it was transformed into non-viticultural activities. The exception, south of Buena Vista, were the vineyards of Jacob Gundlach and Julius Dresel. During the eighties their vineyards, about three hundred acres in total, were in excellent shape, although they had been drooping some in the mid-seventies. An explanation for this situation must wait until the next chapter.

The lower valley, west of the town, is often called El Verano. Nicholas Carriger and O.W. Craig continued and expanded their operations there, as did William McPherson Hill to the north. Between them two important wine operations were under way in the eighties. In 1872 George F. Hooper bought a huge swath of valley and foothill land, 870 acres just west of today's town of Agua Caliente. After returning from a trip to the East Coast in 1879 he made public his view that the demand for California wine in the east was about to explode. He began planting Riesling and Gutedel vines and soon had a small winery. His white wines were good enough to be exhibited at the Paris Exposition in 1889. Years later he sold his Sobre Vista estate to Rudolph Spreckels, the Hawaiian sugar magnate.[1] Near Sobre Vista was George Whitman's 100 acre vineyard operation, which eventually would be part of Senator George Hearst's historic Madrone Ranch.

A far more permanent and historic winery operation was founded in 1885 in the footh Zinfandel and Riesling and was eventually acquired by the California Wine association. The old winery survives today in partial ruin, but the vineyard and its wines are still famous. In 1938 Louis Martini acquired and rejuvenated the old vineyard, and renamed it Monte Rosso. Bottles of outstanding wine bearing the Louis Martini label are still an important part of California's premium wine production.[2]

We have already noted Kohler & Frohling's 1875 move north to complement their huge company's Los Angeles product with the excellent dry table wines of the Sonoma Valley. Charles Kohler bought a huge piece of land that stretched across the valley west of Joshua Chauvet's place. It included a thirty- acre vineyard planted by Jackson Temple in the 1860s. In 1867 author Titus Cronise had stopped by and sampled Temple's wine. He later wrote that it tasted "similar to the famous Hungarian tokay." Vineyards in those days often had distinctive names, and Temple's became Tokay Vineyard. Charles Kohler liked the name and kept it for his three hundred acre spread of vines.[3]

After Kohler died in 1887 the property eventually was controlled by the CWA. In 1910 Jack London bought a large portion of the property. Today it is the Jack London Historic Park on which several structures from the Kohler days have survived.

There was a good deal of continuity between early winegrowing in the Glen Ellen area and developments in the eighties. Chauvet, Justi and several others carried on; Mmes. Warfield, Stuart and Hood continued to prosper. Eliza Hood's brother, James Shaw, had also established a flourishing winegrowing operation a few miles to the north, which he named Wildwood Ranch. Shaw was an early advocate of employing resistant rootstock as a defense against phylloxera. When the Kunde family acquired Wildwood in 1904 they kept some of Shaw's old Zinfandel vines. A few of those vines have survived on the V. riparia rootstock, perhaps the oldest such vines in California.[4]

Just south of Wildwood in 1878 a former British army officer bought a large piece of William Hood's Los Guilicos Ranch. John H. Drummond soon had 150 acres of vines, and what vines! Only Napa's H. W. Crabb of To Kalon fame could rival this gritty Scotsman for the variety and premier elegance of the vine varieties he imported, raised and sold to his Sonoma neighbors.

190

The ruins of John Drummond's Dunfillan Winery, as seen today on the grounds of Kunde Family Estates.

His first vine imports poured in between 1879 and 1880, first from Bordeaux: Cabernet Sauvignon and Cabernet franc from Chateau Lafite and Semillon from Chateau. d'Yquem. Then came the rest of the red Bordeaux varieties: Merlot, Malbec and Verdot from Chateau Cantenac-Brown. There were also Chardonnay and Pinot noir from Burgundy, and Syrah from the Rhône's Hermitage district.[5]

He became famous at the 1883 Viticultural Convention in San Francisco for his Dunfillan wines. Frederico Pohndorff, the European wine ex-

191

pert and assistant to professor Hilgard, wrote up an evaluation of the top wines exhibited. He declared that Drummond's 1882 Semillon was the best wine shown. He also praised the Scotsman's 1882 Cabernet, the 1881 Zinfandel, and the 1882 Syrah, dubbed by Drummond "Oeil de Perdrix." Napa got lots of plaudits, but mostly for varieties like Refosco and Tannat. And there was, as always, Jacob Schramm's delicious Riesling.[6]

Where did Drummond pick up his knowledge of wines and vines that helped him burst from the starting blocks? It's not clear. In a long technical letter to Isaac DeTurk in 1884 he made it clear to any knowledgeable reader that all those excellent wines were not the result of dumb luck. Professor Hilgard was also impressed. He visited Dunfillan in 1885 and was surprised at what he saw. "The general excellence of the wines shown by (Drummond) at the Viticultural Convention proved how far good management and scrupulous care" could overcome the youth and small size of Drummond's facility.[7]

Charles Wetmore, the head of the State Viticultural Commission, had recently planted his Cresta Blanca Vineyard in Livermore, but he wanted to establish his brand before his vines came to full bearing. Thus, in 1886 he bought the best 1884 Cabernet and Syrah he could find, from J. H. Drummond and H. W. Crabb, for a price more than double normal wholesale.[8]

Drummond had tested his wines' ability to travel in 1883 by sending a few cases to friends in England. Soon he was selling wine north and south in the Pacific coastal trade and to Honolulu. By 1889 he was making large rail shipments east. Then suddenly, just before Christmas that year, he died.[9]

His estate was complicated. He had grown children, but had married a widow before coming to California, a certain Mrs. Bioletti. Drummond was generous with all his heirs, but the money he left to his widow had a mysterious condition. At no time could she permit her son, Frederick Bioletti, to reside in any house in which the Drummond children were living. Frederick Bioletti went on to serve as Professor Hilgard's assistant after that scholar's retirement in 1906. From then on he was in charge of the wine and viticulture research at the University of California, first at Berkeley, and then at U.C. Davis until 1935.[10]

Charles Wetmore, mentioned above, and Isaac De Turk came together closely after 1880 through their work in the State Viticultural Commission. Wetmore was its first boss and De Turk was the commissioner for the Sonoma District. The creation of the Commission came in the wake of the new and booming condition of the state's wine industry and in the face of the rising destructive threat from phylloxera. The Commission's task was to perform practical experiments on wines and vines, to fight and control disease, and to further viticulture education. The university's College of Agriculture, under Eugene Hilgard, would independently take charge of scientific research in viticulture and enology.[11]

De Turk's job as commissioner for Sonoma was primarily to collect information on the growth and needs of the county's burgeoning wine industry. This he did diligently, although he often complained that vineyard owners were too often loath to share their data with him. In 1880 the U. S. Census taker could find only about eight thousand acres of wine grapes in the county; De Turk was able to locate almost 10,000. Together these numbers reflect the approximate 20-30% increase since 1876.

About 57% of the vines were alive, some barely, in the Sonoma Valley. About 20% were alive and well in the Santa Rosa area. And about 13% were mostly new plantings around Healdsburg and Calistoga, including the Alexander Valley. The remaining 10% were scattered around Petaluma, Sebastopol and out in Knight's Valley near the Napa County line. It was the large area from Santa Rosa to Cloverdale that saw most of the dramatic expansion of wine grape acreage in the eighties. By 1890 the county total had more than doubled.

The detailed statistics tell us much about the pattern of wine-growing in the county and how it evolved between 1880 and 1890. In the Santa Rosa area below Healdsburg there were 203 vineyardists in 1880. Of these, 74% had fewer than ten acres of vines. From Healdsburg to Cloverdale there were 170 vineyardists, 73% of whom had fewer than ten acres of vines. These statistics support historian Thomas Pinney's observation that Sonoma County then was full of "individual farmers, still unspecialized, who grew grapes among their crops and who. . . sold their crops to nearby wineries." In 1880 the problem for these farmers was transportation. Most outside the Sonoma Valley were at a distance from wineries of any size. Almost all of these were in the Sonoma Valley, twenty-two of which regularly produced ten thousand gallons of wine or more. When Isaac DeTurk built his Santa Rosa winery in 1878, he became, in Professor Pinney's words, 'the King of Sonoma County." He soon had another large facility in Cloverdale; others would soon come onto the scene.[12]

By the early nineties there were between twenty-one thousand and twenty-three thousand acres of wine grapes in Sonoma County. Sonoma Valley still had five thousand, but now in the Santa Rosa area there were about 12,000, and in the Alexander Valley about 3,100. There were also about seven hundred acres south of Santa Rosa, mostly near Sebastopol. Obviously, there had been a huge shift in winegrowing in the county since 1880. And there were sixty-seven Sonoma wineries that were crushing fifty

Isaac De Turk's massive Santa Rosa winery and plant depicted in this 1940s photograph. It is now the centerpiece of the City's Railroad Square restoration, and will soon see commuter and freight trains ride past on the long-dormant tracks. (Courtesy of the Unzelman Collection)

tons or more annually. The county was now really wine country. The wine grape acreage here in the nineties would not be surpassed until 1975, during the modern wine boom.[13]

DeTurk's plant in Santa Rosa eventually covered an entire city block with a million gallon capacity. He sold large amounts of wine to the most respected San Francisco wine houses. But his name was known in all the places Americans drank wine, because a sizeable portion of his output went out in cases of bottles under his own label and name. So well established was his brand that twenty years after his death in 1896, "I. DeTurk" wines were still being marketed by his successors all over the Country.

Among connoisseurs he was famous for the high quality of his best wines. His Cabernet Sauvignon and Zinfandel were probably his best. But unlike almost all California producers he often provided the varietal designation on his front labels. At the 1893 Chicago Exposition Charles Oldham made a special point of the fact that DeTurk's entry in the "Claret" division was "in first class condition, labelled 'Zinfandel.'" In the Medoc division DeTurk's "Cabernet 1891" was "a beautiful, soft wine. . . in perfect condition."[14]

Isaac DeTurk continued to serve Sonoma on the State Viticultural Commission until 1893, when he became its president; he held that office until its demise two years later. He died a bachelor in 1896, and his estate was settled on a small army of relatives.[15] But the winery and business remained intact and operated under Clarence Mann, who had been DeTurk's San Francisco agent since 1889. Eventually the William Hoelscher Co. ran the plant and marketed I. DeTurk wines until Prohibition.[16]

Just north of Santa Rosa was a winegrowing operation like no other in California history. No winery in Sonoma County has had a more interesting history, and few have made better wines. Fountaingrove was a rare survivor of Prohibition under its pre-1919 leadership. And it was unique in that it was founded as a utopian religious colony.

Its leader for seventeen years was Thomas Lake Harris, an English-born religious leader, whose family came to New York when he was five, in

In 1892 Thomas Lake Harris, the mystic prophet and founder of Fountaingrove, left his California legacy to fend for itself after allegation of sexual improprieties at the commune dogged him in the Bay Area press.

1828. By the 1840s he was preaching a Universalist philosophy, but gradually developed an eclectic cosmological view of his own on the relationship between God and mankind. The end result was the founding in 1858 of the Brotherhood of the New Life. For this study its most important element was social rather than religious. In 1861 he founded a colony of followers in Dutchess County, New York. One of these was a Missouri man, E. B. Hyde, who understood winegrowing, which the colony took up in a small way. In 1867 they expanded this activity at Brocton on Lake Erie, and by 1870 had production up to fifteen thousand gallons.

In retrospect Harris's next step seems obvious. He would establish an agricultural colony in California. For him and Hyde the area around Santa Rosa was very attractive, and in 1875 land prices there were rock bottom. On his first trip west Harris took Hyde and a young Japanese man, age twenty-two, whom he had met in Scotland in 1867 and who had become a knowledgeable winegrower at Brocton. Kanaye Nagasawa had left Japan in 1865 under the patronage of a Satsuma nobleman to learn the ways of the western world. When he met Harris two years later he was impressed by the American's communal philosophy and accepted his invitation to live and work at Brocton. The young man learned horticulture and winegrow-

Fountaingrove winemaker Kanaye Nagasawa with poet Edwin Markham, who was a resident at the commune for some time. (Courtesy Kosuke Ijichi collection.)

ing under Hyde, and continued at Fountaingrove, where he supervised the vineyards while Hyde ran the cellar.[17]

Harris's western trip brought him ownership of four hundred acres in the lower foothills north of Santa Rosa, for which he paid only fifty dollars per acre. In these years he always had plenty of money since several of his followers had brought large fortunes with them, which they entrusted to their spiritual master. One Englishman had been a member of Parliament.

The first agriculture at Fountaingrove was dairying on a large scale, but by 1879 Harris had picked up the scent of the coming boom in wine. In 1883 he built a huge stone winery which eventually had a capacity of six hundred thousand gallons. By the end of the eighties the entire estate covered two thousand acres, with four hundred in vines. The winery's first vintage was 15,000 gallons; in 1888 it was 200,000.

Harris had many eastern connections from his New York days. He soon was connected to a New York City office run by Jonathan Lay and Samuel Clark. The business and marketing end of the operation was there, and was always referred to as Lay, Clark and Co., even in California. By the late eighties most of Fountaingrove's wine was marketed on the East Coast, and there were four outlet deports in Britain, located in London, Liverpool, Glasgow and Manchester.[18]

Nagasawa soon learned that first class grape varieties were essential to Fountaingrove's financial success, but he later remarked that their early East Coast success depended "upon the peculiar merits of Zinfandel." There was always an emphasis on red wine production from such as Mataro, Cabernet Sauvignon and Malbec. There was never a mention of Mission grapes. Their whites came from Sylvaner, Gutedel, and Burger for wines in a German style.[19]

In 1892 Harris left Fountaingrove after the San Francisco "Yellow Press" ran a series of salacious articles on communal life at the colony, based on a book by a disgruntled former community member. He never returned, but the local Sonoma press never took part in the personal attacks on him. In 1900 Harris sold the estate to the five remaining members of the community; Nagasawa was the boss for forty-

198

Fountaingrove's famous "Red Barn," which was built in 1899, and can been seen today perched on the hillside off of highway 101 just north of Santa Rosa. (Courtesy of the Unzelman Collection)

two years, from 1892 until his death in 1934, the last survivor of the colony. Harris had died in 1906.[20]

Ernest Peninou believed that "With Nagasawa at the helm, the mood at Fountaingrove changed." He was convivial and liked to entertain. Celebrities were soon making the winery and manor house a destination point. The operation survived and prospered.

Fountaingrove had always been a diversified agricultural operation. It became even more diversified during Prohibition, but not quite as profitable. Under new ownership in 1938 Fountaingrove began producing some truly excellent wines. But the vineyards were decrepit and profits almost nonexistent. The last vines were pulled up in 1954. Today much of the area has been developed and is really part of urban Santa Rosa. The ruins of the great winery survive, but out of plain sight. Travelers heading north

199

today can get a glimpse of history, for they can hardly miss on the hillside the great red round barn that Nagasawa had built in 1899 to house Foun-taingrove's sixty horses.[21]

Before heading north to the Alexander Valley we need to take two important detours, first along the Russian River west of Windsor. Then we should drop over to Dry Creek Valley, just northwest of Healdsburg. The main winegrowing development in both areas took place in the 1890s, but the seeds were scattered in the 1880s.

The Russian River flows south out of Mendocino County, through the Alexander Valley, and suddenly turns west below Windsor and heads for the Pacific. Eons ago it probably flowed on south to the great bay. This region was lumber country in the pioneer days, but as the land was cleared, developers turned to agriculture. The winegrowing pioneers were the Korbel Brothers, who came here in the 1860s from the Czech region of the Austrian Empire. Of the three, Francis was the leader in wine. In 1880 he started planting forty acres of vines near the river east of Guerneville. In 1883 his first vintage of 10,000 gallons encouraged him to expand. In 1884 he began building a large brick winery, which was finished for the 1886 vintage. By 1891 the winery was again expanded, now "a magnificent wine cellar" with an elegant brandy tower.[22] This complex stills looks out on the Russian River and is a necessary destination point for wine tourists today.

Back on the main road at Healdsburg we jog left into the Dry Creek Valley, one of Sonoma's most famous districts today. There may have been a few vines here before George Bloch settled in 1869. Another Frenchman arrived a year later, and Alex Colson joined with Bloch to begin the little valley's first commercial winery. They started operating in 1872, and according to historian Jack Florence, this was the second winery north of Santa Rosa. By the mid-seventies there were sixteen small vineyards in Dry Creek. By 1883 there were fifty-four. Florence counts 807 acres of Dry Creek vines by that year: 49% Zinfandel, and 30% Mission. By 1885 Charles Dunz's 70,000 gallon Laurel Hill Winery was the largest of the valley's seven. It was later the site of the modern Frei Bros. facility.

200

Sixteen-year-old May Queen Isabelle Simi holds court on the family porch.

Dry Creek's first grand winery was built in 1887 by John Paxton, who hired the famed Hamden McIntyre to design his native stone edifice. It was later an earthquake victim in 1906. By 1889 Dry Creek had eleven wineries, whose combined capacity was 350,000 gallons. In these years the typical product was common bulk red wine. Today it is considered one of the county's best fine wine districts.[23]

Returning to the main road north at Healdsburg we almost immediately pass one of Sonoma County's great winery monuments. Today it is the Simi Winery, appropriately named for the brothers who in 1881 bought a little winery located south of today's location. Pietro and Giuseppe Simi had been in the wholesale grape business for several years.[24] In 1884 they joined the wine boom by planting 128 acres of vines. In 1887 they began building their great winery, which was finished in 1890 with a capacity of 200,000 gallons.[25] The brothers came from the Tuscan village of Montepulciano, and that is what they named their winery. It prospered, but the brothers died in 1904. Giuseppe's daughter Isabelle ran the winery until 1970, aided until 1954 by her husband, Fred Haigh. Sixteen years later she sold the winery, but continued working in the tasting room until 1978.

About three miles north of Healdsburg the Alexander Valley opens up to the east and the southeast of the Russian River. Today it is one of California's great winegrowing areas, with about 15,000 acres of vines. In 1880 there were a few scattered vineyards which had to sell their grapes to producers in the Healdsburg area, or in Cloverdale to Isaac DeTurk. But in 1885 there were about eight hundred acres of new vines whose grapes would need

Andrea Sbarboro, second from left, with a group of Italian Swiss Colony investors in 1881, the year of ISC incorporation.

a secure home soon.[26] Two small wineries went up in the mid-eighties near today's Chalk Hill Road, built by Shadrick Osborn and Ludwig Michelson. Several more were built in the nineties out in this part of the valley.

The seeds of a truly large scale operation were planted in 1880 when Augustus Quitzow planted a few vines and built a small wooden winery just outside the then-tiny village of Geyserville. Quitzow went bankrupt in 1886, and Edward Walton, the head of one of America's most important brandy importers, bought the place and proceeded to build the largest brandy operation in California. By 1888 Walden & Co. had production up to fifty-four thousand gallons. By 1893 the company's huge stills were handling the product of one thousand tons of Alexander Valley grapes. Some years later, under new owners, the operation changed its emphasis to bulk red wine production as the Ciocca-Lombarda Wine Co.[27]

Of all the Alexander Valley's winegrowing operations the greatest and most famous, for the longest time, was the Italian Swiss Colony (ISC), established between Geyserville and Cloverdale. The idea for ISC came from Andrea Sbarboro, a long-time San Francisco resident who had success organizing mutual aid societies aimed at helping ordinary folk buy homes, somewhat like today's credit unions. From the beginning Sbarboro and his partners aimed their ISC at winegrowing, which was booming when they signed their articles of incorporation in 1881.

Their hope had been to establish a colony of workers who would eventually own their own vineyards, somewhat like the Anaheim Colony in Los Angeles County. But it didn't happen. The end result was a joint stock company, but the "Colony" term stuck to the operation.[28]

Sbarboro and a committee of directors traveled the state looking for the best place to plant ISC. They settled on a 1,393-acre piece of land in the Alexander Valley. Land was cleared and vines planted during the dormant months of 1882, about 150 acres by 1884. Half were Zinfandel; next came Riesling with thirty-five acres, and a scattering of Mataro, Grenache and Cinsaut. The emphasis was definitely on red wine.[29]

There was actually a small Zinfandel crop in 1884 whose wine was tasted at the State Viticultural Convention that year. It couldn't have been long out of the fermenter, but Frederico Pohndorff declared it an "expressive and full bodied wine," and that it "augurs well for the success of the colony."[30] But for the next two years ISC sold its grapes to other Sonoma wineries; their 1886 crop was 465 tons.[31] But California grape prices dropped sharply in 1886, the result of the heavy planting since 1878. The ISC leaders decided to build a winery. It was finished for the 1887 vintage, a fine two-story building with a three hundred thousand gallon capacity. Other new construction included workers' cottages and a little church. The estate was now called Asti and had its own railroad stop, whose little stone "station" is still standing in good condition.[32]

This first real vintage was a disaster. Scorching hot weather in September and October made it impossible to control fermentations. Sbarboro decided to acquire a winemaker with a solid academic background in chemistry. He hired Pietro C. Rossi, a San Francisco pharmacist with a degree in agricultural chemistry from the University of Turin. He ran the ISC cellar until his death in 1911. From 1888 onward the wines of ISC were known for their high quality.

Part of ISC's quality success came from the large number of vines imported from Italy: the Nebbiolo, Barbera and Sangiovese, particularly the latter, which became the basis for the company's nationally popular Tipo Chianti.

By the 1890s ISC had about one thousand acres in vines, and their wines were available in most of the country's large cities, they also won medals. At a time when the Italian immigrant population had been on the rise, ISC wines found an enthusiastic reception wherever the new arrivals settled. During the decade the company's wines won medals at seven international expositions.

Their financial success moved Sbarboro and Rossi in 1896 to expand into the Central Valley for sweet wine production. By 1897 the company had 1,750 acres of vines and wineries, with three million gallons of capacity. After 1900 the ISC became a powerful part of the California Wine Association. But the nineties were unhappy years for most Sonoma producers. Even ISC had to tighten the belt. The break in wine prices in 1887 was a harbinger of worse days to come. And on top of the financial situation, the phylloxera was still eating its way up the Sonoma Valley. Was there no way to stop it?

Chapter 11 Notes

1. *Sonoma Democrat*, 7/11/1879; PWSR 9/18/1889.

2. Peninou, *CWA*,pp.50-51; *Sonoma*, p.89.

3. Titus Fey Cronise, *The Natural Wealth of California*, San Francisco, 1868, p.171. There has never been evidence of Hungarian varieties here or that the Tokaji production methods were ever used.

4. Peninou, *Sonoma*, pp.106-107; *PWSR*, 1/1/1885; *Sonoma Index-Tribune*, 10/8/1904.

5. *PWSR*, 4/13/1883, 9/14/1883.

6. *PWSR*, 4/17/1883.

7. *PWSR*, 5/22/1885.

8. *PWSR*, 4/19/1886.

9. *PWSR, 6/11/1885, 5/24/1889.*

10. *Sonoma Democrat*, 11/18/1890; *PWSR. 1/8/1890.* I once interviewed a Davis professor who knew Bioletti well. He knew of Drummond's will, but had never heard anything to explain its bitter attack on Bioletti. Kate Warfield was the executor of the Drummond estate, valued at about $2,000,000 in today's dollars.

11. Carosso, pp.120-126.

12. Pinney, *History*, pp.336-340.

13. Board of State Viticultural Commissioners. . ., *Directory . . .Grape Growers, Wine Makers. . .*, Sacramento, 1893, pp.161-182; Isaac DeTurk, *The Vineyards of Sonoma County*, Sacramento, 1893, Peninou, *Sonoma*, pp.297-382. Most of my statistics do not appear in these reports but are derived from their numbers.

14. *PWSR 11/20/1893.*

15. *PWSR, 3/23/1896.*

16. *PWSR, 3/7/1895, 11/30/1902; San Jose Mercury, 8/12/1810;* Peninou, *Sonoma,* PP.112-116.

17. Robert V. Hine, *California's Utopian Colonies,* Berkeley, 1953, pp.12-32. Pinney, *History,* PP.331-335; Peninou, *Sonoma, pp.120-125.* Peninou was the general manager at Fountaingrove in the early 1950s.

18. *PWSR, 8/17/1888.*

19. *Sonoma Democrat, 8/22/1891, 1/2/1892, 6/4/1892.*

20. *American Wine Press,* 1/1901; *PWSR, 12/31/1900. The Sonoma Historian,* 2002, #4, pp.6-14 contains a well-illustrated biographical essay on Nagasawa.

21. *Wines & Vines,* 9/1947, 9/1951; *Santa Rosa Press Democrat,* 3/13/2010.

22. *Sonoma Democrat, 8/3/1883, 10/10/1891.*

23. Jack W. Florence, *A Noble Heritage,* Geyserville, 1993, pp.23-43; Peninou, *Sonoma,* pp.158-164. McIntyre designed many of Napa's great wine edifices, including Inglenook and Trefethen.

24. *Healdsburg Enterprise,* 11/7/1878; Pacific Rural Press, 11/16/1878.

25. *PWSR, 12/2/1890,*

26. *PWSR, 1/16/1885.*

27. *Sonoma Democrat, 8/13/1887; PWSR, 9/8/1889, 12/31/1911.*

28. Jack W. Florence, *Legacy of a Village,* Phoenix, 1999,pp. 42-44. This is the best published history of ISC. My own 1980 in-house manuscript history of ISC can be found in several wine libraries in northern California.

29. Sonoma Democrat 9/19/1883.

30. *PWSR,* 1/3/1885, 3/27/1885.

31. *Alta California,* 12/9/1886.

32. *Sonoma Democrat,* 7/17/1887; Florence, *Legacy,* pp.52-53.

Chapter
12

The Destroyer

1879-1890

The phylloxera has entered this study in several places, but a more fully realized story is needed here for several reasons. It is generally understood that most of the great work in the fight to save the vineyards of Europe and California was performed by French scientists. But Americans were also involved and important, particularly a Missouri scientist and two nurserymen from that state. And so far as the solution to the problem in California was concerned, it was effected by Californians. And of these by far the most important was a Sonoma winegrower, who made it clear through his efforts that the discoveries of the scientists could lead directly to a practical, in-the-vineyard solution.

The phylloxera is a tiny louse, or aphid, whose scientific name today is *Dactylasphæra vitifoliæ*. But in the early years of the struggle it was *Phylloxera vastatrix*, The Destroyer. It is native to the eastern United States, generally the Mississippi and Missouri Valleys. There is no good evidence of its residence west of the Rocky Mountains, certainly not in California, prior to the 1860s. In these eastern regions of America there are many native grape varieties that evolved alongside the phylloxera. Many of these are able to resist the bug's attacks on its root system. But there are also vines, usually considered native, that are not fully resistant. West of the Rockies, particularly in the coastal valleys of California, the chief native vine is the *Vitis californica*, which grows wild in abundance near streams and other waterways.

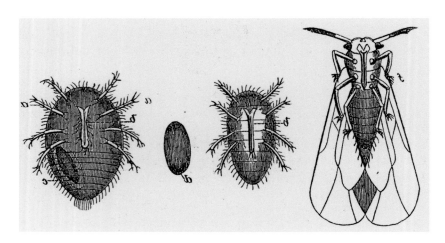

Phylloxera vastatrix (J.E. Planchon). Female specimens, the winged form at the left, and their eggs, all greatly magnified.

In the early 1860s, in the Rhône region of France, in the *département* of Gard, vinifera grape vines began declining, soon dying. This condition spread like wildfire in southern France. It was thought to be a new disease, previously unknown, *"la nouvelle maladie de la vigne."* It took French scientists several years to discover that this affliction was not really a disease. The vines' roots were being attacked by a tiny root louse, and the resulting damage led to infection and death.[1]

A French scientist, Jules-Émile Planchon, finally figured out what was happening in 1869 and gave the bug its first name, "The Destroyer." The first French attempts to solve the phylloxera problem seemed almost endless and were eventually unsuccessful after the investment of huge amounts of time and money. They attempted to defend the vine by attacking its attacker. They tried flooding, various poisons, electric shock. Many approaches today seem downright silly. But the government was offering a huge prize to anyone who could come up with a practical solution. The press was full of stories of the battles between the various advocates of the miscellany of proposals. Meanwhile the spread became a plague. In the Hérault region of southern France, between 1871 and 1879, 320,000 acres of wine grapes were destroyed.

210

At the same time, other scientists worked on discovering where the bug suddenly came from and how it got to France. It was finally and correctly decided that the phylloxera came from America. This discovery was reinforced by the revelation of a well-concealed secret: In 1862 a vineyardist in Gard had imported 154 American vines. They were still alive years later, their roots surrounded and covered by phylloxera, but the plants were in good condition. Planchon reported that, "of the French vines planted in the same ground, a great number are dead or dying. . ."[2]

During the same years an American entomologist based in Missouri had proved that the American phylloxera was the same louse that was destroying the French vineyards. Charles Valentine Riley was soon a hero in France, and worked with French scientists for many years. He and they soon saw the possibility of grafting European vinifera vines onto American rootstock. In fact, Riley was undertaking practical experiments attempting to identify the best species for such an undertaking a few years before the French were able to untangle their various battling adversaries on the subject.

Isidor Bush and George Husmann were Missouri nurserymen who began playing important roles in the quest for the proper rootstock to employ for grafting.[3] Riley worked with them and discovered that some American vines were far more effective than others. By 1872 Planchon and his associates had convinced the embattled vineyardists of southern France that American rootstock was the answer to their problems. Bush's nursery catalogue, developed with Riley's help, was translated into French and sold like hot cakes in the southern *départements.* In the winter of 1872-1873 Bush received orders for more than four hundred thousand cuttings, just from the Montpellier area.[4]

But there was still a lot of work to be done. In the fine wine regions of Bordeaux and Burgundy, growers were not convinced. Many wondered if the American vines would impart their "foxy" flavors to their *grands crus.* The question was answered for many in 1876 by Jean-Henri Fabre's experiments with Aramon vines grafted onto several American varieties. Over four years there was "no alteration in the quality of taste of the wine. . . ." [5]

One of Planchon's observations on the phylloxera's life cycle later explained why Californians could "watch and wait," in a way that Frenchmen could not. In France the development of the winged, egg-bearing female was standard. The winds of southern France made these ladies the principal agents of the phylloxera's high speed, long distance spread. This female form didn't develop in California's long, dry summers. Thus, unless the bugs were brought into a vineyard with other vines, they had to get around slowly on such things as workers' boots and wagon wheels. In California, effective area quarantine could help slow the tiny creatures' gradual migration.

We have already had a good look at the phylloxera's arrival and growth in California, with the center in the Sonoma Valley in the Buena Vista area. Some vines were drooping in the mid-sixties, but that the phylloxera was the cause only became known in 1873. O. W. Craig didn't know for sure what he had found until he sent his samples of the bug to Riley, who confirmed the Californians' suspicions.

Now what to do? Unfortunately no one was even close to knowing an answer to that question. In California, and at almost the same time in France, "What to do?" caused a lot of intellectual turmoil. Actually the situation was more confused in France than in California. In France the various theorists and their supporting factions were at each others' throats for years. In the Golden State there were several forces looking for answers in a fairly amicable manner. Hilgard went straight to work at the university. He started in Sonoma giving moving talks on the danger vineyardists faced. He also sent his assistant into the field to surrey much of California and determine the extent of the infection. The results were shocking. The bug was not limited to parts of Sonoma. There were several places in northern California where vines were already drooping in the presence of phylloxera.

The Viticultural Commission also took steps to promote quarantine throughout the state. It was up to local government to effect a quarantine, but Charles Wetmore appointed more than a hundred inspectors to alert growers of danger. There were seven appointed in Sonoma County. And the northern California press poured out continuous calls for action. But, to do what?

212

The famed Bush & Son & Meissner catalogue, 1875 edition. (Courtesy National Agricultural Library)

The first idea most embraced was defense. Defend the vines by fighting and eliminating the bug. Insecticides, flooding, electricity were all tried, as in France, to no avail. Hilgard believed that the soundest approach any grower could take at the moment was to have a well-cultivated, well-fertilized vineyard. This was an idea that any conscientious grower could accept and follow, but without lasting results.

In Sonoma, Eliza Hood's French winemaker, August Drioton, had been following the news from France for several years. He wrote a short

Julius Dresel

pamphlet, published in San Francisco in 1877, that supported Hilgard's suggestions in detail. Growers must avoid the exhaustion of their soils. Use the pressed grapes as vineyard fertilizer. Cultivate with precision and care. Prune vines closely, leaving fewer buds than normal to conserve the vines' energy and ability to resist infection. In other words, don't over-crop the vineyard. He rejected all attempts to destroy the insect, and argued correctly that it was impossible to cure an infected vine. However good these suggestions, none would ultimately stop The Destroyer.[6]

The answer was being developed both in France and America. If the American vines' roots are resistant to these attacks, graft European varieties onto these resistant rootstocks. Riley was already at work on the idea in the mid-seventies. And two California vineyardists who had kept up on the subject were in contact with Riley and George Husmann.

The first importation of American vines for rootstock was by Napa's H. W Crabb, probably in 1876. Husmann sent him cuttings from the Lenoir, a mysterious vine at first very attractive because its grapes, it was said, made a drinkable wine. This was not true of other rootstocks under consideration. The Lenoir became popular in Napa, since there was no grafting involved. It was a direct producer. It took several years before it became clear that it was only partially resistant. It took less time to discover that the wine made from this variety was of less value than what came from the lowly Mission variety. Napa growers were soon grafting the Lenoir over to vinifera.[7]

The real pioneer in this story was a Sonoma producer noted for the high quality of his wines. Julius Dresel had lived in Texas for many years before coming to Sonoma in 1869 after the death of his brother, Emil. In Texas he had dabbled in viticulture and was aware of Riley's work on resistant rootstock. In 1878 he imported several American vines from Missouri and began experimenting with them, just as Riley had done earlier. Only one vine worked well with vinifera grafts. It was from the *Vitis riparia*, a species usually found near streams and other water sources, as its names implies. It is not clear whether these vines came from Husmann or Isidor Bush. But in later years, after Husmann moved to Napa in 1881, he picked up the credit.[8]

By 1880 Dresel had brought in thirty thousand riparia vines, and by 1885 his vineyard, and that of his neighbor, Jacob Gundlach, had been transformed into the healthy and verdant beauties they had been in the sixties. Some others in Sonoma followed, but not many. What Dresel was doing was expensive, and the spread of the phylloxera was deceptively slow. It was not until 1887 that phylloxera had crept slowly north into the Glen Ellen area and was perceived as a real problem. But Eliza Hood and Kate Warfield had been moving to resistants for several years. By the 1890s, when vineyard planting of any kind had shut down all over Sonoma County due to the economy, there were about 2,300 acres planted there on resistants, that is, about ten percent of the county's vines. A little more than half of these were in the southern Sonoma Valley. In Napa only about five percent of the vines were on resistants.[9]

By 1889 most protected vines in Sonoma County were on *V. riparia.* But there were some there and around the Bay Area who had planted on native *V. californica.* In a few years such plantings were dead. Hilgard, Wetmore and many other leaders had taken it for granted that wild native American varieties were resistant. The californica was thought to be resistant primarily because Almaden's Charles Lefranc had used the native vine for grafting to expand his vinifera imports in the early sixties. These vines were perfectly healthy until the phylloxera made its way into the Santa Clara Valley. When these vines started dying in the nineties, many learned heads began shaking. One of these belonged to Professor Hilgard, who had planted his own vineyard near Mission San Jose on this non-resistant stock. By 1901 he had replanted on *V. riparia.*[10]

It is difficult to look back with any sympathy at the huge majority of Bay Area winegrowers who by 1890 had done nothing to protect their vineyards. Julius Dresel tried to stir his fellow vineyardists in a letter to a local newspaper. Why did they "listlessly stand by, waiting for something to turn up, while the vineyards fall dead?"[11] In his 1890 report on resistant rootstock to Isaac DeTurk, Dresel took a different tack. After he and Gundlach had employed their *V. riparia* in their declining vineyards, the results cried for notice from other producers. "We will be pleasantly

216

remunerated this year by the sale of 50,000 gallons of wine raised exclusively on American stock." [12]

But far too many vineyardists were not in the same financial condition as Dresel. Most had planted between 1878 and 1886. Many had bulging cellars of unsold wine. Most were still paying off mortgages signed at rates and with conditions that no longer reflected current grape and wine prices. The hurt became serious after the 1887 vintage, when prices slid steadily for two years. Trade journals wrote of the growing demoralization in the industry. At first it just seemed to be a little air being released from the bubble puffed up in previous years. When the 1890 crop was large and of excellent quality there was a sigh of relief from the press. But practically nobody was planting vines. From then on it was six years of ups and downs, mostly the latter, declining prices and the phylloxera spreading faster than ever.[13]

The only practical way to combat the Destroyer was by planting new vines on resistants. Virtually no one was planting new vines. And few were even trying to replace the vines that were dead or dying. It was obvious that the country had slid into a cyclical agricultural depression. For California wine producers there were too many grapes. Charles Krug commented that the phylloxera might be seen in a positive light. The bug was helping to hold down grape production.

Thus it stood for the Sonoma wine industry entering the "dismal nineties." Now all agreed that resistants were the answer to their viticultural salvation. But who now had any reason, or the means, to plant a vine? Most folks who had lived through and survived the ugly years of the seventies recalled how everything turned around after 1878. Hang on, they thought; things will improve. They were correct. But until then there would be hard times.

Chapter 12 Notes

1. George Gale, *Dying on the Vine*, Berkeley, 2011, pp.13-15; Christy Campbell, *The Botanist and the Vintner*, Chapel Hill, 2004, pp. 43-46.

2. George Ordish, *The Great Wine Blight*, New York, 1972, pp.28-32.

3. Husmann had a second career in viticulture after he came to California in 1881. For more on his years in the east see my *Companion*, pp.157-158 and my *Napa Wine*, pp.116-188. For his several careers in the east see Pinney, *History*, pp.181-182.

4. Gale,P. 45; Pinney, *History*, pp.183-184.

5. Campbell, p.154.

6. A. Drioton, *All About Phylloxera*, San Francisco, 1877.

7. *Alta California*, 10/4/1875, 10/18/1875; *Pacific Rural Press*, 9/9/1882; *St. Helena Star*, 12/13/1895, 1/13/1905.

8. *Pacific Rural Press*, 9/6/1879, 10/4/1879; *Sonoma IndexTribune*, 1/30/1880, 4/3/1880.

9. DeTurk, *Vineyards of Sonoma*, pp.5-6; PWSR, 6/6/1893

10. Charles L. Sullivan, "U.C. Grapes and Wine," *Wayward Tendrils Quarterly*, 1/2009, pp. 3-5.

11. *Sonoma Index Tribune*, 10/11/1890.

12. State Viticultural Commission, *Report*, 1889-90, pp.74-75.

13. *PWSR*, 8/3/1888, 8/22/1889.

Chapter

13

Hard Times

1890-1900

There was a false dawn for the California wine industry in 1890. Many thought, or rather, hoped, that the downward slide in prices for grapes and wine was ending. Prices were stable in the spring, and there were bright words from the press, pointing out recent lively sales on the East Coast. But these were mostly of California's best wines whose brands had trusted labels, such as I. De Turk, Inglenook and Italian Swiss Colony (ISC). The Inglenook general manager had a very different perspective when he returned from the east after a big sale of his wine. He grumbled that "There is much poor, green, unsound and impure wine dumped on the eastern market as first class California wine." Isaac De Turk agreed. Easterners' trust in most California wine had collapsed. These potential customers were "more and more judging us by our worst commercial wine."[1]

By the end of the summer the black clouds of depression had again rolled in, heralded by the New York stock market collapse in June. By the end of the year nationally 491 banks had closed their doors. No one singled out Sonoma as a source of the "green, unsound and impure" wine being dumped in the east for less than the cost of production. But Sonoma wine was part of the unsold sea of California wine resting in the cellars of local wineries and in those of San Francisco wine merchants.[2]

Phylloxera was not yet holding down production in the wine land around and north of Santa Rosa. In 1892 the Sonoma vintage was huge, almost a record. The large 1893 vintage added to the surplus. ISC

221

Eugene W. Hilgard

crushed four thousand tons of grapes, Walden and Simi 1,500 each, and Fountaingrove 1,200. In self-defense, these large producers now depended mostly on their own vineyards, and bought few grapes from the hundreds of Sonoma vineyardists who depended on such sales to meet their mortgage payments. Many tons of Sonoma grapes were not even picked in 1893. The *San Francisco Examiner* cried, "We raise more wine than we can sell. . . ." This was the problem for Sonoma; it was not a matter of poor quality.[3]

During the eighties one of the California wine industry's best supporters had been the University of California. Professor Hilgard was world renowned as a soil scientist, but in these years he had focused most of his attention on the state's wine industry. He and his assistants were in the field continually, supplying practical information and technical instruction. By 1892 the College of Agriculture had issued forty-one bulletins specifically on wine and viticulture, and sixteen on related subjects such as soil and entomology. This emphasis declined over the next twenty-five years. During that period no subject field was dominant as had been the case before 1893.

By that date Hilgard and his assistants were championing the use of resistant rootstock to protect new vines from phylloxera. They had given up the idea that established vines might be saved by attacking the deadly bug. It was clear that the phylloxera was here to stay in northern California. In promoting resistant rootstock Hilgard gave early and powerful support to the voice and example of Sonoma's Julius Dresel.[4]

One of the bright spots in Sonoma's nineties was the transformation and operation of Madrone Ranch, which Senator George Hearst had purchased in 1888. He did not wait for the phylloxera to finish off his vineyards but ripped most of them up and planted 150 acres to resistant rootstock. Hearst died suddenly in 1891 but his wife, Phoebe Apperson Hearst, lived at Madrone during its conversion and came to know quite a bit about viticulture and winegrowing. She later moved to Pleasanton and in 1897 became a regent of the University of California. There she is probably best known for promoting almost singlehandedly the anthropological work at the university. Far less well known is her very friendly relationship with Eugene Hilgard. She became his steady supporter in the Board of Regents in matters viticultural and successfully pushed his agenda; she understood the issues from her experiences at Madrone. Mrs. Hearst kept the historic estate until 1905.

Unfortunately, relations between the wine industry and Hilgard began to change dramatically when hard times appeared after 1889. No one in these days really understood how the business cycle worked, and

Eugene Hilgard and Charles Wetmore were no exceptions. By the summer of 1889 it was clear that the state's wine industry was in deep trouble. In those months the *San Francisco Examiner* ran a series of articles on the situation and asked readers for their ideas on the causes of the wine depression. Some few were correct in arguing that the problem had been over-planting of vines after 1878. Wetmore, as head of the Viticultural Commission, would not face up to that explanation, since he had vociferously led the planting campaign.

On August 8 Professor Hilgard's answer appeared in the *Examiner* in elaborate detail. Every one of his eleven points was aimed at the large amount of cheap, poorly made wine on the market. But nowhere in his explication did he take into account the fact that large amounts of poor wine had flooded the market during the boom years. It was true that such wine now exacerbated the situation, but it had not caused the depression.

Hilgard's explanation and recommendations targeted the California wine industry in general and set off a running battle between industry leaders, led by Charles Wetmore in opposition to Eugene Hilgard and his crew at the university. The pro-business San Francisco press rose quickly in opposition to Hilgard, as did the wine and spirits trade journals. Only the *Pacific Rural Press* sided with Hilgard, which is understandable since its publisher, Edward Wickson, was a professor of agriculture at the university. Out in the countryside, where the wine was made, in the Sonoma, Napa and Santa Clara Valleys, the university found solid support. The exception was the Livermore Valley, where Wetmore had his Cresta Blanca Winery.

On August 14 Wetmore's answer to Hilgard appeared in the *Examiner*. It was the same tired mantra he would use against the university for the next five years. Simply put, he asked how anyone could trust "the judgement of a college professor rather than the taste and experience of educated, practical men. . . ?" But he answered not one of the professor's specific complaints, merely noting that Hilgard's response in the newspaper had been "illogical."

The *PWSR* was an instant enemy of Hilgard's work at the university. Soon the *Alta California* and the *San Francisco Post* joined in. A typical *PWSR* attack on Hilgard claimed that the professor "cannot point to a single vi-

The San Francisco-based Kohler and Frohling, at the corner of Second and Folsom Street, became the headquarters of the California Wine Associations in 1894. (Courtesy of the Unzelman Collection)

ticulturist who has benefited from his work." The cry soon went up in the press to have the Viticultural Commission take over the university's scientific work relating to wine and viticulture. The whole affair made for good reading in a time of depression when so much of the news was dismal.

Winegrowers in Sonoma and Napa got a different picture from the country press. There the sense had been growing for years that the wine depression was due to the commission's almost mindless advocacy of

225

extended vineyard planting, even after the over-supply of wine became apparent. By 1893 a large portion of the country press was calling for the legislature to end the commission. Wetmore was seen as a tool in the hands of the San Francisco wine merchants. Winery owners believed that the low prices paid them by the large houses were ruining both them and the vineyardists who sold them their grapes. The powerful enmity against Wetmore can be seen in a letter written to Hilgard by George Husmann, who was now living and working in Napa. Wetmore was an "impertinent rascal. . ., who has not even the principles of a dog."[5]

In February 1895 the Napa Wine Growers' Union sent a resolution to the State Legislature calling on it to abolish the commission. On March 27 the legislature did just that. Hilgard's correspondence for the next few weeks was full of the satisfaction he felt at the end of this public confrontation. Before this date, Hilgard's correspondence indicates that he might have left the university if the right offer had come along. Things changed after 1898, when better times came better times came. Then the press began complaining that the legislature was not giving Hilgard enough money for his research.[6]

This grudge fight made public another source of serious conflict in the wine industry. Winery owners saw no sign that the merchants' prices to retail and wholesale dealers had declined anywhere nearly so steeply as the prices paid them for their wine. On top of that, the merchants had cut way back on the amount of wine they were buying from country producers. Part of this was due to the fact that many of the largest houses, such as Kohler & Frohling, owned vineyards and wine production facilities. In the spring of 1894 Korbel's cellar was bulging with 550,000 gallons of unsold wine; Julius Dresel had 300,000. In June of that year a huge producers' conference in San Francisco was chaired by Sonoma's Isaac DeTurk. The conference sessions addressed this conflict, and their resolutions set the stage for the organization of a producers' association later in the year.[7]

Meanwhile the merchants were on the march. In August seven of these large San Francisco wine houses came together to form the California Wine Association (CWA). Kohler & Frohling and B. Dreyfus

& Co. were Sonoma's indirect representation in the new company. The chief goal of the combination was to stem the ruinous plunge in wine prices that resulted from merchants and producers often dumping huge amounts of wine in various eastern markets, especially the New Orleans market, where prices had sunk to ten cents per gallon.[8]

Wine producers and leading vineyardists had correctly foreseen at their June conference that such a massive concentration of capital interests could place them at the mercy of an "octopus" that was potentially more dangerous than the Southern Pacific Railroad. Led by Sonoma's Italian Swiss Colony, in November the producers formed the California Wine Makers' Corporation (CWC). Its purpose was not to do battle with the CWA but to organize wine production and distribution in a way that would avoid dumping and help stabilize prices. From the outset the CWC aimed at selling a large part of their members' production to the CWA. By the end of the year the CWC had fifty-three winery members, about thirty percent located in Sonoma, led by ISC, Isaac DeTurk, P. & G. Simi and Joshua Chauvet. Not all the large Sonoma operations signed up. J. Gundlach and Fountaingrove chose to compete independently.[9]

Through 1895 and until the last month of 1896 the hoped-for stability in wine prices appeared to be something of a reality. The trade press made it clear that the CWA and the CWC were working together. ISC was finally doing well enough in 1896 to pay a dividend to its stockholders. The next year the company built a gigantic five hundred thousand gallon capacity wine vat to hold its large 1897 vintage.[10]

One of the reasons that the two organizations worked for a while in peace was the level-headed leadership provided the CWA by Percy Morgan. Although he only held the official position of auditor at this time, he was the company's de facto CEO. But the peace was broken after January 1897 as a result of the deepening of the national depression. The *PWSR* wrote that "an extreme depression has marked all branches of business." Wine prices were slaughtered and the two great combinations were at each others' throats. In February the *PWSR* announced, "Wine War On."[11]

Percy Tredegar Morgan (Courtesy of the Unzelman Collection)

The CWA won the war. It had the financial muscle and much better leadership. By the spring of 1898 the smoke had mostly cleared, and there were but a few more inconsequential skirmishes. What insured a placid conclusion was the upturn in the national business cycle, which became noticeable in the fall of 1897. In the fight Morgan had taken off the gloves. "No more Mr. Nice Guy," in Thomas Pinney's words. Four years later Morgan admitted that the combatants had rushed toward the precipice of ruin "like a herd of stampeded animals."

The great fact of the moment was that the industry had been able to handle the large wine surplus in 1898 soberly. In fact, vineyardists in Sonoma and Napa were now rushing to replace their phylloxerated vines, many of which had been dark stumps for several years. But before 1898 another conflict had arisen over what rootstock to replant with.[12]

While the merchants, producers and vineyardists struggled financially in the nineties, the phylloxera had continued its slow spread through Sonoma County. In the early nineties the bugs' effects were starting to become apparent in the Santa Rosa area, and the 1896 vintage statistics illustrate how dominant the virtually unaffected areas to the north had become. In a county vintage of 4,600,000 gallons only thirty-nine percent of the grapes came from the historic vineyards in the Sonoma Valley and Santa Rosa areas. The Healdsburg and Cloverdale areas alone had 1,634,000 gallons. The 1897 vintage was even larger, 500,000 gallons of which went into the great ISC wine vat.[13]

By the planting season in 1895 there had been a small but noticeable pickup in vineyard planting in Sonoma and Napa. There was more in 1896 as better times seemed to be on the horizon. Those who did so knew that it would take three years to get a real crop from the new vines. In Sonoma County south of Healdsburg almost all of the new vines went onto resistant rootstock, overwhelmingly onto *V. riparia*, as Julius Dresel's success seemed to demand. In Napa both riparia and Lenoir were popular. Unfortunately for Napa growers there was little rain in 1895 or in 1896, and some of the vines on riparia began drooping, some dying.

229

In 1897, with better times clearly in sight, planting picked up in both counties. By now Hilgard's phylloxera crew at the university under Arthur Hayne had settled on the riparia and rejected the Lenoir as not sufficiently resistant. In 1896 Hayne toured Sonoma beating the drum for riparia, which was doing fine in that county. Later it was understood that the drought was a cause of the riparia's poor showing in Napa. As its name implies, riparian vines had originally evolved near water. In average or wet years both counties had similar rainfall figures, but in dry years Sonoma received significantly more of the reduced rainfall.

Planting in Napa in 1897 took a weird turn. Vineyardists logically abandoned the Riparia, but turned to the Lenoir. The *St. Helena Star* conducted a survey after the spring planting in Napa and found that sixty-eight vineyardists had set out new vines. Of these 65% chose Lenoir. The rest seemed to have learned nothing and planted their vines on their own roots.[14] The Lenoir was the special and well-broadcast choice of George Husmann, now living and working in Napa, where his influence dominated. In 1876 he had first sent this vine from Missouri to Napa's H. W. Crabb. Now in his cranky old age Husmann felt that the university's rejection of Lenoir was a reflection on his work. He began a personal attack on Hilgard and Hayne, who suggested that Californians should acquire their native American resistants from the French, who had been doing most of the scientific work on the question.

The university scientists knew what Husmann and most Napa growers did not: The French had isolated individual varieties of the *V. riparia* and *V. rupestris* species, some of which were far more resistant than other varieties inside these species. Hayne warned against sending to Missouri for resistants, since variations in the favored species had not been identified and tested there. Husmann thought this was a personal attack on his honor and bombarded the press with attacks on the university's advice. Why trust the French when practical experience in local vineyards was all that was needed?[15]

Hilgard had sent Hayne to France in 1896 to observe the French experiments. Hayne published his findings the next year in a College

230

of Agriculture bulletin.[16] Napa's problems with riparia now encouraged Hayne to promote varieties of *V. rupestris.* Of these he decided that the Rupestris St. George was the best all-round resistant for California vineyards. Before the 1898 planting season, nurseries in Sonoma, Napa, Livermore and Santa Clara Valleys were ordering St. George resistants in huge numbers. In Sonoma new vines were now usually being planted onto the soon-to-be victorious St. George, although the riparia was not abandoned. Sonoma growers had followed the advice of Dresel and Hayne from the start and avoided the Lenoir. Husmann finally agreed that the St. George was the best choice, but he never gave up his attacks on Hilgard and Hayne. When the young professor enlisted to serve in the Spanish-American War, Husmann hoped in print that he "would make a better soldier than viticulturist."[17]

In the years to come the phylloxera infestation continued to work its way north to the Alexander Valley. But now Sonoma growers did not hesitate grafting their new vines onto the soon-to-become almost ubiquitous St. George stock, which is still the favorite today among the county's Zinfandel growers.

From 1898 to 1900 it was obvious that the hard times of previous years were things of the past. The CWA had won the Wine War, but the producers were not vanquished. By 1899 the CWA was buying CWC wine at a price acceptable to the winery owners. The next year the CWC was out of business, and the ISC and several other independents had become associated with the CWA. Good prices for grapes and wine prevailed, aided by a very short Sonoma vintage in 1899.

The consumer did not see any great change in the wine they bought after the near monopoly was established. The wine houses that came together did not give up their brands. It appeared that there were still as many in the competitive field as there had been before, although there were also several distinct CWA brands as well. The manner in which the CWA enforced quotas and established prices was obviously a restraint of trade under the terms of the 1890 federal anti-trust legislation. But even after 1901 when the Sherman Act was finally vigorously enforced, there was no move by Theodore Roosevelt's Justice Department against the CWA. Nor was there any great voice raised by California wine producers for such action. Percy Morgan and his followers were no "robber barons," an image often associated in the popular mind with trusts and monopolies. His stated policy was "fair dealing with all, coupled with a strong hand."[18]

CHAPTER 13 NOTES

1. *Pacific Wine & Spirit Review (PWSR),* 1/8/1890, 2/22/1890.

2. *PWSR,* 6/13/1890

3. *PWSR,* 6/27/1893, 8/5/1893, 10/5/1893.

4. Sullivan, "U. C. Grapes & Wine."

5. Hilgard's correspondence is on file at the Bancroft Library, University of California, Berkeley.

6. *PWSR,* 2/20, 8/5/1893; 3/21, 4/6/1895; Pinney, *History,* PP.350-353; Sullivan, "U.C. Grapes & Wine."

7. *PWSR,* 5/5, 6/6/1894.

8. *PWSR,* 8/20/1894; Peninou, *Sonoma,* PP.27-30.

9. *PWSR,* 11/20/1894.

10. Jack W. Florence, *Legacy of a Village,* Geyserville, 1999, PP.63-65; *PWSR,* 2/27, 7/8 1895; 4/23, 11/9/1896.

11. Thomas Pinney, *The Makers of American Wine,* Berkeley, 2012, PP.95-98; *PWSR,* 1/8, 2/22/1897.

12. *American Wine Press,* 7/97, 6/98, 2/99; *PWSR,* 5/24, 6/24/1897, 2/24/1898, 12/31/1902. For Sonoma activities see 9/30/1898.

13. *PWSR,* 10/23/1896.

14. *St. Helena Star,* 5/25/1897; *PWSR,* 6/11/1897.

15. Sullivan, *Napa Wine,* PP.116-118.

16. Arthur P. Hayne, *Resistant Vines,* Sacramento 1897, PP.15-16.

17. *Napa Register,* 8/12/1898; Ag. Soc., 1899, PP.104-111; *PWSR,* 5/31, 12/31/1899. Frederick Bioletti, "Bench Grafting Resistant Vines." College of Agriculture Bulletin 127, 1900.

18. Pinney, *Makers of American Wine,* PP.96-100. Morgan is one of the thirteen "Makers" in Professor Pinney's excellent study.

Chapter

14

Prosperity

─────◦⟨⟩◦─────

1900-1915

After the successful 1900 vintage many Sonoma producers concluded that larger wine grape crops and more vineyard acreage would be necessary to meet the steadily rising demand for California wine since 1897.
Carl Dresel, and his father Julius before him, had been steady opponents
of the mindless over-expansion that had led to the wine industry's economic suffering in the seventies and nineties. Now even he voiced a happy
optimism about expansion and the future, as did his Gundlach-Bundschu
neighbors at Rhinefarm.[1]

Two forces added to the sense of security among Sonoma's growers
and producers. The most obvious was the huge California Wine Association (CWA), in 1900 only six years old and the clear victor in the recent
wine war. Most of the association's previous opponents were now in league
with that company. At the turn of the century only three large independent
wine houses were still in the field. These were Lachman & Jacobi (Lac-
Jac), C. Schilling & Co., and the Italian Swiss Colony (ISC). By 1901
CWA owned at least fifty percent of the stock in all three. But the ISC and
Lac-Jac continued to operate for a while as separate, integrated companies,
whose products remained competitive with those of the CWA. In fact, ISC
was the second powerful force in Sonoma that helped promote the sense of
stability and prosperity in the county's wine industry.[2]

Consolidation was the order of the day after 1900 in the Sonoma
wine country. This large scale process meant that more and more produc-

tion facilities came under direct CWA control or by affiliation through contracts. These plants dotted the landscape from the lower Sonoma Valley to the Alexander Valley, the most important among them the Madrone, DeTurk, Trenton and Geyserville Wineries. The CWA also constructed huge production plants at Windsor and Geyserville. The ISC also spread its wings, acquiring the Sebastopol, Fulton and Cloverdale Wineries before 1902.

Small scale expansion and consolidation was also important during this time. Notably in the Windsor, Forestville, Occidental and Cloverdale areas, small producers expanded their facilities or bought up the operations of their neighbors.[3]

The power of the CWA and ISC was felt by all in Sonoma County who produced grapes and/or made wine, whether they were part of the larger corporate structure or not. Both set prices for grapes that established the pattern for all vineyardists, except for the very few who might have a special lot of Riesling or Cabernet for sale. It was truly a tyrannical system, but a benevolent one. There was a certain amount of grumbling expressed in the country press from time to time, but there was not a hint of the type of battle that had rocked the industry before 1898. The motto of the CWA's president, Percy Morgan, was "fair dealing for all." Historian Thomas Pinney, obviously ill at ease with the CWA's power and rigidity, still has written that Morgan's managerial concepts were then "operating nicely."[4]

Sonoma growers were always most interested in the established price for Zinfandel grapes. By 1900 Sonoma County was the country's number one producer of high quality dry table wine, and most of this was red, and Zinfandel was the base for most of that. There was one curious exception. From the earliest days at ISC the Zinfandel had been the company's number one variety. The ISC's red Tipo Chianti by this date was the country's most popular brand. But the base wine for that tasty blend was the Italian Sangiovese (San Gioveto) variety. These vines had been imported from Tuscany in the late 1880s.[5]

It is important to know how the American consumer was able to buy California wine before Prohibition, since the process from grape

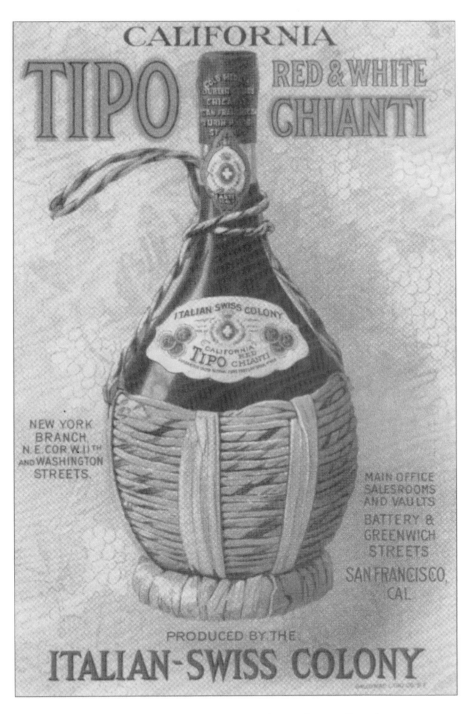

A 1950s advertising postcard from ISC. (Courtesy of the Unzelman Collection)

to bottle was almost totally different then than it is today. The process varied from region to region in the state, but the Sonoma process was typical. About half the wine grape acreage in the county was owned by independent vineyardists. About thirty percent was owned by wineries not owned by large wine houses. About twenty percent was owned by large wine houses whose headquarters were concentrated in San Francisco and whose wineries were in the country.[6] Fully ninety percent of all wine leaving San Francisco and the state was shipped in bulk, to be bottled in the east, the midwest or in other West Coast cities. The CWA also sold its wines nationally under many different brand names, such as Greystone and Vinecliff.

There were other wines bearing the names of its members, such as I. De-Turk and Schilling. There were still some independent producers who were able to market their wine directly on the West Coast and east of the Rockies. In Sonoma such notable exceptions were Gundlach-Bundschu, Dresel, Fountaingrove, Korbel, Louis Kunde and William Lehn. ISC also qualifies as a de facto exception, although it was part of the CWA organization.

The geography of this system was logical only in one sense- the historical one. The system that had developed since the 1860s resulted in numerous huge cellars concentrated in San Francisco, from which enormous amounts of wine were shipped out by sea or across the bay to Oakland for transportation east by rail. In 1905 no one had the money, power or bravura to reform a commercial geography that required almost every barrel of wine traveling out of Sonoma County for San Francisco to leave its wagon or railroad car and go to sea to get across the bay. But in April 1906 the power of nature provided an obvious path to reform.

The earthquake that rocked northern California on April 18, 1906 might have been called the Santa Rosa Earthquake had there not been a great city sitting atop the peninsula to the south. The quake's epicenter was just off the Sonoma coast, and the county's chief town of six thousand souls was reduced to rubble. It was not the quake but the subsequent fire that caused San Francisco's destruction and the almost total obliteration of the wine industry's physical presence there.

On April 22 Charles Bundschu, the founder of Sonoma's Gundlach-Bundschu Wine Co., wrote a letter to his brother describing events on the fatal day. Less than an hour after the quake a crew at their great cellar on Bryant Street was able to fill two wagons with books, business papers and other items. Before the sun had set the huge building was destroyed by the advancing inferno.

Later the whole Bundschu family took a steamer to Tiburon and went on to Rhinefarm. "Now the children and grand-children are gathered around the old vineyard home to seek shelter and rest from the turmoil of heart rending afflictions." When they returned to the city on the twenty-second, where their home had stood was "a barren waste."

Bundschu thought his family's life work in wine was doomed. "I shall never forget the thunderbolt of wrath smashing the last hope of my life forever. . . . Such a business cannot be redeemed by bright hopes for the future. . . . Our future was bright for everyone interested. We never had a better assortment of wines- never a larger stock. . . every nerve strained in offices and cellar to promote the good work- and now? It means despair."[7]

Bundschu's dark pessimism soon cleared. In a short time his historic business would be functioning profitably, as was the business of almost the entire wine industry. But at the end of April the visible hurt to the industry in San Francisco and Sonoma was awesome.

Bundschu's experience was typical. There were twenty-eight large cellars in San Francisco in 1906, and all but one were destroyed. The subsequent fiery holocaust changed the history of wine in California. About fifteen million gallons of commercial wine were lost, well more than half of it in cellars owned by the CWA. [8] The one cellar that survived, along with two million gallons of wine, belonged to ISC.

It had been built in 1903 at Battery and Greenwich, near the railroad and waterfront. During its construction a spring had been found on the property, and P. C. Rossi had a well dug. On the morning of the quake Andrea Sbarboro and several ISC employees raced down from Asti, and by the afternoon the ISC president was leading a band of fire fighters. They set up a fuel-oil pump at the well and spent long hours drench-

Following the 1906 quake, the once magnificent San Francisco California Wine Association headquarters lay in "a chaos of hoops and debris." (Courtesy of the Unzelman Collection)

ing the huge building. Sbarboro later wrote, "We fought unceasingly for three days and three nights." He also had a line of hoses extended to the waterfront and was able to save several other buildings in the area. After the fire the ISC spring was one of the few sources of fresh water in the city. The many histories of the Earthquake and Fire have not remembered the ISC well and Sbarboro's band of heroes.

Of the nine counties that make up the Bay Area, Sonoma was the hardest hit by the quake. There it was the great shake, not fires, that did the damage. The million gallon De Turk Winery in Santa Rosa was a total loss. Practically every winery in the Sebastopol area was heavily damaged. The Lehn Winery in Forestville lost several hundred

242

thousand gallons. Dry Creek's Paxton Winery was destroyed. No area escaped heavy losses. But some wineries went almost unscathed. ISC's Asti plant reported no damage of importance, except that its great wine vat was cracked. But just down the road, the CWA's Geyserville facility was battered. At Buena Vista the great winery buildings survived, but three of its historic tunnels collapsed. Despite the damage to the Sonoma wine industry's capital plant, the county's 1906 vintage came through without serious problems. Of course, the vineyards had suffered not at all.

The wine industry was well insured against loss by fire though earthquake insurance was almost unheard of. It took a while to prove that fire not quake was the great culprit in the city, but eventually about eighty percent of the San Francisco wine industry's losses were covered and paid off. It took a while; the CWA did not cash its last check until 1910.

Another financial plus came from the fact that in April 1906 most of the wine from the 1905 vintage in northern California counties was still in the country wineries. If the quake had come in July or August, the loss of wine in San Francisco might have been double. Still there was an immediate national shortage of wine, and prices rose. But the CWA and ISC launched a California campaign to avoid steep increases; Morgan and Rossi put forth the idea that such price increases would open the gates for a flood of Ohio and New York wine into markets normally controlled by California interests.

What was permanently destroyed by the quake and fire was the historical geography of the California wine industry. The destruction of San Francisco's great commercial cellars meant that never again would almost every barrel of wine destined for blending and shipping outside of northern California have to first travel by water to and from the city.

It is not clear whether Arthur Lachman or Percy Morgan took the first steps to move his company's large scale blending and storage facilities off the peninsula in the direction of the wine country. Lachman & Jacobi had bought land in Petaluma for such a facility before the quake, after

April 18 the concept of Lac-Jac's future operations there moved from sizeable to massive. At Petaluma the wines from their Sonoma wineries could be processed and shipped. But the four million gallon plant was not designed to function as a winery.

Percy Morgan took longer to settle on a site for the new CWA plant, but it was better located than the Lac-Jac Petaluma facility. Morgan and his board finally bought a forty-seven-acre piece of land across the bay, on the water west of the town of Richmond. It had easy access to the transcontinental railroad and the Central Valley where wine production had been booming since the nineties. The plant was named Winehaven and on September 2, 1907 it was dedicated. Morgan predicted the ten-million-gallon facility would be the "Bordeaux of the Pacific." It began production with the 1907 vintage. Prohibition later brought an end to its wine operations, but its sturdy and well-preserved remains can still be seen just north of the eastern end of the Richmond-San Raphael Bridge.

The story of the halcyon years for California and Sonoma wine from 1900 to 1915 is easily and accurately expressed with the words "prosperity and stability." For Sonoma several more specific themes deserve notice.

The spread of the phylloxera on ungrafted vines continued into the 1920s, but new planting on resistant rootstock was the rule. Calculations of the county's grape acreage are mostly guesses until the twenties, but in the years just before Prohibition total acreage probably averaged between twenty thousand and twenty-three thousand acres, about one third of today's total. Nevertheless, there was a similar ratio then and now of red to white varieties, about two to one.

An important change in Sonoma's ethnic landscape had been taking place since the nineties. More and more Italian-Americans were taking up winegrowing. By the twenties probably half the county's wine grape vineyards were owned by Italian immigrants or their descendants. Soon after Prohibition *Wine Review* published a directory of California wineries. Of the persons identified as registered owners of Sonoma wineries, sixty-four percent had Italian last names. In the *Wines & Vines* directory of 1961 the number was seventy-one percent.

244

Workers unload grapes at Santa Rosa's Martini and Prati Winery. Ca. 1905

San Francisco's business leaders began working in 1909 to get the congressional nod to hold the Panama Pacific International Exposition in their city. The official unifying theme for the 1915 event was to be the previous year's opening of the Panama Canal, but all northern California knew that the most powerful idea behind the expo was to show the world that the city by the Golden Gate had risen from the devastating effects of the 1906 Earthquake and Fire.

July 14, Bastille Day, was Wine Day at the PPIE. An international jury was on hand to evaluate hundreds of California wines on exhibit. Visitors could taste most of them at the sampling room in the large scale and elaborate California wine exhibit building. There were judges from all over the world. Officially Fountain grove's Kanaye Nagasawa represented both Sonoma and Japan. They handed out medals by the bushel. A total of fifty-

Promotional poster for the 1915 Panama-Pacific International Expo.

nine awards were given as "Grand Prizes" and Medals of Honor," before the 167 gold medals, the third-highest award.

The big Sonoma winner was ISC with five grand prizes, three for sparklers, and one each for red Tipo and "Chablis." Gundlach-Bundschu also won a top award for its Cabernet Sauvignon, labeled "Chateau Gundlach." Korbel won a grand prize for its Zernosek wine, made from a Czech variety, and a Medal of Honor for its Grand Pacific Champagne. Dresel won five golds for its white wines and one for its Cabernet. DeTurk also won seven golds. The highest award for a wine specifically labeled Zinfandel was a gold medal to Louis Kunde's Wildwood Vineyards. There were lots of Sonoma wines in-

246

cluded in CWA's thirteen awards, but the association's brand names give few hints as to the wines' sources.[9]

One might expect that CWA's huge Winehaven plant across the bay would have taken center stage in the industry's self- image portrayed at the expo, but the highlight for more than one hundred thousand visitors to the California wine exhibit was a movie produced by Horatio Stoll, ISC's former publicist. He had been enthusiastically backed in this project by Andrea Sbarboro. The two men were concerned by prohibitionists' attacks on wine producers, which likened them to the distillers and brewers of the liquor and beer industries.

Stoll had traveled throughout the state gathering shots of life among the vines and cellars of California's ordinary winegrowers. The movie was carefully edited to represent wine and viticulture in their purist state of innocence. Who would think to deprive these happy, industrious families of their livelihood?

Wine industry leaders had no interest in spreading an image of massive industrial wine plants producing millions of gallons of fortified sweet wines and brandy. The specter of prohibition was hovering over the California wine industry. Employing the newly legalized tools of initiative and referendum, prohibitionist forces had just narrowly lost an attempt to make the state bone dry. Another effort was already under the way for the 1916 election. California voters could and did defeat such efforts, but they could not control the drive for national prohibition.

On December 22, 1914, just a few weeks before the PPIE opened, the House of Representatives voted 197-190 in favor of just such an amendment to the Constitution that would outlaw the production and sale of alcoholic beverages. It was sixty-two votes short of the necessary two-thirds. but when the PPIE opened, every California wine leader understood the significance of this failed but threatening harbinger.

CHAPTER 14 NOTES

1. *PWSR*, 10/31/1900.

2. Ernest Peninou and Gail Unzelman, *The California Wine Association . . . 1894-1920*, Santa Rosa, 2000, PP.79-91.

3. *Op. cit., PP.137-168.*

4. Pinney, *Makers*, PP.98-100.

5. Other than identifying the wine's basic variety, Rossi never disclosed the exact composition of his Tipo.

6. These imprecise generalizations are taken from the extensive individual statistics in Peninou, *Sonoma.*

7. For the entire letter and a more complete story of the quake and the wine industry, see my "The Great Wine Quake," *Wayward Tendrils Quarterly,* January and April 2006.

8. Almost miraculously, much of the wine in one CWA cellar was pumped out and down to barges on the waterfront. From there it went to a brandy distillery near Stockton.

9. *PWSR*, 6/30/1915.

Chapter
15

Sonoma Dry?

1900-1933

Concerns about the potential evils of strong drink have been a part of American history since colonial times. In the nineteenth century the idea of temperance dominated most of the conversation, its proponents stressing a positive approach to moderation for the resulting mental and physical health benefits.

By 1900 a strong movement to prohibit the production and sale of alcoholic beverages developed in many southern and midwestern states. The word "Dry" became the common term to describe the movement's supporters and their policies. The first target of the Dry campaign in America was the saloon; strong opposition to this institution could be found all over the United States.

Dry sentiment in California had a peculiar geography. Southern California, the counties south of the Tehachapi Mountains, had a strong and growing Dry sentiment after 1900. The southern counties had had a population explosion after 1880, primarily due to immigration from the Midwest, and these newcomers were mostly Protestant and conservative. All over the Southland new towns with powerful temperance sentiment grew up, even in places where winegrowing had been a tradition.

In the state's northern areas, especially in the San Francisco Bay Area and the nearby wine-producing counties, a far more diverse population had been developing since the Gold Rush days. In Sonoma and Napa Counties the population had a large German and Italian background. Overall the Bay Area counties were predominantly Roman Catholic.[1]

The most powerful force in the California and national Dry movement after the nineties was the national Anti-Saloon League (ASL). With local chapters all over the state, it was a single-issue political pressure group, the first of its kind and scope in American history.[2]

Before 1900 many towns in Southern California had established Dry ordinances on their own, but there was not, as yet, a state law supplying guidelines or official authorization for local option. In northern California there had been little support for such laws, but in that year the ASL surprised many in the Bay Area when its all-out support for such an ordinance in Berkeley was successful. Of particular importance was the State Supreme Court's validation of the ordinance.[3]

Meanwhile a powerful reform movement inside the Republican Party was gathering steam nationally after Theodore Roosevelt became president in 1901. In California these Progressive Republicans took control of the state

A postcard used in the campaign against Prohibition. (Courtesy of the Unzelman Collection)

252

party in 1910 and elected Hiram Johnson as governor, along with a solidly Progressive State Legislature. Johnson and the Progressives did not follow the ASL's prohibitionist line, but most of them were opposed to the "evils of the saloon" and were willing to make it easy for local areas to go Dry.

In 1911 the Wylie Local Option Law legally formalized a simple process by which local communities could go as dry as they desired, even Bone Dry. Now "Dry" meant an end to saloons; "Bone Dry" meant that a couple could not even have a glass of wine with their meal in a restaurant. Such local option campaigns got nowhere in Sonoma and Napa Counties. Sonoma did pass a county ordinance that outlawed saloons on county roads, which meant the end to their infamous roadhouses. But none of the local option votes in any of the Sonoma towns was successful.

The ASL's next move was to take advantage of one of the Progressive movement's most popular reforms. Voters, through the new initiative process, could pass laws and even amend the state constitution, by collecting enough signatures on petitions and placing their propositions on the state-wide ballot. In 1914 the ASL went all out to make California Bone Dry.

It was a move that Andrea Sbarboro had seen coming much earlier. He was convinced that hard liquor was probably doomed all over the country. In 1904 he had spoken to a large winegrowers group in Sonoma and warned that the future of wine in California depended on being able to separate it from whisky and other ardent spirits in the voting public's mind. It was well known that the leadership of the CWA was in league with the brewers and distillers who controlled most of California's saloons. He called for wine men gradually to make a separation by condemning the evil effect of the saloon. But this call was met with disdain by the wine industry leaders.[4]

For now Sbarboro concentrated his efforts, and those of his ISC publicist, Horatio Stoll, on the many local option elections taking place in Sonoma County. They personally visited each of the towns, successfully speaking against the various prohibition ordinances up for a vote. One of their most telling arguments was the Jeffersonian idea that wine was really a temperance drink, and if used in moderation was a useful tool in the fight against alcoholism. They noted correctly that this affliction was less common in wine-drinking areas than in those in which hard liquor was the favored drink.

They also worked successfully to organize the county's wine men to counter the ASL's propaganda. Throughout the county such organizations were formed whose stated aim was to protect the wine grape grower, his family and his vineyard. By 1909 there were "grape protective" organizations in Windsor, Cloverdale, Fulton, Healdsburg and Santa Rosa.[5] Sbarboro also led in the formation of several statewide wine grower groups, culminating in 1914 with the formation of the California Grape Protective Association (CGPA), just before the ASL launched its petition campaign to put a Bone Dry proposition on the ballot.

Sbarboro could now take some pride in the CGPA's mild announcement in favor of strong statewide *control* of saloons, but not their outlaw. The organization's "Vote No" campaign was led by Sbarboro and Napa winegrower Theodore Bell, who had been Governor Johnson's Democratic opponent in 1910. Non running for re-election, Johnson attacked the ASL as "Dry fanatics."[6]

The California 1914 Dry initiative was soundly defeated 61%-39%. Even Los Angeles County voted "NO" and, San Francisco voted "No" by five to one. The margin in Sonoma and Napa Counties was about the same as the statewide numbers.

So far as California wine men were concerned, the people of California had made it clear that they had no intention of killing the wine industry. When we consider the effectiveness of the CGPA campaign emphasis, it might be more accurate to conclude that the people of California had no intention of ruining California's vineyardists. It was clear that Sbarboro's prescient advice to separate wine from the saloon in the public mind was now the wine industry's accepted ideology.

The ASL was not daunted by defeat. For the 1916 statewide election they came up with a double-headed initiative. Two propositions made the ballot. One was Bone Dry; the other would bring an end to the saloon. Bell and Sbarboro wanted the CGPA to support the anti-saloon measure to emphasize the new separation between the wine and liquor interests, but the industry leaders would have none of it. It was one thing to advocate

254

Save California's {WINE GRAPE / RAISIN GRAPE / TABLE GRAPE} Vineyards
Vote "NO" on Both Prohibition Amendments
ON THE BALLOT NOVEMBER 7, 1916

"PROHIBITION. Initiative measure adding Article XXIV to Constitution. Defines alcoholic liquor. After January 1, 1920, prohibits the manufacture, sale or possession of same, except for medicinal, sacramental, scientific and mechanical purposes under restrictions prescribed by law. Prescribes and authorizes penalties. Declares payment of Internal Revenue Tax prima facie evidence of violation. Declares this amendment shall not affect prohibitory liquor laws, or ordinances, enacted before such date, or be construed as in conflict with Article XXIV-A of Constitution if latter article is adopted, and that this amendment supercedes that article on that date."

Yes ___
No X

STAMP "X" HERE

"INITIATIVE AMENDMENT, ADDING ARTICLE XXIV-A TO CONSTITUTION. Defines alcoholic liquor; after January 1, 1918, prohibits its possession, gift or sale in saloon, dram shop, dive, store, hotel, restaurant, club, dance hall or other place of public resort; prohibits sale, accepting or soliciting orders anywhere, except in pharmacies for certain purposes and by manufacturers on premises where manufactured, under delivery and quantity restrictions. Owner or manager of all such places to prevent drinking therein. Restricts transportation. Payment Internal Revenue Tax prima facie evidence of violation. Prescribes and authorizes penalties. Neither repeals nor limits state or local prohibition, or Article XXIV of Constitution."

Yes ___
No X

STAMP "X" HERE

—CALIFORNIA WINE ASSOCIATION.

[P.W.&S.R., 5.31.1916]

California Wine Association advertisement. 1916. (Courtesy of the Unzelman Collection)

stricter controls on saloons, another to outlaw them. And only voices from the Dry side of the issues would point out that saloons in California sold huge amounts of fortified sweet wines and brandy.

The CGPA put together an enormously effective campaign against both initiatives. Both were defeated, but by closer votes than in 1914. If the San Francisco vote had been subtracted from the totals, the anti-saloon measure would have carried. Again, both Sonoma and Napa were solidly No on both propositions.

Events in 1917 made these lively wins for the wine industry next to meaningless. In April the U.S. declared war against Germany, an event that called for greater efficiency and sacrifice from everyone. For the ASL it provided issues that would not have mattered so much in peacetime. Foodstuffs could not be wasted on booze. Our "boys" in uniform everywhere had to be protected from the evils of drink. And when the "boys" were "over there," the home front had to be protected from the drunkenness and violence associated with the saloon. Congress adopted the 18th Amendment in December and submitted it to the states. Three-fourths of the state legislatures (thirty-six) needed to approve it for the entire nation to go Dry. It was slow going in 1918, but in January 1919 twenty-five states came aboard. The 18th Amendment would become the law of the land on January 16, 1920. Prohibitionists everywhere felt secure from the fact that no amendment to the Constitution had ever been reversed.

In Sonoma after 1915 the vines kept producing grapes and wineries still made wine, whatever was happening in legislatures or at the ballot box. Wine and grape prices kept rising as the European war steadily cut off wine imports from Germany, Italy and France. And as the threat of prohibition increased, so did the demand for California wine in the eastern states. There was even a growing demand for California grapes from eastern wine producers.

Eastern shipments of grapes grew steadily after 1913, reaching 10,741 railroad carloads in 1916.[7] Most of these shipments were from

Onlookers crouch and drink near a wine-dark creek, into which Foppiano Vineyards was forced to empty its tanks by raiding federal agents. 1926.

the Central Valley, but some Sonoma grapes went east. Here the leader was Samuele Sebastiani, who regularly shipped grapes to Michigan wineries after 1915.[8] But there was virtually no talk among wine industry leaders or in the press to suggest that shipping wine grapes across the Rockies to home winemakers might save California's vineyards if the Dry movement was successful nationally.

Vintage 1918 was a miserable one in the north bay wine country. The early and numerous rainstorms would have spread gloom in former years, but the vineyards were full of pickers, rain or shine. School days were shortened in Sonoma and Napa. All the pickers were wearing masks for fear of the deadly influenza epidemic sweeping the country. And the high grape prices brought good money to everyone involved. Another event, on November 11, brightened faces when the Armistice ended the fighting in Europe, although it did not end the legal state of war. That fact caused anxiety in the wine country, since Congreshad earlier outlawed the production of alcoholic beverages as of July 1, 1919. This "wartime prohibition" was to last until President Wilson announced the end of mobilization. The still-confused situation in Europe precluded his making such an announcement yet.

By the spring of 1919, almost like magic, almost everyone involved in winegrowing suddenly saw the potential of shipping wine grapes over the Rockies for home wine makers. When the vines were starting to leaf out, Sonoma and Napa saw a stream of fresh fruit brokers with contracts to offer growers for the fall vintage, when it seemed wine production would be illegal. That eventuality ended in the summer when the IRS informed Theodore Bell that it was not equipped to enforce the new federal law that year, so far as wine production for sale was concerned. Thus, there would be a quasi-legal vintage in Sonoma in 1919.

In the years before Prohibition families had been allowed to make up to two hundred gallons of fruit juice at home. There was nothing in federal enforcement procedures about letting the juice ferment, and this was the approach of the federal government's enabling law for the 18th Amendment. This was the infamous Volstead Act, which set the allowable alcohol content on commercial beverages at one-half of one percent. What the home winemakers did with their fermented fruit juices in their homes was of no interest to the Treasury Department's enforcement officers. Of course, such fruit juice, fermented or not, might not be sold or even leave the family's place of residence.[9]

But there was no clear sense as yet that the state's wine grape interests were safe. Many winegrowers in Sonoma and Napa had begun interplanting the rows in their vineyards with orchard crops. In Sonoma prunes and apricots were favored, in Napa prunes and walnuts. For many it was simpler just to rip up their vineyards. This was particularly true north of Santa Rosa for older vineyards not yet wiped out by phylloxera.

The CWA leaders had seen the handwriting on the wall and announced in December 1917 that the Association's pursuit "of a business with a future so uncertain is not wise." Stockholders were warned that steps were being taken "for liquidation of the affairs of the Association. . . ."[10] This meant selling the capital assets associated with the production of wine and brandy. An example in Sonoma was CWA's Windsor Winery, which soon became a cannery. The leadership did have the foresight not to begin dumping vineyard property, whose value was soon skyrocketing.

Since 1915 the ISC had been part of he CWA. After P. C. Rossi's death in 1911, his son Edmund had risen to a high position in the Association, and in 1918 he began putting together a deal to buy ISC from the CWA. When Edmund's twin brother Robert returned from the war, the brothers combined with Enrico Prati, the ISC superintendent, and winegrower Eduardo Seghesio, to form Asti Grape Products, which then would own the old Asti plant and most of the old ISC Sonoma vineyards.

After the 1919 season proved the lucrative financial prospect of what came to be called "The Fresh Grape Deal," the partners bought the Cloverdale Winery from the CWA. This would be the plant for producing the thousands of wooden lug boxes that they and their neighbors would be using to send grapes east during the 1920 vintage. Everyone knew that there would be no beverage wine produced for sale after January.[11]

Rossi thought, as did most others in the wine industry, that producing grape concentrate for home winemakers would be more efficient than shipping lug boxes of grapes across the country. ISC did have some success

258

selling its Moonmist Zinfandel and Riesling syrup. But overwhelmingly, home winemakers in California and across the country wanted to examine the grapes and make their own wine.[12]

In 1918 and 1919 thousands of carloads of wine grapes headed east by rail. Grapes that had previously sold for $20 per ton were now bringing the grower close to $100, and the broker/retailer at the end of the line was collecting close to $200. The whole operation was messy and highly complicated, but by 1922 there was something of a system in place that organized the transfer of lugs of wine grapes from the grower to rail car and thence to cities in the east or California, particularly San Francisco.

Among American home winemakers, Sonoma County's name became firmly attached to high quality wine grapes, particularly Zinfandel. In Boston, Zinfandel was as popular as it was in San Francisco. Today the Zinfandel connection persists for wine consumers throughout the country. It is a rather astonishing fact that Sonoma County growers in 2011 received more than $200 per ton more for their Zinfandel than for their Cabernet Sauvignon. At the same time, Napa Cabernet sold for almost two thousand dollars more than Napa Zinfandel.

The "Fresh Grape Deal" of the twenties became organized in Sonoma as in no other California county. A California Grape Exchange was put together to establish a rational system of getting the state's grape to eastern markets. At first, no more than half of the Sonoma County crop went into channels organized by the Exchange, which also set minimum prices below which members were pledged not to go. Under this system the state's growers prospered until 1926, but there were always ups and downs. Bad weather could mean a short crop and higher prices. But bad weather in September and October could leave grapes hanging on the vine, or picked and mouldering in their lugs and worthless by the time they reached their destination.[13]

Before 1926 the other half of the Sonoma crop did not head east but stayed near to home. Horatio Stoll estimated that 30,000 families in the San Francisco Bay Area made their own wine in 1919. By 1922 that number had doubled.[14] Sonoma's contribution to this home market was greatly indebted

Fountaingrove's Namco brand concentrated grape juice was supplied to home winemakers during prohibition.

to the Rossi's' work at ISC, or Asti Grape products, as it was known until the company got its old name back from the CWA in 1924.

The ISC's remarkable scheme would not have been a success without the assistance of the Northwestern Pacific Railroad. It had run from the docks in Marin County through Santa Rosa to Cloverdale and north since 1914. There was even a little station at Asti. Edmund Rossi developed a system for shipping grapes down the NWP to the docks at Tiburon or Sausalito, where the loaded cars were hauled aboard barges and shipped to the San Francisco waterfront and the rails there on Drumm Street.

Rossi also acted as a broker for other Sonoma vineyardists. The most common and profitable grape variety headed east out of California as a whole was the Alicante Bouschet, dull in flavor but dark in color, which the eastern customers admired. But the Alicante had no following among San Francisco's Italian North Beach connoisseurs, who considered the variety little better than a junk grape. Only three varieties came down from Sonoma in any amount: Zinfandel, Carignane and Petite Sirah (Durif). In Napa the Alicante and Petite Sirah were the top shippers.

Between 1915 and 1918 wine grape acreage in Sonoma declined well below Twenty thousand acres, but there were no pullups after 1919. About two thousand acres were added before 1926. The state's total wine grape acreage after 1919 soared at a much higher rate, by the tens of thousands of acres. This explosion was mostly in the Central Valley, where the wine grape crop after 1926 became a severe drag on the eastern market.

A small portion of today's oldest and most valuable Sonoma vineyards was created during these years. During the Dry years Zinfandel was the county's mainstay for flavor, vinosity and adequate color. But many vineyardists were not loath to add a few Alicantes to their vineyards, most vines mixed right in with the other reds. The Petite Sirah was also popular in Sonoma for its color and flavor. Such mixed vineyards that have survived today are prized. A good example of such vines in Sonoma today are three recent vineyard designated Zinfandels from Ridge Vineyards. They average seventy eight percent Zinfandel in various mixtures of Petite Sirah, Alicante, Carignane and Mataro (Mourvèdre).

The carloads of Sonoma wine grapes to the east began their trip at several county stations. A count of refrigerated cars shows a total of 872 leaving the county for the east in 1921. The main stations and the number of carloads sent that year were: Healdsburg (156), Santa Rosa (150), Cloverdale (78), Geyserville (64), and Windsor (60). Of course, more than half of the county's wine grapes were sold to home winemakers in the Bay Area. Only four cars headed east from Asti. ISC grapes on their way to the San Francisco market, if all went well, didn't need refrigerated cars.[15]

The top eastern destinations for California wine grapes and the number of carloads shipped in 1925 were: New York City (13,365), Chicago (6,917), Boston (3,817), Philadelphia (2,847), Pittsburgh (1,669) and Cleveland (1,488). Only 715 carloads were dispatched to the entire south, half of those going to New Orleans and Louisville.[16]

The superiority of Sonoma grapes in the minds of San Francisco and peninsula home winemakers was well established by 1923. At first, trains coming down from Sonoma had such names as "Asti," "Healdsburg," and "Santa Rosa" chalked on their cars. Shippers sending Central Valley grapes to San Francisco were soon chalking the same towns on their cars. It was not long before wary San Francisco buyers would not take grapes from any cars not permanently stenciled "NWP." Even though railroad companies often traded cars, the Rossis insisted that their railroad employ only NWP-designated cars for the fall grape runs.

ISC also set up a small station near the waterfront tracks with a little crushing plant for customers. The buyer could borrow barrels and receive advice from an ISC employee, who would later visit the amateur winemaker's home to see that the fermentation was proceeding properly. There was always a supply of SO2 powders available and their use demonstrated, so that the end product might not be vinegar.[17]

The "Fresh Grape Deal" began to falter after 1925. The huge Central Valley vineyard expansion began taking its toll in two ways. Supply began to exceed demand, pushing down wine grape prices about fifty percent by 1927. And the early arrival on the East Coast of grapes from the torrid

Central Valley was beginning to cause a huge and almost uncontrollable backup of cars loaded with unsold, often unsaleable, grapes. In 1926 forty-five thousand carloads of wine grapes headed east from California, an amount the market could no longer digest.[18]

Sonoma growers' prosperity was hurt by the general decline in wine grape prices after 1926, but they were in better condition than those in other Bay Area counties. Even Napa had a special hurt from its over-dependence on the Alicante, which had almost no market in the region.

The steady national decline into depression after the 1929 New York stock market crash accelerated the decline of demand for wine grapes and the deterioration of prices. Between 1928 and 1930 California wine grape prices dropped forty-three percent prunes were down only twenty-two percent. This fact helped accelerate the conversion of wine grape acreage to prunes, where farmers could afford it. In the Central Valley about twelve thousand acres of wine grapes were pulled up in those years.

However low the prices, Sonoma's position in the San Francisco wine grape market became even more dominant. So many Sonoma grapes were part of 1929's 2,202 cars sold in San Francisco, that for the first time Napa, with half the acreage, sent more grapes east than its western neighbor. In 1930 Sonoma sent only forty-six cars of Zinfandel east. The year before it had shipped only 209, for then an all-time low since 1920.

Horatio Stoll thought the San Francisco wine grape market belonged to Sonoma. He also thought that about the equivalent of forty carloads a day left the county by truck during the vintage with grapes to sell to other parts of the Bay Area. He described the Drumm Street tracks loaded with cars full of grapes surrounded by enthusiastic buyers "a wild place."[19]

The hard times after 1929 cured Sonoma and Napa vineyardists of their occasional wry comments on the evident financial benefits of Prohibition. By 1932, California and the nation were ready to repeal the 18th Amendment. But one national party was not. When the Republicans renominated President Herbert Hoover in June 1932 the convention delegates voted 690-460 against repeal. A few days later, before nominating Franklin D. Roosevelt for the presidency, the Democrats voted 934-213 for repeal.[20]

Just after the end of the 1932 vintage all but one of California's fifty-eight counties voted for FDR-Sonoma and Napa overwhelmingly-but he did not take office until March.

The vintage had been a disaster for Sonoma vineyardists, with prices for the best grapes hovering between ten and fifteen dollars per ton. The people of Sonoma joined the rest of a desperate nation in the winter of 1932-1933 as the Great Depression bottomed out. They were correct in thinking that things surely could not get worse.

After it convened Congress went right to work on repeal. On February 20 both houses together sent the 21st Amendment to the states for ratification. This would take several months, but Congress could change the law defining an "intoxicating beverage," and did on April 7. Now beer was legal at 3.2% alcohol-and, to the dismay and opposition from California wine producers, so was wine!

Californians began gearing up for Repeal and produced a lot of wine in 1932, although it could not yet legally go onto the market until December 1933, when the new amendment became law. At first the 3.2% limit was seen as something of a joke by potential California wine producers. How could anything be called wine with that level of alcohol? But W. V. Cruess and his food technicians at the University of California had been developing a low alcohol wine drink for just such an occasion. By June the Rossis had a slightly sweet, slightly effervescent, pink 3.2% drink on the market, as did Healdsburg's Scatena Winery, which called its product "Sparkling Clairette." Stoll tasted both and wrote that they "proved a real surprise. . . better than soda pop."[21]

There weren't many 3.2 wines made after the 1933 vintage. Before the vintage began everyone was fairly sure that Repeal would go into effect before the end of the year. After December 5 real wine would be legal. But there was a lot of work to be done before an almost-ruined wine industry was back on its feet.

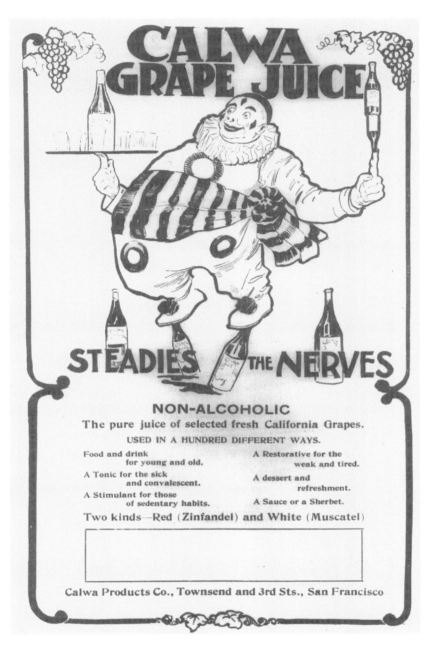

1910 California Wine Association ad for their multipurpose Calwa Grape Juice.
(Courtesy of the Unzelman Collection)

Chapter 15 Notes

1. Pinney, *History,* PP.425-434; Gilman Ostrander, *The Prohibition Movement in California. . .,* Berkeley, 1957, PP.63-88
2. Peter Odegard, *Pressure Politics . . .,* New York, 1928.
3. *PWSR,* 12/31/1900.
4. *American Wine Press,* 8/1904.
5. *Santa Rosa Republican,* 5/19/1909, 7/31/1909.
6. *American Wine Press,* 3/1914, 7/1914, 12/1914; Ostrander PP.124-126.
7. *American Wine Press,* 4/1917.
8. *American Wine Press,* 7/1916.
9. Ostrander, PP.178-180.
10. *PWSR,* 2/18/1918; Peninou, *CWA,* P.120.
11. Edmund Rossi, oral history, Bancroft Library, 1971, PP.40-42, 45-47; Florence, *Legacy,* PP.156-158; *California Grape Grower,* 5/1919. Horatio Stoll turned his CGPA newsletter into this publication. Several years and titles later it became *Wines & Vines.* Hereinafter all these publications will be cited *Wines & Vines.*
12. *Wines & Vines,* 6/1920, 11/1920, 5/1922.
13. Thomas Pinney, *History of Wine In America,* Vol. 2, Berkeley, 2005, PP.18-24.
14. *Wines & Vines,* 12/1919.
15. *Wines & Vines,* 7/1922.
16. *Wines & Vines,* 11/1925.
17. Rossi, oral history, PP. 51-55; *Wines & Vines,* 8/1926, 10/1926, 10/1927.

18. Pinney, *History,* Vol. 2,PP. 25-32.
19. *Wines & Vines,* 10/1930, 12/1930, 4/1931.
20. David Kyvig, *Repealing National Prohibition,* Chicago, 1979, PP.168-177.
21. *Wines & Vines,* 3/1933, 5/1933, 6/1933.

Chapter

16

Repeal, Depression, War

1933-1943

California wine producers and vineyardists were faced with a messy and confusing state of affairs when Repeal became a fact in December 1933. The wine they had made that year was legal, but the state and national governments were understandably slow in developing legal avenues for its distribution and sale. If these had been prosperous times the situation would have been daunting. But all government was focused on dealing with the problems specific to the Great Depression, now in its fifth year.

The IRS ruled that grape growers who had made dry table wine, from grapes they had grown themselves in 1933, could sell it without bond by paying the Treasury Department ten cents per gallon. It was also made clear that the bonding process for wineries in coming years would be simple and inexpensive.[1]

There was still plenty of home winemaker demand for wine grapes in California and east of the Rockies. Average prices paid growers tended to cover costs, just barely, so the carloads of grapes kept rolling east, but at only about half the volume as before. For Sonoma growers the Bay Area market was still very important. In 1934 most of the 1,385 carloads sold on Drumm Street came from Sonoma.[2]

By the end of 1934 it was reported that there were close to a hundred registered wineries in Sonoma County. Many of these undertakings were operated by grape farmers who had never made wine commercially before, and they were rarely prepared to take on the task. Published records of these operations are not wholly reliable, but a fair picture of the situation going into the 1935 vintage appears below.

There were, of course, several well-established producers in the county to whom the smaller operations sold their wine, usually to be blended with better-made wines. Some of this wine was sold at retail at the wineries or to local and regional retailers. But most went in bulk to wholesalers, again to be blended and eventually bottled, usually after making a trip by tank car or by barrel in box cars to the intended market. Overwhelmingly the wine from Sonoma was red table wine, almost all the white varieties there having been pulled up or grafted over to shipping varieties during the Prohibition years.

California consumption of commercial wine in the 1930s was huge. Statistics are not trustworthy for the early thirties, but by 1936 it was clear that California's wine drinkers were buying twenty-five to thirty percent of all the wine consumed in the United States.[3]

Before 1937 much of this wine was purchased in "barrel stores," which sprang up in 1934 in virtually every town and city of any size in the state. The customers could fill their own jugs, which they probably had acquired in such a place earlier; they could even bring in small barrels. They could fill up with dry or sweet wine at bargain prices.

Usually consumers could take a few sips and make their selections. The greater Los Angeles area and the San Francisco Bay Area were simply loaded with such stores. On one block on Howard Street in San Francisco there were seven barrel stores. Wine industry leaders, but not small scale producers, saw these places as a nuisance, as did the California Department of Health, eventually. A *Wine Review* critic in 1935 contended that "the wine industry has suffered incalculable loss of public opinion from the mismanagement of barrel stores," but the public liked them and appreciated their low prices. My young parents had several stores to choose from in Santa Monica, where they paid about fifty cents for a gallon of muscatel.[4]

A few Sonoma wineries were able to profit by marketing their wines under their own brand names. Italian Swiss Colony (ISC) was one of the first on the market. The Rossis had pre-Repeal wine stored up and had made about 200,000 gallons in 1933. They put on a huge celebration at the winery in November for the first trainload of wine that headed east from their Asti Station. Students from Cloverdale High School were invited to take part, and some of the girls were outfitted in red, white, and green uniforms. The newspapers were on hand, as well as Pathé newsreel photographers, as two of the girls rolled the first barrel onto the waiting boxcar.[5]

Hoping for and expecting Repeal, ISC in 1927 had begun replanting their Sangiovese vines. The wine from this variety had been the backbone of ISC's famed red Tipo Chianti before Prohibition. Thus they were early able to bring out that famous brand, which by the summer of 1934 was on the wine list of every major San Francisco hotel, along with the winery's Zinfandel and Riesling.[6]

From Guerneville there was again a steady flow of Korbel Sec, the sparkling wine made famous before Prohibition under the eye of wine master Jan Hanuska, who was still in charge of production in the thirties. Fountaingrove made wine through 1935, but Kanaye Nagasawa's death in 1936 brought a temporary end to production. Still, there was enough good wine on hand to keep the brand and its good reputation alive until the new owner took over in time for the 1937 vintage.

The DeTurk brand was still alive at Santa Rosa, where the wine was being made at the Joseph T. Grace Brewery and sold again through San Francisco's Wm. Hoelscher firm. For several years DeTurk wine and Grace Bros. beer were produced in the old winery building.

Samuel Sebastiani also sold wine in bulk and under his own label. That California wine production in the early thirties was well over sixty percent sweet/fortified wine attracted Sebastiani and ISC to expand into the Central Valley, where the hot weather was best suited for such production. But there was also a small amount of sweet wine produced in Sonoma County itself. In 1936 there were seven wineries there licensed to produce brandy as a beverage or for fortification: ISC, Sebastiani, Fountaingrove, DeTurk, Pagani Bros. (Kenwood), Prima Vista (Healdsburg) and Korbel. The latter was soon known for the high quality of its beverage brandy.[7]

Two Healdsburg wineries worth noting were gaining special attention for red wines by the bottle. Scatena Bros. had been out first with a 3.2 wine

The landmark Korbel Brandy Tower, which was built by founder Francis Korbel as a sym-bol of the freedom he found in America: the tower is a replica of one which he could see from a Prague prison cell he occupied in the 1940s. (Courtesy of the Unzelman Collection)

272

in 1933, but their Zinfandel brought them local fame in later years. Their Healdsburg operation was acquired in 1949 by Geyserville's Seghesio Winery, today considered one of Sonoma's premier Zinfandel producers. Even more famous for a while were the reds from the Simi Winery. After her father and uncle died in 1904, Isabelle and other family members ran the winery for a few years. She married local businessman Frederick Haigh in 1908, and the couple ran the ranch in subsequent years and went into winemaking again in the thirties. By the end of that decade their late-released Zinfandel, Carignan and Cabernet were famous; they were still winning Bay Area wine tastings in the seventies.

Other important bulk producers with a local retail following were the Foppiano Winery near Windsor, Lee Morelli's Lemorel Winery at Occidental, Frei Brothers in Dry Creek Valley, and the Petri Winery at Forestville. Felicien Vadon's 175,000-gallon operation near Cloverdale also had a local retail trade. On a small scale he also produced well-received cuvées of sparkling wine.

The federal government helped winegrowers by lowering the wine tax from ten to five cents per gallon in 1935. Earlier, Mrs. Roosevelt had made a helpful but symbolic gesture by announcing that only American wines would be served at White House dinners. In the Department of Agriculture wine producers had a supporter in Assistant Secretary Rexford Tugwell, who believed in promoting a friendly national policy toward producers of dry table wines.

California wine producers had a real friend in Tugwell, but the New Deal depended on the support of southern Democrats. Many of these were dry sympathizers, and they were instrumental in blocking Tugwell's policies. The 21st Amendment was also a problem for wine producers since it laid aside Congress's specific control of interstate commerce and gave individual states a free pass to enact virtually any law that might hinder commerce in all alcoholic beverages.

There was little on the national political scene that affected Sonoma winegrowers except for the New Deal actions to raise consumer buying power. As it rose gradually after 1933, up twenty-seven percent by 1937, so did wine grape and wine prices, but at a slower pace. Actually the wine-grower's income was more affected by the weather. A short crop from frigid spring temperatures usually meant better prices for sound dry wine grapes. Two very large crops in a row could mean disaster.

Through the thirties the consumption by Californians of their state's wine stayed high at about twenty-million gallons per year. Per capita consumption here, at more than three gallons, was seven times the national average, which has never, to this day, topped the California numbers of the thirties.

After 1936 we finally have a good picture of Sonoma wine producers. In 1937 *Wines & Vines* published a fairly comprehensive list containing eight-five county wineries. This number is somewhat smaller than that usually cited, "about one hundred." The data below also contain material supplied me by the Treasury Department in 1993 on microfiche of the records on California wineries from 1933-1988. Many question marks appear below where neither the *Wines & Vines* chart nor the Treasury's data gave a number or a date.

Sonoma Wineries in the 1930s

Proprietor/Winery Name End of Business/Successor	Bond #	Capacity
CLOVERDALE		
E. Bandiera Stonegate 1996	3998	75,000
H. Black Cortz 1964	328	167,000
E. De George 1942	325	10,000

P. Dehay 1938	4039	150,000
J. Ferrari 1942	764	30,000
W. Furber ca. 1946	1447	120,000
A. Ghotti 1954	1739	55,000
C. Giannechini 1941	327	25,000
C. Haehl 1945	364	40,000
Italian Swiss Colony/E.&R. Rossi National Dist. 1944	1589	3,400,000
R. Lotti 1946	834	10,000
C. Mazzini 1951	326	?
C. Pastore ?	2960	?
S. Ratto 1960	311	18,000
A.Seghesio	56	100,000
W. Sink 1959	885	100,000
A. Trusendi ?	4891	?
F. Vadon 1946	853	175,000
G. Ziller ca. 1946	338	25,000

FORESTVILLE/GUERNEVILLE/OCCIDENTAL

E. Barsotti/Santa Nella Korbel 1953	259	150,000
F. Korbel A. Heck 1954	74	400,000
F. Martinelli 1960	1824	?
L. Morelli/Lemorel Winery 1964	1067	50,000
Petri Wine Co. Allied growers 1953	2268	1,250,000

GEYSERVILLE

P. Domenichelli 1946	345	50,000
F. Fredson 1987	658	150,000
L. Lombardi ?	699	?
F. Nervo 1994 Geyser Peak	350	250,000
E. Norton ?	400	?
J. Pedroncelli	113	175,000
J. Rose ?	906	?
G. Stefani 1943	362	50,000
I. Vasconi ?	1732	?

| L. Zanzi | 3129 | 25,000 |
| ca. 1944 | | |

GLEN ELLEN/KENWOOD

B. Behler	250	12,000
1943		
F. Duggan	4053	?
1950		
C. Kunde/Wildwood Vineyards	202	200,000
F. Mancuso	3664	87,500
ca. 1964		
A. Pagani/Glen Ellen Winery	872	200,000
1963		
Pagani Bros.	978	189,000
to Kenwood Vineyards 1969		
J. Weise	1402	?
1953		

HEALDSBURG

B. Bacchi	487	?
Pedroncelli 1944		
F. Bella	4065	?
?		
S. Bignano	656	?
?		
J. Cambiaso	4052	100,000
Domaine St. George 1987		
L. Foppiano/ Riverside Winery	312	400,000
W. Frei/ Frei Bros. Winery	1114	600,000
Gallo 1961		

Healdsburg Wine Co.	303	?
1944 Alta Vineyard		
E. Oneta	4177	20,000
1957		
E. Passalacqua	35	?
1952		
W. Passalacqua	4125	?
?		
S. Pieroni	653	?
?		
L. Rosasco	95	750,000
1950		
A. Rafanelli	4013	?
1943		
Scatena Bros. Winery	56	1,000,000
Seghesio 1949		
D. Schieck	248	?
?		
Simi Winery/ F. & I. Haigh	2331	1,000,000
Russell Green 1970		
Soda Rock Winery/ A. Ferrarri	3662	80,000
Ken Wilson 2009		
A. Sodini	316	50,000
1961		
Sotoyome Winery/E. Commisky	687	125,000
1949		

SANTA ROSA

M. Bettini	3985	?
1941		
P. Dehay/Prima Vista	4039	150,000
1938		

De Turk Wines/J.T. Grace	15.1	750,000
1944 to Hiram Walker		
A. Bossa	1937	?
1941		
Fountaingrove/E. MacBoyle	1051	400,000
1955		
G. Frati/ Mt. Olivet	4053	?
1943		
M. Galeazzi	1066	?
?		
A. Lagomarsino	989	135,000
1957		
J. Marsh	292	?
?		
H. Meese	1258	15,000
1953		
J. Peterson	903	?
?		
G. Rocco	4010	?
1942		
Santa Rosa Wine Co/J O'connor	3011	25,000
1965		
P. Tenti	3851	?
?		

SEBASTOPOL /PETALUMA

L. Dioguardi	3678	?
?		
A. Hodges	3843	?
1941		
G. Rafanelli	578	?
1943, 1974 to BW 4679		

P. Rossi	1199	12,000
?		
R. Theiller	255	?
1941		

SONOMA

A. Bianchini	1164	?
?		
S. Sebastiani	35	1,000,000

WINDSOR

A. Baldocchi	3179	?
1943 to Vercelli		
N. Chisholm/ Chisholm Farms	907	150,000
ca. 1955		
A. Crevelli	4043	?
ca. 1946		
R. Martini Wine Co.	1881	1,300,000
1943 to Hiram Walker		
Sonoma Cooperative Winery	4138	750,000
1965 to Gallo		

From these data it is clear that a large number of small wineries quit making commercial wine during and just after the war years. These small wineries did not cease production before 1946 because of the business climate between 1940 and 1945. With grape prices rising in those years, it was far more efficient and profitable to sell their grapes to larger wineries. Sonoma grape prices stabilized before the war but soared after 1941. Grower return per acre between 1938 and 1942 rose seventy three percent.

Frank Schoonmaker, pictured here, wrote of Sonoma in his 1964 book Encyclopedia of Wine, *"One of the most important wine-producing regions of Northern California, and on the whole one of the best."*

The threat of war in Europe after 1938 prompted several eastern wine merchants to look to California as a future source of high quality table and sparkling wines. The most important for this study was Frank Schoonmaker, who had been importing European wines since 1935. He toured California in 1939 and contracted for wines from several producers noted for high quality. These were then marketed in a manner that reflected his powerful beliefs about commercial wine. The consumer should be able to tell from the label where the grapes were grown and from what variety the wine was produced. Terms such as "Chablis" and "Burgundy," almost standard on California wine labels, were not seen on his selections. This varietal labeling was not new for a few California producers, but it was opposed for several years by most wine industry leaders. Schoonmaker's principles, reflected in his wines, and his books

The packed entrance of the Golden Gate International Exposition, 1939.

and articles, directly influenced the development of higher standards for California wines after World War II.[9]

Schoonmaker's first selections were all from Bay Area producers. Among others there were Wente and Concannon from Livermore, Inglenook and Larkmead from Napa, Fountaingrove and Korbel from Sonoma.[10]

The selection of Korbel's sparkling wine was no surprise, but Fountaingrove's Cabernet Sauvignon and Pinot noir need some explanation. Mining magnate Errol MacBoyle had visited Fountaingrove before Nagasawa's death, but then as a collector of Japanese art. In 1937 he bought the huge ranch and engaged E. C. Romeno as its manager and wine maker. Romeno was a graduate of Italy's Royal Enological College and the former general manager of southern California's giant Italian Vineyard Company. For MacBoyle the estate's main attraction was its four hundred acre vineyard, which contained "all the most 'aristocratic' varieties." He intended to produce the best wines California producers could offer the public. In the years before MacBoyle's death in 1949, few lovers of California's wines would have argued that his goal had not been met.[11]

At the State Fair in 1939 Korbel won gold medals for its Sec and Pink champagnes, as did Fountaingrove for its Riesling. Later, at San Francisco's Golden Gate Exposition, where few golds were awarded, Fountaingrove won silver for Riesling, Zinfandel, Cabernet and Burgundy. Other awards went to Glen Ellen Winery, ISC, Korbel, Santa Rosa Winery and Scatena Bros.[12]

When Schoonmaker toured Sonoma, what many later thought were the county's greatest red wines had not yet been released. Fred and Isabelle Haigh at Simi Winery were convinced that proper aging and strict varietal designation were essential for establishing a reputation for the best table wines. Starting in 1935 they produced varietal Cabernet, Zinfandel and Carignan. The first two won gold medals at the 1941 State Fair. Later that year the famed Hotel Del Monte in Monterey began featuring Simi wines under the hotel's label.[13]

As California entered the war in December 1941 the picture of the state's wine production was clear, and Sonoma was very much out of step. More than seventy-four percent of California's wine production was sweet/ fortified, while Sonoma's production was eighty-nine percent dry table wine, overwhelmingly red. Napa's numbers were similar.

These percentages were destined to change after January 1942. In fact, World War II might be used as a text for studying unintended consequences for the California wine industry. The January event was the War Production Board's order that California raisins were now going to be food to support the war effort. Among other uses, they became almost famous as a standard part of the G.I.'s K rations. This development assured a steep decline in Central Valley wine production, particularly wine of the port-sherry-muscatel sort. In 1941 wine and brandy made with raisin grapes had amounted to about forty-five percent of the state's total grape crush. That percentage would plummet in 1942. As a result, the value of Sonoma wine grapes went straight up during the three wartime vintages.

Another consequence of the war was a sudden shortage of tank cars used to transport bulk wine. By mid-1943 half the huge fleet of cars was solely in government service. This helped promote a practice we take for granted today, wine "bottled at the winery," or "estate bottled," if the winery owned the vines.

Related to this situation was the Office of Price Administration's decision to cap the price of wine in interstate commerce, but not the price of wine grapes. Wineries with higher-priced wine in their product line in 1941 were allowed to sell all their wines at these high prices. Such a policy was of great benefit to such as Fountaingrove and Simi. Another twist was that bulk producers such as Frei Bros. and Foppiano could sell their wines to any winery in the state at any price. If the sale was to a premium winery, that wine could be sold at a premium price.[14]

American distillers had to convert most of their production to industrial alcohol for the war effort. Whisky production ended in November 1942. Distillers now needed something else alcoholic to produce and sell. Wine was the answer. Four large distillers, Schenley, Seagram's, Hiram Walker and National Distillers, began scooping up mostly large Central Valley operations. Sonoma was also affected when Hiram Walker bought the million gallon R. Martini Winery near Windsor. Historically far more

284

important was National Distillers' acquisition of Italian Swiss Colony. The main target was La Paloma, the company's huge sweet wine plant near Fresno. The Asti winery was a sidelight of the transaction. Over the years the historic winery passed from one corporate giant to another. In the years after the war Asti's large tasting room became a celebrated tourist stop. But the ISC brand was never again a guarantee of excellent red table wine.[15]

The war years brought more than economic stability to some Sonoma wine producers. The region's growing reputation as the source of some of California's best wines was solidified. There was Simi at Hotel Del Monte, and numerous other local wines were on hotel wine lists up and down the coast. Hotels on the East Coast now had Sonoma wines on their wine lists as never before. A good example was the Waldorf Astoria's list in 1943, which had varietal table wines from Simi and Fountaingrove and sparklers from Korbel and Fountaingrove.[16]

Many Bay Area wineries were now placing a very special emphasis on limited production of very high quality table wines. Some were revivals of older premium producers like Freemark Abbey in Napa (1895 Lombarda Winery), Los Amigos near Mission San Jose (Grau & Werner 1888) and Martin Ray in Saratoga (Paul Masson 1896). Others like Inglenook, Wente and Korbel had excellent pre-Prohibition reputations they were working to restore.

There were very few before 1946 who started winegrowing from scratch-actually only one who didn't move into an old abandoned winery. That was Chaffee Hall (1941) in the Santa Cruz Mountains. In Napa, Lee Stewart moved into the 1884 Rossini Winery, which became Souverain Cellars. Jack and Mary Taylor took over Napa's long-empty 1885 Fischer Winery, which became Mayacamas Vineyards.

In Sonoma in 1943 a newspaperman and his wife acquired an even older abandoned winery whose huge structures dated back to 1863, but they saw no need to change the winery's name. Why should they? It was almost forgotten, but not by the few who knew something about the origins of the California wine industry.

Chapter 16 Notes

1. *Wines & Vines,* 6/1934.

2. *Wines & Vines,* 11/1934.

3. *Wines & Vines,* 1/1938.

4. *Wine Review,* 7/1935.

5. Florence, *Legacy,* PP.166-167.

6. *Wines & Vines,* 6/1934.

7. *Wines & Vines,*10/1936.

8. These data also contain material supplied me on microfiche by the Treasury Department in 1993 of the records for California wineries from 1933-1988

9. Thomas Pinney, *The Makers of American Wine,* Berkeley, 2012, PP.149-170.

10. *Wines & Vines,* 12/1939; Pinney, *History* II, PP.119-123.

11. *Wines & Vines 5,* 1937; Adams, P.232.

12. *Wines & Vines,* 10/1939.

13. *Wines & Vines,* 9/1941, 10/1941. These Simi wines can still be found for sale on the internet for $500-1,000. My personal experience with all these wines in the seventies and eighties confirmed their excellent reputation.

14. Pinney, *History* II, PP.131-135.

15. Leon Adams, *The Wines of America,* Boston, 1973, PP.198-201; Pinney, *History* II, PP.126-129.

16. *American Wine Merchant,* Spring 1944. In 1940 Hanns Kornell became Fountaingrove's champagne maker. He later established his own winery in Napa.

Chapter

17

Bart at Buena Vista

1943-1968

On a beautiful fall day in November 1943, Frank and Antonia Bartholomew drove up to a friend's ranch near Glen Ellen for a Sunday afternoon luncheon. He, always called "Bart," was home for a few days from the war in the Pacific, where he was the supervisor of the United Press's (UPI) corps of war correspondents. Their host, Howard Makelim, in a "casual remark," told the couple of a large ranch east of the town of Sonoma that the State of California was about to auction off.

On their way back to San Francisco, Makelim took the Bartholomews over to view the property. Bart later wrote, "I was immediately entranced by the quiet beauty of the ranch." He and his wife decided to submit a bid for the property and ended up with the high number of $17,600, about equal to almost $200,000 in 2012 constant dollars.

Bart had to return to Australia and "presented the ranch to my wife as a birthday gift." Actually, the couple had quickly decided that Antonia would take charge of the ranch for the duration of the war and supervise whatever improvements they decided to initiate. She was well suited for the task.[1]

Her husband's twenty years as a newsman made it easy for him to help direct his wife's efforts in learning about the property. Their first discovery was that their new acquisition had a name, Buena Vista, and that it was "one of the great legends of the wine industry." Antonia knew that there was no reason to rush into any venture without careful preparation. So at

Frank Bartholomew, some years after the sale of Buena Vista.

first she was interested in getting a close picture of their newly-acquired almost five hundred acres.

"I was alone - just me and my horse Tula Vista." She rode the estate off and on for several weeks and decided that she "couldn't stand to see all this land idle." At the same time she had gradually picked up historical information on Buena Vista, partly from old- timers in the area. (One of her early visitors was the ninety-one- year-old owner of the place in 1905.) She also contacted the Viticulture and Enology Department at the Davis campus of the University of California. Professor Albert Winkler perked right up when she described the land and the great structures on it. He had a hopeful idea of what the couple had actually bought. He came over and toured the property with Antonia. It was surely the great Buena Vista! He gave her some ideas to improve her knowledge of the place, directing her to The Wine Institute in San Francisco. There she got a copy of a 1939 master's thesis written at U.C. Berkeley which had a whole chapter on Buena Vista and its remarkable Hungarian founder, Agoston Haraszthy.[2] It was also loaded with other sources of information for additional study.

There was no person in the country better suited than Professor Winkler to gauge the winegrowing potential of the newly purchased property. He told her that the land wasn't much good for anything but grapes, and he impressed upon her the great and glorious history of the place as the center of the Bay Area's original wine industry. They also found an acre of very old Zinfandel on the estate, well removed from the old winery buildings. The weeds were so high that they obscured the vines. Later writers' claim that they had been planted by Haraszthy are laughable, since they were on resistant rootstock.

Winkler suggested they plant Riesling and Sylvaner for their white wines and Cabernet Sauvignon for the red. That sounded fine to Antonia. "I was practically weaned on Riesling," her father's favorite wine.

The Bartholomew's next expert connection was one that would last for more than twenty years. In 1944 Bart came home on leave again and was invited to attend a meeting of "The Brotherhood," that is, the monthly luncheon meeting of the Napa Vintners' Society. There he met André Tchelistcheff, who had come from Russia via Paris to Napa's Beaulieu Vineyards in 1938. By 1944 he was already gradually developing a great reputation for his wines there. The tiny enologist was immediately attracted to Bart's hopes for re-establishing winegrowing at Buena Vista. A few days later he drove over to Sonoma and spent some time at admiring the historic estate. He was convinced that the old buildings could be put back to work as a winery, and he knew a stonemason who could do the job. He also knew that he could get expert help in re-establishing a vineyard of premium varieties on the property. Always the bubbling enthusiast, Tchelistcheff offered to buy into the coming operation as a partner and consultant. Bart accepted the proposition and Buena Vista's new history was under way.[3]

Bart had also met Louis Martini, Sr. at the Napa luncheon. That connection led Antonia to hire Jim Lyttle, Martini's vineyard foreman, to supervise the planting of the new vineyard. It was spring 1945, the war was still on, and labor was scarce. Lyttle was able to hire some of the older boys at the nearby Glen Ellen State Home. He also got a crew of sailors from the Mare Island Navy Yard at Vallejo. The varieties were Cabernet Sauvignon, Riesling, Sylvaner and Chardonnay. The last two were accidentally planted together.[4]

Work on getting usable working space for winery operations in the 1864 winery building had to wait until 1946. The great 1863 Press House was in worse shape, and for many years would be used only for storage. When Bart came home late in 1956, on Jim Lyttle's suggestion he hired Antonio Maretti to supervise the vineyard. He was able to restore some of the little Zinfandel vineyard on the property. Bart also bought a tiny Barbera vineyard on a piece of land adjacent to the property. Most of these vines Maretti grafted over to Gewürztraminer. A few years later grapes from these vines did much to solidify the special Buena Vista reputation for high quality German-style white wines.

Before the first new Buena Vista estate wines went on the market in 1949, Bart and Antonia read everything they could find about Buena Vista and its founder. They wanted to use the history to help promote their wines. "We had become Haraszthy aficionados through study of every bit of history we could find of the old stone buildings, and the enormously colorful life of their builder. . . we determined to return the great name of Haraszthy to the wine trade. . . ."

The general picture they developed of Buena Vista's fame in the 1860s and 187 was fairly accurate. I can find no evidence that they succumbed to

André Tchelitscheff

the bold and ignorant claims that later flourished in the columns of wine writers and in books by non-historians. The best example is that they did not claim that Haraszthy founded the California wine industry. They did accept the idea that Haraszthy had brought the first Zinfandel to California from the Hungarian portion of the Austrian Empire in the 1850s, but that was what practically everyone writing on the subject believed before the 1970s.

Leon D. Adams, known as the dean of American wine writers.

Bart's understanding of Buena Vista history *after* Haraszthy's departure in 1867 was not at all accurate. When Bart wrote his memoirs in 1982 he still believed that the winery had operated on through the nineteenth century and had only been shut down after the 1906 earthquake. Readers of this study know that this view is off by twenty-three years.

Virtually all published material on the new Buena Vista dates its wines from the 1949 release. These were estate wines, produced from grapes grown on Buena Vista property. But hidden in André Tchelistcheff's oral history are facts that help explain how Bart won silver medals in 1947 at the Los Angeles County Fair for his "Rhine Wine" and at the 1949 State Fair for his well-aged Pinot noir.[5]

After they formed their partnership, André convinced Bart that there was no reason to wait for his young vines to produce a vintage. Why not buy some good wine made elsewhere and release it under the Buena Vista label, a perfectly legal and customary practice throughout the California wine industry. The two men took a visit to the Alexander Valley's Soda Rock Winery and tasted through their unbottled wines. They ended up buying five gallons of Riesling and Pinot noir. The wines were transferred to the old winery and André supervised their preparation. André later said that these wines had good "personality" and asked Leon Adams to try them. Adams, the co-founder of the Wine Institute and later California's greatest wine chronicler, according to André, declared the white wine the best California Riesling he had tasted. I doubt if he said "ever." The Zinfandel was at least partly an estate wine, some of it made from grapes whose vines Antonia and Professor Winkler had found on the property.[6]

In 1950 Buena Vista joined the small but growing group of small scale newcomers dedicated to the production of first class dry table wines with an emphasis on varietal labeling, the Chateau Wine Growers. Original members also included such names as Stony Hill, Mayacamas, Souverain, and Hallcrest, but there were no premium old-timers likeInglenook, Almaden or Wente. Bart was one of the organization's officers.[7] Most of these small wineries were enthusiastic participants in California's two important wine competitions, the State Fair in Sacramento and the Los Angeles County Fair at Pomona. In the fifties Buena Vista captured dozens of medals in these competitions.

Bart wasn't able to enter his first, most successful wines, at least not under the names he put on the labels. Vine Brook was a tasty blend of Chardonnay and Sylvaner grapes, that had been unintentionally interplanted in 1945. Rose Brook was a pink wine, a rosé, made from Cabernet Sauvignon. Although Bart gradually became a true believer in the varietal designation of wines, his first gold at the State Fair was a "Chablis" made from French Colombard, whose grapes he bought from a neighboring grower. Sonoma was red wine country for a long time, nine-to-one over white in 1943, but only four-to-one in 1947. Only one good white variety, the French Colombard was grown enough to be in the county records. Thus did the familiar term "chablis" make it onto a Buena Vista label, and as a category of competition at the fairs.

A good part of the Buena Vista success in the fifties was due to the work of winemaster Albert Brett. He came aboard and ran the cellar until his retirement in 1974. He had previously made wine at Oakville's Napa Wine Co. For much of this time Buena Vista also benefited from the expert knowledge of André Tchelistcheff. Not long after André entered his partnership with Bart he had to pull out due to personal financial problems. Frank did not hesitate when André explained the situation. He returned the investment but kept his old partner as his consultant on a generous monthly salary. André liked the arrangement. After all, as he said, Bart was a rich man and a good friend.

Bart made sure that his best wines got plenty of attention at the state's big fairs through the late fifties. His white varietals were the outstanding performers by far, particularly the Riesling, Sylvaner and Gewürztraminer. Between 1950 and 1956 these wines won fifteen gold and silver medals at Sacramento and Los Angeles. Here we can see the Tchelistcheff hand. He was an ardent promoter of cool fermentation techniques to improve white wine quality. He was also helping the Mondavi Brothers at Charles Krug in the same way. Their medals for these wines at the big fairs were just as numerous as Buena Vista's. Bart's success with red wines in these events was more occasional, such as when his Zinfandels won gold medals in 1954 and 1955.

After 1957 a storm of protest developed over the judging at the State Fair and over the professional ability of many of the judges. Most of the concern came from small, quality producers like Buena Vista. For a while U.C.Davis refused to supply judges for the State Fair. Changes were made, but by 1960, for one reason or another, wines from small scale premium producers were rarely seen on the premium lists from either large fair.[8]

Buena Vista stayed with Los Angeles longer than most, winning its final L. A. gold in 1959. Bart had good reason for having placed special emphasis on his entries there. He was convinced that the Los Angeles market was a virtually untapped source of potential customers. There was a large and rapidly growing population, and the southern California press gave good coverage to medals awarded at the county fair at Pomona. There was also

296

Robert Lawrence Balzer, as pictured on the dustcover flap of 1948's California's Best Wines.

good reason to believe that customer interest in California's premium wine was rising just as steadily there as it was in the San Francisco Bay Area. His conviction dated from 1949, when Robert Lawrence Balzer visited Buena Vista. Balzer was a successful Los Angeles wine merchant who eventually became a regular wine writer for the *Los Angeles Times*. In 1948 his first book, *California's Best Wines*, was published, based on his research since the war. At this early date he had to concentrate on established wineries which were producing excellent table wines, such as Inglenook, Wente and Fountaingrove. But he was soon seeking out serious newcomers like Hallcrest, Stony Hill and, of course, Buena Vista.[9]

In a later book Balzer described his 1949 visit to Buena Vista in glowing detail. He pulled no punches in describing the Bartholomew's achievement since 1943. Buena Vista "has risen phoenix-like from its own ashes, to a glory surpassing anything it had ever known in the days of its founder. . . ."[10] Balzer was particularly fascinated by the rosé from Cabernet Sauvignon labeled "Rose Brook." He featured this wine and the Vine Brook at his store. Los Angeles demand for these two almost depleted Bart's inventory in those wines.[11]

Buena Vista's rise to fame in the fifties is ironic, since Sonoma County statistics between 1946 and 1966 suggest that winegrowing there was dying. In 1946 Sonoma had 22,235 acres of wine grapes. Five years later there were only 14,772 acres, and by 1962 the total bottomed out at 10,600 acres. The basic cause for this fall was the declining profitability in the county of growing grapes for wine. In 1946 growers received on average $125 per ton for their grapes there. By 1955 their gross receipts showed an average price of $55 per ton. At the average yield that year of 2.3 tons per acre, their take per acre was only $125. The average yield per acre from 1943 to 1956 was 2.05 tons.

There were several more attractive crops that encouraged vine pull-ups and discouraged more planting. Chief among these were prunes. From 1950 to 1958 Sonoma prune growers brought in an average of $227 per acre.

Making wine was just as unprofitable as raising and selling grapes. There were sixty-six bonded wineries in the county in 1946. By 1964 the number had dropped to twenty-eight.[12]

Following the 1950 vintage Edmund Rossi, who had helped rebuild Italian Swiss Colony after Prohibition, gave an address to the Sonoma County Wine Growers Association, "to enthusiastic applause." His thesis was that American wine consumers did not know the name "Sonoma," and those who did "rarely associate it with the idea of quality wine." He pointed out the declining acreage and the almost non-existence of premium wine grape varieties in their vineyards. He told them to put "Sonoma" on their wine labels and put better wine in their bottles.[13]

That his warnings were justified was emphasized by the end of Fountaingrove. There was much lamenting the demise of what many thought was the producer of Sonoma's best table wines. The handwriting was on the wall after Errol MacBoyle died in 1949. There was no money to replace the old vines, many of which dated back into the previous century. The great vineyard was allowed to fall into neglect. By 1955 the vines had been pulled. The two thousand acres, as cheap as farm acreage was then, were more valuable to the new owners than trying to make a profit from them growing grapes and selling wine.

Nevertheless, beneath Sonoma's sad statistics and dead wineries were some hopeful signs. In 1952 on a hillside north of Sonoma James D. Zellerbach had begun planting a beautifully terraced vineyard of Pinot noir and Chardonnay. His little winery was a small copy of Burgundy's Clos de Vougeot. He hired Bradford Webb as his winemaker.[14]

Zellerbach was the U.S. Ambassador to Italy at the time, and to the embassy in Rome went part of his first Chardonnay vintage in 1956. In the next years the Hanzell wines were a sensation. Webb had aged the wine in new French oak barrels, and the result was a triumph of elegant flavor. Leon Adams considered the Hanzell wines to have encouraged "scores of America's leading vintners to make an important change in the flavor of their wines."[15]

In 1958 *Consumer Reports* published its first suggested list of California table wines; its evaluation gave Buena Vista a big boost. Bart's was the only Sonoma County label to make the grade. Nine Buena Vista wines were suggested, the same number posted by Beaulieu and Beringer. Actually, two other Sonoma wines were recommended, but under the label of a Napa producer. These came from Louis Martini's Monte Rosso Vineyard in the hills above the Sonoma Valley.[16]

The dismal wine grape acreage reports for Sonoma County in the fifties and sixties did not give a complete picture of some positive changes taking place. For example, in 1957 the county had 450 acres of new vines planted, but pull-ups of old vines were about the same, so no gain was noticeable. This process of vineyard improvement continued into the sixties. Then some encouraging numbers appeared. Between 1964 and 1968, total wine grape acreage in the county expanded by almost two thousand acres. In 1964 there had been eighty-nine acres of Cabernet Sauvignon; whatever the Pinot noir, Chardonnay or Sauvignon blanc acreage, it was too small to make the official statistics. But in 1968 1200 acres were devoted to those four premium varieties, and five hundred more acres were added the next spring. That brought the Cabernet Sauvignon total to 742 acres. Buena Vista had been adding to these statistics since 1962, when Bart began planting heavily to Riesling, Chardonnay, Gewürztraminer and Pinot noir. He would retain all these vines when he sold Buena Vista in 1968.

The change in the pattern of wine consumption in California and the nation was also favoring the production of fine table wine. Since the 1930s fortified sweet wines, the ports, sherries and muscatels, had led the consumption of dry table wine, often with a ratio of higher than two to one. That ratio began changing in the fifties, and in 1963 in California the ratio tilted in favor of table wine. On the national scene table wine took the lead in 1967.

A revolution in California wine was on the way. It was the result of changes in habits by perhaps twenty percent of the national population, for, as a whole, Americans were not wine drinkers. Most of those represented in the growth numbers for table wine were looking for fine wine to go with the fine food that was a great part of this change in national habits. Thus came the sixties' small rise in the acreage of world class wine grape varieties in Sonoma, and in the Livermore and Napa Valleys.[17]

Bart and Antonia sensed these changes. He was approaching seventy and had his hands full staying on top of his successful but relatively small 15,000 case operation. His rise to the position of board chairman of UPI did not simplify his life. Much of his time was spent in the east, but on the phone continuously with Albert Brett and André Tchelistcheff.

Perhaps his greatest asset in Southern California was Young's Market Company, which distributed his wine there. Company president Vernon Underwood loved Bart's wines and was even more impressed by the way the Buena Vista brand had risen to prominence in the fifties. He also knew the

Buena Vista Vineyards

ESTABLISHED JANUARY 1857 BY COUNT AGOSTON HARASZTHY

SONOMA, CALIFORNIA 95476 • P.O. BOX 311 • [707] 938-2244

January 25, 1975

Frank Bartholomew's letterhead clearly shows the value he placed on Haraszthy's name and its association with the property.

importance of the great old winery as a destination point for the small but growing number of tourists heading to the California wine country.[18] He knew the revolution in California wine was coming and gave Bart an offer he couldn't refuse.

Underwood would take the old winery, some surrounding acres, and the Buena Vista brand. Bart kept most of the recently planted vineyard acreage and might continue calling them Buena Vista Vineyards and using the Haraszthy name. Underwood agreed to buy his grapes. The deal was closed in 1968. All this and the huge monetary settlement left the Bartholomews free to stay a part of the wine world in any manner they chose.[19]

Underwood and his team at Young's were well aware of André Tchelistcheff's almost passionate belief in the viticultural future of the Carneros region. In 1961 he had induced Beaulieu to buy 160 acres on the Napa side. Los Carneros is an area of flatlands and rolling hills encompassing the lower reaches of the Sonoma and Napa Valleys just above San Pablo Bay. In Underwood's mind this region was to be the key to Buena Vista's future growth.

301

Chapter 17 Notes

1. Frank H. Bartholomew, *Bart, His Memoirs,* Sonoma, 1983, PP.113-130. This autobiography is overwhelmingly devoted to the author's 57 years of service with UPI, but there is a detailed section on the couple's 25 year Buena Vista experience. This material was published verbatim in *Wines & Vines,* 11/1984, PP.34-38, which is far more accessible that the long- out-of-date autobiography.

2. Herbert B. Leggett, "Early History of Wine Production in California," Wine Institute, 1941. PP.35-44.

3. André Tchelistcheff, Oral History, Bancroft Library, 1983, PP.105-106.

4. *Wines & Vines,* 3/1945.

5. Fair results appeared annually in the September or October issues of *Wines & Vines.*

6. Tchelistcheff oral History, P.106.

7. *Wines & Vines,* 12/1950, 2/1952.

8. *Wines & Vines,* 7/1956, 3/1958.

9. Balzer, *California's Best Wines,* Los Angeles, 1948.

10. Balzer, *Pleasures of Wine,* New York, 1964, P.112, PP.226-342.

11. Bartholomew, P.119.

12. Wine industry trade publications tended to veil the enormity of this decline, but Treasury Department records told the unhappy story.

13. "Selling Sonoma County," *Wines & Vines,* 11/1950, P.11.

14. Webb was nominated to the Vintners' Hall of Fame in 2012.

15. Adams, 1973, PP.188-189,P. 191.

16. *Wines & Vines,* 12/1958.

17. Pinney, *History* II, 227-231; Leslie Brenner, *American Appetite,* New York, 1999.

18. My wife and I first visited the Sonoma wine country in 1961. Our first stop was Buena Vista; we were thoroughly impressed by the setting and the wines offered.

19. Adams, 1978, PP.253-254.

Chapter

18

"Boom and Bust" or "Revolution"

1968-1980

Leon Adams has written the best chronicle of the great changes in this country's production and use of wine between the 1960s and the 1970s. It is particularly well focused on the origins of these changes, since the first two volumes of his *Wines of America* were published in 1973 and 1978. In 1979 he gave a talk to do the Wine Industry Technical Seminar and chose the word "revolution" to characterize the events of the previous years. The word suggests fairly permanent change, but the events of the seventies also suggest a return to the "boom and bust" cycle the California wine industry had experienced in the 1870s and 1890s.

For this large group of wine scientists and technicians Adams ticked off the most important recent factors affecting this revolution: the quadrupling of national consumption of table wine, the decline in the importance of fortified dessert wines, the spread of gourmet cooking, the massive growth in the number of wineries and their new focus on wines from world class wine varieties, and the dramatic rise in wine quality. He contended that after World War II the typical bottle of California table wine was not palatable. Most Americans were not wine drinkers, but those who did drink wine with their meals were not about to select an unpalatable wine over a well-regarded foreign wine, whatever the cost. If this situation had not changed, he said, the revolution would not have taken place. So to the question, "Who caused the wine revolution?" he answered his assembled listeners, "You changed wine. You made it palatable!" [1]

At $3.00, 1970s vintage Simi Cabernet was an excellent example of "reasonably priced good wine."

My personal experience and my years of research in American history bring me to a different conclusion. I believe this revolution in American wine consumption would have taken place even if the typical bottle of California wine had remained mediocre. I left the army in 1957 and returned to grad school at Berkeley, a non-wine drinker. My wife and I were soon drawn into the beginnings of the revolution. The first wines we favored were German whites and red Bordeaux. We were not seduced by the gradual improvement of California wines; we simply learned that there were a few very good ones in the Santa Clara, Sonoma and Napa Valleys. We were soon all over the northern California wine country. Meanwhile, my wife's copy of Julia Child's' famous 1961 cookbook began its process of deterioration. Our focus on the regional food scene was sharpened in the seventies by the fact that our three sons all worked at Berkeley's Chez Panisse while attending the university.

For me this regional and national transformation was a broad cultural phenomenon, which would have occurred even if there had been no good California wine. But largely thanks to Adams' technical heroes there was good wine, lots of excellent wine and, in those days, lots of reasonably priced good wine.

The revolution in Sonoma was a year-by-year development. A person taking a yearly flight over the county would have hardly noticed the expansion of vineyards each year. The move toward better wine varieties would certainly not have been apparent, but what would have caught the eye was the almost total transformation of the aforementioned Carneros area.

Over the coming years this vast region at the foot of the Sonoma and Napa Valleys was transformed agriculturally from dairying and raising fodder crops into one of California's most prominent fine wine regions, covered by thousands of acres of world class wine varieties. In 1983 the U.S. Treasury Department officially designated and established borders for Los Carneros, as a 39,200 acre viticultural district (AVA). It is unique since is covers large parts of two counties. To date most of the vineyard development has been on the Napa side, but the work of the new owners of Buena Vista made their spread the largest in the AVA.

Heartily encouraged by André Tchelistcheff, Buena Vista in 1969 acquired the six-hundred acre Ramal Ranch a few miles southeast of the old winery. They bought the land a few months before Beaulieu's Carneros land had its first large vintage, which included a wonderful crop of Pinot noir. This event moved the Buena Vista owners to begin planting the following spring.[2]

The man in charge of Buena Vista's Carneros project was a good friend of Tchelistcheff's. René Lacasia had met the Beaulieu winemaker at a 1965 U. C. Davis viticulture conference. His experience in Chile made him a seasoned expert on wines and vines. There he was the head of research in the viticultural department of the State Ministry of Agriculture. Within a year Lacasia was a Buena Vista employee in charge of the winery's pre-Carneros vineyard expansion. In the spring of 1970 he was in charge of converting the Ramal property to vineyard.[3]

The cool Carneros climate meant that most of the Buena Vista vines would be Burgundian or of German origin: Pinot noir, Chardonnay, Riesling and Gewürztraminer. But both Lacasia and Tchelistcheff knew that there were some exposures on the Ramal property where Cabernet Sauvignon would ripen. To insure enough water for the thin soil, a huge drip-irrigation system covering 192 miles of tubing was constructed, with a 120-acre-foot reservoir built on nearby Huichica Creek.[4]

While waiting for their Carneros vines to produce their first crop in 1974, the winery's new owners moved quickly to advance the Buena Vista brand influence and to expand their wine offerings. When my wife and I visited in 1971 there were fourteen table wines available, nine of them varietals for sale at an average price of $2.60 per bottle, (about $14.77 in current dollars) There were also three dessert wines and two sparkling wines. Part of this production came from purchased wines and grapes, but Buena Vista still had access to Frank Bartholomew's vines until 1973, when Bart opened his Hacienda Wine Cellars nearby on Castle Road.[5]

Just across the road from the northern Carneros border another historic winegrowing operation came back to life. In 1968 the Bundschu family began replanting the famed Rhinefarm vineyards, and 1973 the old winery was restored, again doing business as the Gundlach-Bundschu Winery. Some of its three hundred acres of vines had once been part of the historic Dreyfus Vineyards. Not all the GB grapes went into GB bottles at first. For a while the Sebastiani Winery had a contract for one hundred acres of GB vines. This situation illustrates another aspect of the Sonoma wine revolution.

308

August Sebastiani

Samuele Sebastiani had founded his winery east of Sonoma in 1904, predominantly a bulk wine operation. After his father's death in 1944, son August took over and gradually changed the direction of the family's wine business. In 1954 he introduced wine under the SS label, and by the 1960s was moving more and more to the production of high quality varietal wines. In 1969 the medals for these wines began pouring in. Over the next five years Sebastiani won medals at the Los Angeles Fair for nine different varietals, including golds for Barbera and Cabernet Sauvignon.

There were several other veteran wineries which modified their operations, prospered and survived to the present . Korbel, under Alfred Heck since 1954, expanded and revitalized its sparkling wine production, and in 1956 brought its brandy back onto the market. By 1975 Korbel was producing 150,000 cases of sparklers. Its fine old winery at Guerneville soon rivaled Buena Vista as Sonoma's premier historic destination point for wine tourists.

Simi had continued operations on a very small scale in the sixties under Isabelle Simi Haigh. She and her husband had earlier converted a twenty-five-thousand gallon wine tank into a cozy tasting room and tiny museum, a Mecca in these years for California wine connoisseurs. In 1970 she sold the winery to oil-man and Alexander Valley vineyardist Russell Green. He modernized the old winery and made history by hiring Mary Ann Graf as winemaker, the first woman to receive an enology degree at U.C. Davis. In 1973 the medals began pouring in.

In Dry Creek Valley in the fifties the enormous Frei Bros. Winery began selling huge amounts of red table wine to the Gallo Winery in Modesto. In 1976 Gallo bought the two million gallon operation. Since then it has been the locus of Gallo Sonoma's huge expansion into the varietal wine market.

Non-wine-oriented corporate ownership of large Sonoma wineries was not so successful. The great and beautiful Souverain of Alexander Valley winery, built in 1972, remained in the ownership of the Pillsbury flour milling company for only four years, before it was acquired by a group of North Coast grape growers. The Joseph Schlitz Brewing Company bought the historic Geyser Peak Winery, also in 1972, and transformed the ramshackle old edifice into a modern showplace winery. That company lasted until 1982, when the winery was purchased by Sonoma banker and vineyardist Henry Trione.

Since the sixties Sonoma and Napa have developed a reputation for fine table wine unrivaled by any other region in the western hemisphere. Much of this reputation in both counties derives from the success of numerous small and medium-sized wineries that began dotting the landscape by the hundreds in the seventies. Obviously this study cannot cover them individually. For readers interested in the details of individual wineries I suggest using any of Leon Adams's *Wines of America* volumes. My own *Companion to California Wine* is a historical encyclopedia of the state's wine history and has an entry for almost all existing wineries operating in the years of the revolution. For specific newspaper and periodical articles, the Sonoma Wine Library's "winefiles.org," gives internet access to appropriate references with short abstracts, but not the articles themselves. For example, there are 340 entries for Buena Vista.

To get a broader and more complete picture of the revolution we need to look at the years from 1968 to 1980 statistically. The story that emerges is rather exciting in two ways. For a short while what happened in the vineyards looked like a classic boom, a speculative bubble very much like the over-expansion of the 1880s, whose hardships for winegrowers lasted eight years. But there was an important difference. That early bubble popped in the face of a coming national depression, with the consequent inability of consumer demand to digest the surplus wine of the boom. In the 1970s the bubble seemed to pop, but subsequent years saw demand and consumption soaring.

Sonoma wine grape acreage grew from 12,365 in 1968 to 24,440 in 1975. Before 1971 the total was almost flat, although large numbers of world class varieties were planted to replace old vines pulled up. By 1971 there were 1,629 acres of Cabernet Sauvignon. Pinot noir acreage grew to 709 acres, mostly in the Carneros, where two hundred acres of Chardonnay had also been planted. Nevertheless, the big three reds from Prohibition days did not disappear. In fact they declined to only about five hundred acres between 1968 and 1971. In that year they totaled almost seven thousand acres, led by Zinfandel (3,821), then Carignane (1,787) and Petite Sirah (1,311). In 1971 there were also a lot of good white wine varieties, other than Chardonnay (480). In 1968 Sauvignon blanc, Semillon, Chenin blanc and Riesling had not even registered in official statistics, but by 1971 there were a total of about 1,000 acres of these world class varieties in Sonoma vineyards.

There is no doubt that expected profits fueled the early boom. In 1968 the average ton of Sonoma wine grapes brought the grower $132 ($870 in current dollar). In 1971 the take averaged $342 ($1,939 today). The total value of the crop rose from about four million dollar to almost twelve million.

The real planting explosion in Sonoma began in the spring of 1972. By the end of the planting season there were 2,469 acres of Cabernet Sauvignon, 1,190 of Pinot noir and 743 of Chardonnay. Of these, sixty-five percent of the vines had yet to bear a crop, a hint at the wave that would hit in three years. There was already some talk of a coming over-supply of Sonoma wine grapes by the spring of 1974. Later that year the wave would crest in Sonoma with 6,433 acres of newly planted vines, 2,700 of which were planted in 1974. Due to "unfavorable" weather the wine grape crop was barely a record in 1974, and in 1975 the tonnage actually dropped from the previous year. But the flood of grapes and the backlog of wine was crushing to prices, which had fallen forty-three percent by the end of the 1974 vintage; in 1975 they were down another twenty-three percent

Wineries that owned their own vineyards were hurt by escalating inventories of unsold wine in their cellars. Unless under strict contract, wineries were reluctant to pay better than rock bottom prices to growers. The average price of a ton of Sonoma grapes dropped fifty-three percent between 1973 and 1975; The bubble had popped. But consumer interest in fine varietal wines was virtually unaffected and consumption figures continued their hurried upward pace.6

Actually, consumers benefited from wineries' willingness to cut prices. In 1975 August Sebastiani made history by bottling Sonoma Cabernet and Chardonnay in half- gallon jugs, with cork closures. The two-and-a-half "fifths" in these jugs cost the consumer only about a dollar each. (A regular bottle now holds .750 of a liter, about an ounce less than the old "fifth" of a gallon.)

The over-planting did not cause a continuing disaster in wine prices. Nature helped by keeping the Sonoma wine crop manageable in 1976 and 1977. These were the two worst drought years since the 1890s. Thus, even though thousands of wine grape acres in the county were coming into bearing, production was fairly stable and grape prices rose back to the 1972 level. Growers' incomes continued to improve but not as much as one might

"Premium California" Chablis in a can, produced by Geyser Peak Winery in the late 70s under the Summit brand. (Courtesy Sonoma County Library)

have expected, since the drought caused tonnage per acre to drop almost twenty-seven percent from the average of the previous four years. Another factor that softened grower prosperity for the five years after the drought was the rapid rise of price inflation. Grape prices rose steadily through 1982, but when corrected for inflation 1982 prices were not quite as high as they had been in 1979.

An important factor in Sonoma growers' favor in these years was the steady advance in vineyard productivity after 1977. Yield before that year was rarely more than 2.5 tons per acre. From 1978 to 1982 the average was 3.32 tons, up twenty-nine percent from the previous five years' average. This number is almost exactly the same as Sonoma's ten vintages from 2002 to 2011.

Even though Sonoma wine grape bearing acreage stabilized at about twenty-four thousand between 1977 and 1982, there was an important change in the color of the grapes growing in those vineyards. In 1972 white wine vines accounted for about twenty-five percent of total acreage; in 1982 that number had risen to forty-six percent, Three years later red and white were almost exactly even. In recent years red wine has again attained its two-to-one advantage.

The growth in Sonoma white wine production in the seventies was almost entirely in five premium varieties. However, the nation's "white wine craze," as it was often called, cut across all aspects of California's table wine production. It was a time when a glass of California "chablis" or Chardonnay became a standard bar drink, and a jug of same in the refrigerator supplied a tasty glass of something before dinner without the kick of gin or vodka. In my household we took up Sauvignon blanc.

Sonoma's big five whites by 1982 were Chardonnay (5,629 acres), Riesling (1,392), Sauvignon blanc (1,388), Gewürztraminer (1,249) and Chenin blanc (1,104). (The state's generic chablis and sauterne came mostly from the Central Valley.) In 1982 there were a thousand more acres of Chardonnay than Cabernet, in this normally red wine county. After 1975 a large part of the growth in premium white acreage came from growers grafting over red varieties to white. This is why Cabernet acreage declined and then stalled after 1975. The Sonoma farm advisor estimated that this kind of transformation five hundred acres per season, for good reason. In 1978 Sonoma growers were paid seventy-one percent more per ton for Chardonnay than for Cabernet. By 1982 the price of Chardonnay grapes was double that of Cabernet.

The revolution which eventually converted Sonoma in 2012 into the home of almost sixty thousand acres of wine grapes obviously did not end in 1982. For the next ten years the county averaged adding a respectable 570 acres per year. But it was in the next twenty years that the truly great expansion took place. Between 1993 and 2012 the county's wine grape acreage grew at

314

an average of 1,304 acres per year. California statistics show that in 2012 only San Joaquin County's Lodi area had more wine grapes than Sonoma.

Buena Vista's new Carneros winery had been ready for its first vintage in 1976. Most of the new vineyard's 620 acres of vines were now bearing, with a remarkable 150 acres of Cabernet Sauvignon. There were also 130 acres of Pinot noir and one hundred acres each of Chardonnay and Gewürztraminer. Even though the massive drip-irrigation system had protected the vines from the drought, yields per acre were less than expected. Nevertheless, by 1979 production had topped 100,000 cases, and storage capacity had risen to 900,000 gallons.

The complex operation was still supervised by René Lacasia, who in 1977 officially held the offices of vice president, technical director, winemaker and vineyard manager. Young's Market Company had done well on its 1968 investment. President Vernon Underwood was thus taken by surprise by the events of the spring 1979. "They came to us. We had no idea of selling the winery until they approached us six months ago. We were very pleased with what we had accomplished. But they made us an offer we could not refuse." His investigation of the potential buyers suggested that the German firm would continue "our tradition of fine quality wine." He was correct, and the A. Racke Co. took over the operation of Buena Vista at the end of the year.[7]

CHAPTER 18 NOTES

1. "Who Caused the Wine Revolution?" *Wines & Vines,* 2/1979, P.38.
2. Redwood Rancher, 12/1972, 10; *Wines & Vines,* 2/1970, P.26.
3. *Wines & Vines,* 9/1973,P. 50.
4. *Wines & Vines,* 2/1972, PP.49-50; *San Francisco Chronicle,* 11/6/1979, 10/14/1981.
5. Adams, 1978, P.254.
6. *Wines & Vines,* 2/1975, 2/1976.
7. *San Francisco Chronicle,* 11/6/1979; *Wines & Vines,* 12/1979, P.18.

Chapter
19

Passing the Baton

1980-2011

After the Bartholomews sold Buena Vista to Young's Market Company in 1968, the winery passed through five owners before it was finally acquired by Boisset Family Estates in 2011. By far the longest stretch of ownership in these years was under the A. Racke Co., which bought the estate from Young's in 1979. Then in 2001, after twenty two fairly successful years, Racke passed the baton. Over the next ten years there was a flurry of exchanges that did not add luster to Buena Vista's grand history.

Racke had a long history dealing with wine and spirits in Germany. The Racke family aimed with this purchase to effect an aggressive growth in production and a vigorous program to increase the quality of Buena Vista wines. Nevertheless, continuity was stressed for the next three years. René Lacasia continued to direct vineyard and cellar operations, with a special charge to bring along to the peak of perfection the Chardonnay, Cabernet Sauvignon and Pinot noir wines of the 1977 through 1980 vintages. As usual, André Tchelistcheff would continue to serve as Buena Vista's consulting enologist.[1]

The Buena Vista labels underwent a very gradual change for several years, and the winery began publishing a widely distributed and very handsome publication with News of Buena Vista's winery activities, its people and its wines. It first appeared as "Buena Vista News," then "Carneros Chronicle."

The emphasis on Carneros in all Buena Vista activities became a given under Racke. Eventually the term "Buena Vista Carneros" greeted the eye

Jill Davis, pictured in 1984

on company stationery. In 1983 the entire Carneros area was granted official Treasury Department status as a viticultural area. Buena Vista was instrumental in getting the final petition approved, and also instrumental in seeing that it was not based on the original petition proposed by several Napa wineries in 1980, which would not have included Sonoma.

Buena Vista's new energy and direction after 1983 began gradually in 1981 when Marcus Moller-Racke took over vineyard operations. He was the twenty-seven-year-old son of the Racke family, with a solid background

320

in viticulture. The next year Lacasia retired, and a few months later Marcus became Buena Vista president. He then appointed his wife, Anne, to succeed him as vineyard director.

The third youthful cog in the new Buena Vista engine was a 1978 U.C. Davis graduate in fermentation science, fresh out of a remarkable apprenticeship at Beringer Vineyards. Jill Davis's mentor there had been Myron Nightingale, one of California's greatest winemakers. She came to Buena Vista in 1982 as assistant winemaker, and took control of the winery's cellars the next year, and for the next eleven vintages. The future of Buena Vista was now in the hands of a talented threesome, each with but a few years of experience, and with an average age of twenty-seven years. It was really a four person team, since Davis met weekly with André Tchelistcheff.

Davis was backed up with wines from the 1979-1981 vintages that would be used to focus a quality spotlight on the Buena Vista brand. In 1983 the winery won eight gold and nine silver medals for these wines at eight different competitions. The champion of these eleven wines was the 1979 Special Selection Cabernet Sauvignon, which won six golds. At the San Diego Del Mar competition it was named the very best of the 112 Cabernet entrants.[2]

In 1984 Buena Vista won eleven golds and twenty-three silvers. Four of Davis's 1983 wines were then medal winners, golds for the Pinot noir rosé and for the Gamay Beaujolais. Two of the new winemaker's wines had a personal stamp, both winning silvers. The Pinot Jolie was a low alcohol, slightly sweet Pinot noir. The Carneros Spiceling was unique. The market for Riesling and Gewürztraminer had been slipping. Marcus set Davis the task of producing a blend of these two varieties. The result was "Spiceling," at first a critical success, which "choreographs two negative players into a dazzling dance of success," then a solid marketing success.[3]

Chardonnay (48%) and Pinot noir (37%) dominated Buena Vista's 1983 vintage, with Cabernet Sauvignon at 7%. Yields from the 150 acres of Cabernet vines were still low, but it was wine from this variety which was bringing the winery the largest share of its awards and critical publicity. In a few years production would be up to 20,000 cases.

With sales soaring in 1984, Buena Vista went on its next Carneros planting campaign. The primary target was the huge Tule Vista dairying farm to the east of their established vineyards. That purchase, and several smaller ones, added about a thousand acres of land to the Buena Vista Carneros estate. Anne Moller-Racke supervised the extended planting, which by 1988 brought the company's vineyard total to more than 800 acres. Then came a gradual rise in production and profits. Eventually the estate was producing enough grapes to sell fruit to other producers, especially Acacia, Etude and Sterling, among others. When Racke sold Buena Vista in 2001 the Tule Vista vineyards were retained by the family, still under Anne Moller-Racke's supervision.

Coincident to the vineyard expansion was Racke's large scale renovation project of the old winery buildings, particularly the historic Press House, which had been in no shape to receive visitors for the last hundred years. In fact, 1983 marked the hundredth anniversary of Buena Vista's retirement from the world of winegrowing under the Johnson family. The 1864 winery building had held Buena Vista's modest visitor center since the 1950s. Now Racke renovated the more historic Press House into what greets the visitor today.[4] (For a more detailed description of this $350,000 renovation see Chapter 6. Since 2011 an even grander renovation project had been begun by Boisset. This project is covered in the next chapter.)

To take care of the vineyard expansion through 1988, the irrigation system had to be enlarged and modified. When this task was finally accomplished there were five reservoirs and 450 miles of tubing. All the planting had been arranged to handle Buena Vista's special approach to harvesting. Practically all the vines were harvested mechanically and at night. This process guaranteed that Davis could begin her fermentations with cool grapes.[5]

A special vineyard problem developed for vineyardists in the North Coast region in the 1980s. It was particularly severe in Napa and in both sides of the Carneros. All the new planting in Napa and Sonoma since the 1950s had been on resistant rootstock, mostly onto a stock named AxR1, a hybrid developed in France in 1879. It was a cross between the resistant wild American *Vitis rupestris* and the very non-resistant vinifera wine variety

322

From right, André Tchelistcheff, Frank Bartholomew, Leon D. Adams, and Buena Vista president Hubertus von Wulffen toast the reopening of the Press House at its May 15, 1982 ceremony.

Aramon. It eventually was rejected in France as being not sufficiently resistant to attacks from the phylloxera. But after World War I it became the darling of U.C. Davis scientists, who believed it was resistant enough for the California environment, and it gave excellent yields. Virtually all new planting in Napa after the fifties had been onto the AxR I. In Sonoma there was more rootstock variety in the new plantings. The St. George, a perfectly resistant stock, had always been popular in Sonoma.

323

In the early eighties the decline on vines on the AxR I caused little concern, and for some time the scientists at U.C. Davis came up with various explanations that missed the point that Professor Andrew Walker eventually made clear: the AxR I "is not a resistant rootstock." Growers in the Napa Valley and all over the Carneros had to come to grips with the idea that all the vines on the AxR I would soon be dead. A massive but gradual replanting of vineyards took place in the nineties.

Buena Vista was also affected, although Anne Moller-Racke had not depended solely on the now proscribed rootstock. On the plus side, she was able to reshape the older vineyards better to fit modern standards not realized twenty years earlier. The most obvious modification was the move to closer planting.[6] She eventually replaced more than 400 acres of vines.[7]

Buena Vista made a solid move toward Zinfandel in 1989 when it bought the Haywood brand, a Sonoma winery noted for its production of this varietal wine. Two years later they bought the Stemmler brand, noted for its Pinot noir. The first of these brands was by far the more important, eventually accounting for 130,000 cases in 1996. By that year all Buena Vista wine totaled 320,000 cases.[8]

In 1991 most of the region's growers and producers came together to form the Carneros Quality Alliance. Anne Moller-Racke and Jill Davis were instrumental in the formation of this unique two-county promotional organization. The first meeting was held at Buena Vista. Although the 1983 Treasury ruling creating the Carneros Viticultural Area had allowed producers to label their wine "Sonoma Valley" or "Napa Valley," by 1991 it was generally agreed that "Carneros" was their appellation. Later the group's name was changed to "Carneros Wine Alliance."

Between 1993 and 2001 Buena Vista narrowed its offering of wines and, with one exception, limited all wines under its label to those made from grapes grown in the Carneros. The exception was their Lake County Sauvignon blanc, which had become noted for its concentrated and distinct varietal flavors.

Production by the end of the nineties had risen to about 500,000 cases. Sometime later in this period Racke decided to sell Buena Vista.

Marcus and Anne Moller-Racke

The company announced its intentions in 2000. The *San Francisco Chronicle* quoted a company representative saying that the winery had become "a very small large company," and that they were looking for a new owner who "could fully realize Buena Vista's potential." [9]

In June 2001 A. Racke, now Germany's largest wine distributor, sold Buena Vista and the Haywood brand to Allied Domecq, the British wine and spirits giant. The price was $85.5 million, which, according to one newspaper, was far less than Racke had hoped for.[10] Racke kept the Tule Vista land and its vineyards, which Anne Moller-Racke continued to oversee, as the Donum Estate. Allied now had wineries in Sonoma's Alexander Valley, the Carneros, Napa Valley and Riverside County, with a total production of 2.5 million cases. An Allied representative stated that the Carneros location was central to their decision to buy the estate.

Allied's hold on Buena Vista was short, beginning what one newsman called the game of "musical brands" being played among industry giants for established winery brands. At the end of 2004, Paris-based Pernod-Ricard began negotiating for a huge list of brand purchases. It ended up a three-way deal including Allied and Fortune Brands. In April 2005 the $14.2 billion transaction was done, Pernod buying Allied's wine brands and selling them to Fortune. Wineries were only part of the curious combination of transactions, which included such properties as Dunkin' Donuts, Togo's and Baskin- Robbins. The press focused on Sonoma's Clos du Bois as the key to the winery deal. Readers were led to believe that Buena Vista was just a "high-volume wine brand," tossed in incidentally.[11]

The baton then changed hands even more quickly. In 2007 Constellation Brands, the world's largest wine company, bought seven of Fortune's wine properties from that company's Beam Wine Estates division. Fortune needed to raise cash to pursue the acquisition of Absolut vodka. Again the winery plum was Sonoma's Clos du Bois and its growing 1.8 million case production.[12]

The following year the Constellation CEO declared that the company was "streamlining its wine portfolio by eliminating duplication and excess production capacity." They kept Clos du Bois and sold off a Sonoma package that included Buena Vista, Geyser Peak and Gary Farrell. A news report indicated that Buena Vista was "not central to Constellation's plans."[13]

The new owner of Buena Vista was Ascentia, itself a new company with headquarters in Healdsburg. When its flurry of buying ended it had acquired the trio of Sonoma wine operations and three wineries in Washington and Idaho. The entire package cost Ascentia a reported $209 million, most of that sum heavily leveraged. Heavy debt acquired in 2008, as the Great Recession was taking on a full head of steam, was far too much of a burden for the new company's survival. By the fall of 2010 Ascentia was doomed and began consolidating its Sonoma properties and selling others.

Consolidation meant ending wine production at Buena Vista Carneros and producing all that was left of the brand's wine at the Geyser Peak Winery. The industry press groaned "Bye, Bye, Buena Vista," and pictured the new situation as "Mothballing Buena Vista."

The situation was an attractive one for Jean-Charles Boisset, the head of Boisset Family Estates in this country. His company had already acquired working wineries in Sonoma and in Napa (DeLoach Vineyards in Sonoma's Russian River Valley, which it purchased in 2003, and Raymond Vineyards in Napa's Rutherford AVA, which it purchased in 2009). Now he had the opportunity to buy historic Buena Vista and its brand. In April 2011 he did just that. The Buena Vista Carneros Winery production facility on Ramal Road was already in other hands, as were the Ramal Ranch vineyards.

The original historic winery on Old Winery Road was central to this final passing of the baton. For almost a half century the historic buildings had been incidental to the numerous changes of ownership. Jean-Charles and his family had vacationed in California when he was eleven. The family visited several wineries, and Buena Vista had been the first. After the purchase he stated that he had never forgotten the image of Buena Vista as he grew up, assisting his father, Jean-Claude Boisset, assemble their collection of wineries in France and California. "I had always been charmed by the oldest stones of the California wine world. I've admired its amazing sense of place and revered its history as California's oldest premium winery." Within a year of the 2011 exchange, visitors to Buena Vista would begin experiencing the manifest actualization of Boisset's long-held historical dream.

CHAPTER 19 NOTES

1. *Wines & Vines,* 12/1979, 18; 6/1980, p.71.

2. *San Francisco Chronicle,* 8/17/1984, *Wine Country Review,* i 3/3-/1984.

3. *Wine Country Review,* 3/30/1984.

4. *Wine Country Review,* 8/23/1985.

5. *Wines & Vines,* 10/1988, p.21.

6. *Gourmet Magazine,* 6/1991, p.40.

7. See, ". . .The Non-resistant Resistant," in my *Napa Wine, 2nd ed.,* 368-374, for documentation of this sorry viticultural episode. The best article on the subject appeared in the *New York Times,* 10/17/1993, copied by the *San Francisco Chronicle,* 10/31/1993

8. *Sonoma Business,* 10/1996, p.36.

9. *San Francisco Chronicle,* 11/11/2000.

10. *Napa Register,* 6/7/2001.

11. *Los Angeles Times,* 4/22/2005.

12. *Wine Spectator,* 11/12/2007.

13. *Wine Spectator,* 6/11/2008; *Santa Rosa Press Democrat,* 6/6/2008.

Chapter

Restoration & Revival

2011-

The Boisset purchase of the historic Buena Vista estate in 2011 might have appeared at first glance to have been another passing of the baton, with the formidable stone buildings no more than an incidental token in a large scale financial game. A closer look at subsequent events indicates a very different scenario.

Boisset is one of the largest wine companies in France, and has had a growing stake in the California wine scene since 1980. The company dates from 1961, when eighteen-year-old Jean-Claude Boisset began a négociant business in Burgundy, buying wines from four appellations in the Côte d'Or. Three years later he planted his Les Evocelles vineyard near Gevrey-Chambertin in the Côtes de Nuits. By 1980 Jean-Claude was running a 900,000 case operation in Burgundy, with a fully automated winery in Nuits-Saint-Georges., with a presence on wine lists in more than a dozen countries. (See Appendix I for a complete explanation of the worldwide holdings of Boisset Family Estates.)

In 1980 Jean-Claude began operations in California, establishing a wholly-owned importer - Boisset America. The company also bought a vineyard near Rutherford in the Napa Valley. Thereafter small amounts of Napa wine were produced for a few years at a nearby custom-crush facility.[1]

In the 1990s the Boisset began a more serious commitment to developing a portfolio through the acquisition of two established Sonoma wine operations, William Wheeler and Lyeth, employing their brand names to market high quality wines.

331

Jean-Charles Boisset

In 1992 Jean-Charles Boisset, Jean-Claude and Claudine Boisset's twenty-two-year-old son, took charge of the company's California operations. Since his childhood he had been close to the family's wine business. He had grown up almost around the corner from Burgundy's Clos de Vougeot and had worked summers in the family's vineyards and cellars. In the previous chapter I discussed his first and powerful impression of California, particularly of Buena Vista, when he visited the Golden State with his family in 1981. Now in California on an intermittent, but eventually permanent basis, he began graduate studies in business at UCLA and then entered the graduate program in business and finance at the University of San Francisco, receiving his MBA in 1992.[2]

Reflecting the company's Burgundian origins, Jean-Charles's goal was to acquire a well-established Sonoma winery specializing in wines made from Burgundian wine grape varieties. He found just such a property in Sonoma's Russian River Valley. DeLoach Vineyards, since its founding in 1975, had developed into what wine expert Charles Olken has termed "a leading Pinot Noir and Chardonnay producer in the region." In 2003 Boisset bought DeLoach Vineyards from founder Cecil DeLoach. The purchase also included the twenty-two acre home estate and the winery on Olivet Road.

Boisset soon had converted the estate to organic and bio-dynamic farming practices. The vineyards were replanted and Greg LaFollette was hired as consulting winemaker. The wines from DeLoach have since won numerous awards as has the winery itself.

It was only natural that Jean-Charles would next look toward Napa for the family's next premium winery, to add strength and balance to their California collection. The acquisition of Raymond Vineyards in 2009 gave the company an established Cabernet producer and 300 acres of prime vineyards, centered in Rutherford, one of the Napa Valley's most honored appellations. It also gave Jean-Charles an opportunity to expand on his interest in California wine history, since the Raymond/Beringer Family had the longest tenure of any family of winegrowers in the Napa Valley. One of his first projects at the winery was the creation of an elaborate "Theater of Nature" on the estate. This and several other newly built tasting and educational environs have made Raymond Vineyards quite a bit more than a tasting room stop for visiting wine lovers.[3] Special emphasis was given to biodynamic principles applied to winegrowing and soon Raymond's Napa vineyards were certified organic and biodynamic. In the cellar, change came in the form of winemaker Stephanie Putnam, formerly of Far Niente and Hess Collection, and consultant Philippe Melka.

The Buena Vista revival had two basic programs. The first would be quickly observable to the Sonoma wine community and by consumers in general. No longer would the historic physical estate be treated as an incidental by-product of a larger transaction. Boisset's early goal was to remind the public of Buena Vista's great history in the 19th century and to focus public attention on the historic role of its founder in the origins of Sonoma's and California's early commercial wine history. To this Boisset added the obvious. It was not enough just to remind the world of the estate's former greatness. Its physical presence today and its operations now and in the future should be a clear reflection of a continuity with that past. In Jean-Charles's words, he is "committed to continuing the imaginative vision and unrivaled legacy first created 150 years ago."

There had developed a great amount of mythic information about Agoston Haraszthy after his death in 1869. But, as we have already seen, stripped of this non history, Haraszthy's powerful influence on the California wine scene, and his innovative and flamboyant professional and personal life style, gave Boisset good reason to make Haraszthy's story an integral part of the modern Buena Vista image.

The Hungarian nobleman became the center of several theatrical performances at the winery in 2012, illustrating life at Buena Vista in the 1850s and 1860s. Visitors were also offered informational tours of the estate led by Haraszthy himself, or better, by an actor dressed as the articulate master of Buena Vista, whose presentation was loaded with interesting history. The new owners also gave emphasis to the Hungarian connection by establishing a sister-city relationship between Sonoma and Tokaj, the center of that country's historic sweet wine industry. Haraszthy's name and his various honorifics have taken their place on several new Buena Vista wines. There is now a red wine blend honoring the "Count" and another that commemorates Haraszthy's position as the first sheriff of San Diego county. Later there may be the "Colonel," or perhaps even the "Commissioner."

At the end of the summer of 2012 Jean-Charles organized a gigantic party celebrating the reopening of the estate to the public. Shortly thereafter *Wines & Vines,* America's leading wine trade journal, named the Boisset pur-

334

Actor George Webber regularly channels "The Count of Buena Vista" for tasting room guests.

chase and revival at Buena Vista one of the top ten wine stories of 2012.[4]

Jean-Charles made it clear that Buena Vista was to be a solid part of the Sonoma community as a whole. His contribution to and active support of local causes have been numerous: the Sonoma Harvest Wine Auction, the Sonoma Museum of Art, the Sonoma Historical Society, the Sonoma Film Festival, and the Sonoma Greenbelt Alliance are but a few examples. That he and his wife, Gina Gallo, live in and are raising their family in the North Coast wine country, gives convincing evidence of where the feet of the new master of Buena Vista are firmly planted.

The physical revival of the Buena Vista estate was the central aspect of the Boisset resuscitation program. The two stone wineries, dating from 1862-1864, were still intact, but the 1864 winery was showing the ravages of time. The 1863 Press House had been brought back to life by the Racke

335

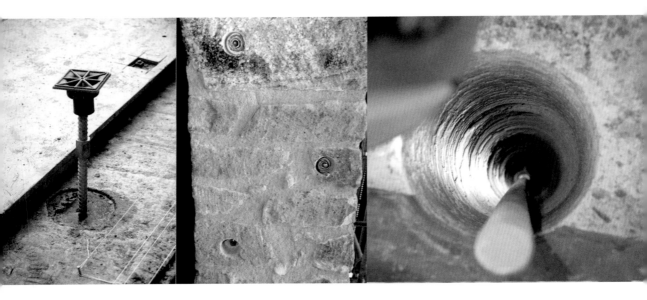

Central-core drilling the 150-year-old walls of Buena Vista Winery.

Company in 1981-1982 with a commodious tasting room. Its walls were secure. The huge 1864 winery next door, often earlier and again today named the Champagne Cellars, had been used long ago by the Bartholomews to make wine, with a small tasting room. But Boisset wanted it to serve again as a real winery, as it had until 1883.

The great stone walls looked as if they might last another 150 years, but their appearance was deceiving; they were quite fragile. The answer to the situation was supplied through a technological breakthrough known as "center-core drilling," developed by engineer Dennis Cox.

The beauty of this technique is that it gives great strength to the exterior walls with no visible evidence. Meticulously calibrated equipment drills a hole from the top to the bottom of the wall. Then a single rod of reinforced steel, averaging about five inches in diameter, is slid and grouted into the length of the core. The rods are spaced fairly close together, about four feet apart. The reinforced walls should stand for generations.

The new owners also felt it necessary to re-grout the outer layers of mortar around the stonework. A natural hydraulic lime was employed which was a perfect match to the original mortar. Stonemasons also filled

336

in the gaps that had developed in the stonework over the winery's almost 150 year lifetime.

Visitors to Buena Vista today cannot miss the changed look of the Champagne Cellars. It had been almost totally covered with ivy, now all removed to give stonemasons access to the outside walls. Much of the arboreal mass that surrounded the area was cut back to open the space around the building and bring more light to the area. My wife and I have been visiting the estate off and on for more than half a century. For the first time in decades, one can really see the great old building.

The spring and summer of 2012 saw a burst of activity in the work of restoration and renovation at Buena Vista. But even though there was work still to be done, it was obvious that August 20 almost had to be a day of celebration; it was Agoston Haraszthy's 200th birthday. Everyone worked frantically to polish the new and restored look around the two old cellars. It was a great day of celebration, topped off by Jean-Charles Boisset sabering the cork on a bottle of Buena Vista sparkling wine in honor of the founder's birthday and the reopening of the Champagne Cellars.

Visitors now walk up to the Press House and its remodeled tasting room through the "Festival Plaza," newly finished with 150-year-old Belgian paving stones. On the left they pass the "Heritage Garden," planted in four sections, each of which highlights a time period in Sonoma horticultural history. The first contains plants native to the region before the coming of the mission padres in 1823. For the mission and rancho period there are examples of grain, vegetables and fruit, such as wheat, tomatoes, peppers, olives and figs. Examples of plants representing the Gold Rush period and the early days of California statehood are cabbage, onions, berries, apples and citrus.

The fourth plot is dedicated to the work of Luther Burbank, one of America's greatest horticultural experimenters. He came to settle in Sonoma in 1875, later declaring the area "the chosen spot of all this earth so far as nature is concerned." Several vegetables are planted, including Burbank's famed Russet potato. There will also be two of his famous fruit trees, the Santa Rosa plum and Elberta peach.

Between the Press House and the Champagne Cellars the land will be terraced with seating for events such as the Sonoma Shakespeare Festival. The area in front of the Cellars has been made into a courtyard with a new fountain, the Vortex, which provides a fascinating, rhythmical water display.

The symbolic and celebratory activities at Buena Vista since 2011 will interest and excite visitors, but the major story is the restoration of the 1864 winery building and the return of winegrowing and wine production to the historic estate.

The ground floor of the Champagne Cellars holds the new winery equipment. On entering visitors first see six beautiful open-top French oak fermenting vats, that Boisset brought from Burgundy. These are sealable and will also be used to store wine after fermentation. Beyond the fermenters large portions of the two old caves have been restored, tunneled into the mountainside. The deeper of the two is lined with oak barrels brought from Europe, the handiwork of French and Hungarian coopers. The walls clearly reveal the efforts of the Chinese workmen who hewed the cellar's stone walls. Their pick marks form regular and rather personal patterns.

The tunnel cave reminds me of those I saw years ago in Tokaj. Where the similarity ends is the lack of thick mold on the walls and ceiling, thought to be an essential part of the winemaking process in Hungary. There it is encouraged for what is thought to be its symbiotic relationship with the cooperage. The winemakers of Tokaj insist that this mold partially explains their wines' high quality and their unique, special flavors.[5]

The second and third floors of the Cellars are still works in progress. However, the top floor is destined to be a historic museum for vineyard and cellar equipment brought from the Boisset collection in Burgundy. It will also include New World equipment, particularly items collected in Sonoma.

The new estate vineyard will be planted on the sloping area adjoining the Press House. Planting was well underway the spring of 2013. This is not a large area, but an interesting future has been planned for it. The land here is protected in such a way that would make it difficult to ripen grapes for hearty red table wines. The goal is to plant several white

338

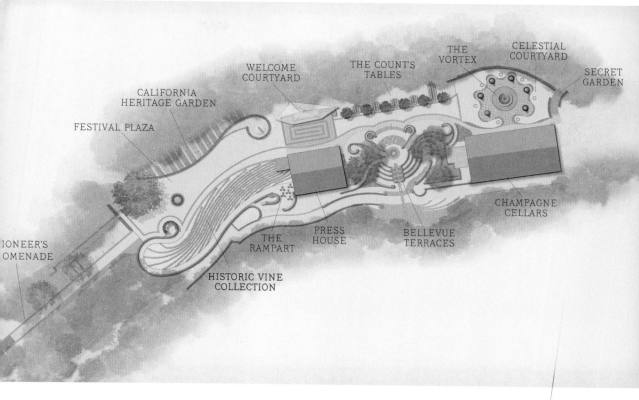

Overhead view of the new Buena Vista grounds.

Labels on image:
THE VORTEX
CELESTIAL COURTYARD
SECRET GARDEN
THE COUNT'S TABLES
WELCOME COURTYARD
CALIFORNIA HERITAGE GARDEN
FESTIVAL PLAZA
IONEER'S OMENADE
THE RAMPART
PRESS HOUSE
BELLEVUE TERRACES
CHAMPAGNE CELLARS
HISTORIC VINE COLLECTION

wine varieties whose grapes will be blended to produce a light, slightly aromatic table wine, in a style for which this part of the Sonoma Valley became famous in the 1860s.

A huge number of varieties are being considered, many of which were present in the vine collection Haraszthy brought here from Europe in 1862. These include the Riesling, Sylvaner and Traminer. Several of the candidates have a slight muscat character and are rarely seen in California. White table wines produced in California's North Coast area in the 1860s and after often had their flavors perked up with a touch of muscat. Among the rare varieties being considered that could provide this touch are the Olivette blanche, Malvasia bianca, and Madeleine Angevine. Also under consideration are white varieties famous in their home areas but rarely seen

339

The tasting room in Buena Vista's famed caves.

elsewhere. Examples are the Vernaccia (Tuscany), Picpoul blanc (Rhône), and Furmint (Hungary).

Should the Furmint catch on here, Buena Vista may make some additional history. It is the variety responsible for the Tokaj Aszú of Hungary, one of the world's greatest dessert wines. As in Sauternes the grapes hang late in the season and acquire their special character from the development of *Botrytis cinerea* mold, the so-called "noble rot."

In Hungary the wine is produced through a complicated and very special process which Haraszthy knew well. He even made a sweet wine in this fashion at Buena Vista from Mission grapes, which was very well received. But the process was far too costly to make the wine a commercial item. Haraszthy had brought five distinct selections of Furmint from Europe in his 1862 collection, but there is no historical evidence of their fate. The experts at U.C. Davis believe the Furmint can be grown successfully in Sonoma, but only with the most meticulous viticultural care.[6]

It takes about seven years from the planting of the vine to a bottle of Tokaj Aszú, often longer. But visitors to Buena Vista need not wait to discover this wine. Boisset imported a shipment of 1999 Tokaji Aszú from Hungary and has it on sale at the tasting room under the Buena Vista label. "Puttonyos" is the Hungarian term that suggests the quality and determines the price of Tokaj Aszú. The highest rating is "6 Puttonyos," which is the quality rating of the Buena Vista import.

Buena Vista was center of the Sonoma phylloxera infestation in the early days. That grapes had not been planted for many years in the immediate area around the winery did not mean that the deadly louse was gone. Thus the new vineyard will be planted on resistant rootstock, either Schwarzmann or 101-14. Both are crosses of *V. riparia* x *V. Rupestris,* native American species that are 100% phylloxera resistant. They are considered excellent alternatives to the St. George rootstock, which historically has been a favorite in Sonoma County since the 1890s.

The fall of 2012 marked the first real vintage at Buena Vista since the Bartholomew days, but actually a few boxes of French Colombard were fermented there in 2011. There was just enough to produce fifty cases of a wine rarely seen in California anymore.

Like Buena Vista vintages of the future, the grape sources for the first vintage were various. Of particular importance were the grapes from the White-Perry Vineyard immediately adjacent to Buena Vista today and on land that was part of the original estate in 1857. The varieties included Carignane, Zinfandel, Pinot noir, Chardonnay and Charbono. The total crush from all sources was 43.4 tons, enough to make a little more than 6,000 gallons of wine.

Other grapes were secured from the Carneros Ramal Ranch vineyards. Earlier the large winery there had been part of the Buena Vista Carneros operation; it is still used for custom crushing by Boisset. Buena Vista intends to continue sourcing grapes from the Ramal Ranch and other noted

Carneros and Sonoma vineyards. (See Appendix II for more information on all Buena Vista wines.)

It is clear that the changes at Buena Vista since 2011 reflect the new owners' commitment to continuing the imaginative vision of the winery's founder. Haraszthy's financial failures do not diminish the accuracy of his prescient view of the future of California wine. Virtually every aspect of the measures he publicly advocated regarding California wine, even close vine spacing, have become a part of the Golden State's wine world. "The future is our past" is the new Boisset motto for Buena Vista. Such a pledge is a promise of good things for all Sonoma wine.

CHAPTER 20 NOTES

1. *Wines & Vines,* 5/30/1985, 54.

2. *Santa Rosa Press Democrat,* 8/13/1992; *Wine Spectator,* 9/30/1992, 2/15/1993.

3. *Wines & Vines,* 8/30/2010, 9/29/2011, 11/30/2011.

4. *Wines & Vines,* 9/30/2012, 12/31/ 2012.

5. For an excellent photo of such a mold enshrouded cave see, Jancis Robinson, *Oxford Companion to Wine,* Oxford/New York, 1994, 973.

6. *Hilgardia,* February 1944, 657. Professors Winkler and Amerine did not recommend the variety but found their test examples "full-bodied and soft, delicate in flavor and mildly distinctive in aroma."

Books and Articles

Adams, Leon, *The Wines of America*, 1973, and three later editions.

Allen, J. Fisk, *Practical Treatise on the Culture and Treatment of the Grape Vine*, New York, 1855.

Amerine, M. A. and M. A. Joselyn, *Table Wines. . .*, Berkeley, 1970.

Baegert, Johann, *Nachrichten von der Americanischen Halbinsel Californien*, Mannheim, 1772. Published by the University of California Press in 1952 as *Observations in Lower California*.

Balzer, Robert, *California's Best Wines*, I Los Angeles, 1948.

Bancroft, H. H., *History of California*, San Francisco, 1886-1890.

Bartholomew, Frank H., *Bart, His Memoirs*, Sonoma, 1983.

Bean, Walton, "James Warren. . . California Agriculture., *Pacific Historical Review*, December 1944.

Biesta, Frederico, "The State of California. . . 1856, *California Historical Society Quarterly*, December 1963.

Bioletti, Frederic, *"Bench Grafting Resistant Vines,"* University of California College of Agriculture, Bulletin 127.

Brace, Charles Loring, *The New West, California in 1867-1868*, New York, 1869.

Brenner, Leslie, *American Appetite*, New York, 1999.

Brown, Madie, "The Vineyards of Gen. M. G. Vallejo," *California Historical Society Quarterly*, 1937, 241-249.

California, Board of State Viticultural Commissioners, Directory. . . *Grape Growers, Wine Makers*, Sacramento, 1893.

California, *First Annual Report of the Board of State Viticultural Commissioners*, 2nd Ed., revised.

California, Isaac De Turk's, *The Vineyards of Sonoma County*, Sacramento, 1893.

California, *The Vineyards of Sonoma County*, Sacramento, 1893.

Campbell, Christy, *The Botanist and the Vintner*, Chapel Hill, 2004.

346

Carosso, Vincent P., *The California Wine Industry. . .1830-1895*, Berkeley, 1951.

Chen, Sucheng, *This Bitter Soil*, Berkeley, 1986.

Cronise, Titus Fey, *The Natural Wealth of California*, San Francisco, 1868.

Drioton, A., *All About Phylloxera*, San Francisco, 1877.

Frederickson, Paul, *"One More River,"* unpublished manuscript in my possession.

Florence, Jack W., *A Noble Heritage*, Geyserville, 1993.

-------- *Legacy of a Village*, Phoenix, 1999.

Gale, George, *Dying on the Vine*, Berkeley, 2011

Gregory, Tom, *History of Sonoma County*, Los Angeles, 1911.

Gudde, Erwin G., *California Place Names*, Berkeley, 1998.

Hague, Harlan and David J. Langum, *Thomas O. Larkin*, Norman, Oklahoma, 1990.

Haraszthy, Agoston, *Grape Culture and Wine-Making*, New York, 1862.

Hardy, Thomas, *Notes on Vineyards of America. . .*, Adelaide, 1885.

Hayne, Arthur, *Resistant Vines*, Sacramento, 1897.

Hine, Robert V., *California's Utopian Colonies*, Berkeley, 1953.

Kyvig, David, *Repealing National Prohibition*, 1979.

Lavender, David, *Nothing Seemed Impossible*, Palo Alto, 1975

Leggett, Herbert B. *"Early History of Wine production in California,"* Wine Institute, 1941.

McGinty, Bryan, *Strong Wine*, Stanford, 1998.

---------*A Toast to Eclipse*, Norman, Oklahoma, 2012.

McKee, Irving, *"Historic Sonoma County Winegrowers,"* California Magazine of the Pacific, September 1955.

Menefee, C. C. , *Historical and Descriptive Sketchbook. . .Sonoma*, Napa City, 1873.

Munro-Fraser, J. P., *History of Sonoma County*, 1879.

Odegard, Peter, *Pressure Politics*, New York, 1928.

Omsted, F. L. et al, *The Production of Wine in California,. . . Buena Vista*, San Francisco, 1865.

Ordish, George, *The Great Wine Blight*, New York, 1972.

Ostrander, Gilman, *The Prohibition Movement in California. . .,* Berkeley, 1957.

Palmquist, Peter E., *Pioneer Photographers of the Far West,* Stanford, 2000.

Peninou, Ernest, *History of the Sonoma Viticultural District,* Santa Rosa, 1998.

Peninou, Ernest and Gail Unzelman, *The California Wine Association. . .1894-1920.,* Santa Rosa, 2000.

Pinney, Thomas, *A History of Wine in California,* Berkeley, 1989 and 2003.

-------- *The Makers of American Wine,* Berkeley, 2012.

Reports of the Board of Trustees. . .of the Buena Vista Vinicultural Society, San Francisco, 1863-1865.

Sandefur, Timothy, "Charles V. Stuart. . .," *Pacific Legal Foundation, Economic Liberties Project.,* Sacramento, 2008.

Solnit, Rebecca, *Infinite City,* Berkeley, 2010.

Robinson, W. W., *Land in California,* Berkeley, 1979.

Smart, Richard, "Vine Density," *The Oxford Companion to Wine,* Oxford, 1994.

Sparks, Edith, *Capital Intentions,* University of North Carolina, 2006.

Sullivan, Charles L, *A Companion to California Wine,* Berkeley. 1998.

----------"*A Man Named Agoston Haraszthy,* Vintage Magazine, April, 1980.

--------- *Like Modern Edens. Winegrowing in the Santa Clara Valley. . .,* Cupertino, 1982.

---------*Napa Wine, a History,* San Francisco, 1994.

---------"Wine in California, 1696-1846," *Wayward Tendrils Quarterly,* April, July and October, 2010.

-------- *Zinfandel, a History of a Grape and Its Wine,* Berkeley, 2003.

Tchelistcheff, André, Oral History, Bancroft Library, 1983.

Teiser, Ruth and Catherine Harroun, *Winemaking in California,* New York, 1983.

Transactions of the California State Agricultural Society, Sacramento, 1858-1911.

Wait, Frona Eunice, *Wines and Vines of California,* San Francisco, 1`889.

Webb, Edith, *Indian Life in the Old Missions,* Lincoln, Nebraska, 1952.

Winkler, A. J. *General Viticulture,* Berkeley, 1962.

Newspapers and Periodicals

Alta California (San Francisco)

American Wine Merchant

American Wine Press (New York)

Atlantic Monthly

American Journal of Enology and Viticulture

California Farmer

California Grape Grower

California Star

California Wine, Wool and Stock Journal

Cloverdale Reveille

Gourmet

Harper's New Monthly Magazine

Healdsburg Weekly Enterprise

Los Angeles Star

Napa County Reporter

Napa Register

New York Times

Pacific Rural Press (San Francisco)

Pacific Wine & Spirit Review (San Francisco)

Redwood Rancher (Santa Rosa)

St. Helena Star

San Francisco Bulletin

San Francisco Chronicle

San Francisco Evening Bulletin

San Francisco Merchant

San Jose Mercury

Santa Rosa Democrat

Santa Rosa Republican

Santa Rosa Press Democrat

Sonoma Business

Sonoma Democrat

Sonoma Historian

Sonoma Index-Tribune

Wayward Tendrils Quarterly (Santa Rosa)

Wine Country Review

Wines & Vines

Wine Spectator

Wine World

Appendix

The Global Holdings of Boisset, La Famille des Grands Vins

CALIFORNIA

DeLoach Vineyards,
Russian River Valley
www.deloachvineyards.com
1791 Olivet Road, Santa Rosa, CA
95401
707.526.9111

Raymond Vineyards, Napa Valley
www.raymondvineyards.com
849 Zinfandel Lane, St. Helena, CA
94574
707.963.6929

Buena Vista Winery, Sonoma
www.buenavistawinery.com
18000 Old Winery Rd Sonoma,
California 95476
800.926.1266

JCB by Jean-Charles Boisset
www.jcbwines.com

Lockwood Vineyard, Monterey
www.lockwoodvineyard.com

Lyeth Estate, Sonoma County
www.lyethestate.com

Amberhill
www.amberhillwines.com

FRANCE

Domaine de la Vougeraie, Burgundy
www.domainedelavougeraie.com
12 Rue de l'Église, 21700 Premeaux-
Prissey, France

Jean-Claude Boisset, Burgundy
www.jcboisset.com
Les Ursulines, 5 Quai Dumorey,
21700 Nuits-St.-Georges, France

Bouchard Aîne & Fils, Beaune,
Burgundy
www.bouchard-aine.fr/en/
Hôtel du Conseiller du Roy, 4, bou-
levard Maréchal Foch, 21200 Beaune,
France

Mommessin, Beaujolais
www.mommessin.com
Le Pont des Samsons, 69430 Quincié-
en-Beaujolais, France

Chateau de Pierreux, Beaujolais
www.mommessin.com/en/vin_1.php
Pierreux, 69460 Odenas, France

Jaffelin, Beaune, Burgundy
www.boisset.fr/en/corp-familles/m-
dat-jaffelin.php
2 Rue Paradis, 21200 Beaune, France

Ropiteau, Meursault, Burgundy
www.caves-ropiteau.com
Caves Ropiteau Frères - Cour des
Hospices - 21190 Meursault, France

Antonin Rodet, Mercurey
www.rodet.com/en/
Grande Rue, 71640 Mercurey, France
J. Moreau & FILS, Chablis
www.jmoreau-fils.com/en/
La Croix St Joseph
Route d'Auxerre
89800 Chablis
France

LOUIS BOUILLOT
www.louis-bouillot.com
rue des Frères Montgolfier, BP 102,
Nuits-Saint-Georges 21703, France

Grandin, Loire Valley
www.boisset.com/en/corp-familles/
m-mht-grandin.php?PHPSESSID=84
8e7439dc44aa6e51f89282b1757a46
Caves de la Bouveraie
6, rue de la verrerie - BP
Ingrandes-sur-Loire 49123
France

CHARLES DE FÈRE
5, quai Dumorey, BP 102
Nuits-Saint-Georges 21703
France

SKALLI and Fortant de France
www.skalli.com
www.fortant.com
Avenue Pierre de Luxembourg, B.P. 5,
Châteauneuf-du-Pape 84231 France

LOUIS BERNARD
www.louis-bernard.com/en/
Le Village - 84190 Gigondas — France

CANADA
Neige, Quebec
www.appleicewine.com
La Face Cachée de la Pomme
617 Route 202
Hemmingford (Québec) Canada
J0L 1H0

Additional resources:
http://www.boisset.com/en/infor-
mations-contact/contacts-maisons.
php?cle=mht

INDEX

INDEX